Ce.

Early in 1971 Jonathan Aitken stood in the dock of the Old Bailey accused of offences under the Official Secrets Act 1911. The charges related to a newspaper article published in the *Sunday Telegraph* which had quoted extracts from a British diplomat's report on the Nigerian Civil War. The other defendants were Colonel Douglas Cairns, a former member of the international team of Military Observers in Nigeria; Mr Brian Roberts, the Editor of the *Sunday Telegraph*; and the Sunday Telegraph Ltd.

The trial lasted for three and a half weeks and made legal and political history. It ended with the acquittal of the accused on all counts, followed by the almost unique direction of the judge that the defendants' costs should be paid out of public funds. In his widely acclaimed summing up Mr Justice Caulfield suggested that section 2 of the Official Secrets Act 1911 (which celebrates its sixtieth birthday this August 1971) 'should be pensioned off' in the interests of free speech.

The Conservative Government, which had inherited this state prosecution from its Labour predecessors, swiftly accepted this judicial advice and set up a committee of inquiry into the Official Secrets Act under the chairmanship of Lord Franks. This committee is expected to makes its report before the end of the year, and legislation amending the present Act will soon follow.

The *cause célèbre* which led to this dramatic *dénouement* had many fascinating ramifications. As the principal defendant in the case Jonathan Aitken is in a unique position for unravelling the military, political and journalistic aspects of what has become known as 'The Scott Report Affair'.

Officially Secret

But although much of this book is a narrative account of an historic legal struggle, *Officially Secret* is more than a contemporary chronicle. Jonathan Aitken devotes six chapters to the history of the Official Secrets Act up to 1970 and shows that his case was the inevitable collision between the growing pressures by the Civil Service for greater secrecy and the public right to know. In the final chapter the author argues the case for radical reform of the Official Secrets Act and discusses the various legislative alternatives.

Jonathan Aitken was educated at Eton and Christ Church, Oxford. He works as a journalist for the *Evening Standard* and has frequently appeared on television. As a reporter he has specialised in covering international events, and was a war correspondent in Vietnam and in Biafra. His writings on the Nigerian Civil War led to his prosecution last year (1970) under the Official Secrets Act. In 1966 Jonathan Aitken was, at 23, the youngest Conservative Parliamentary candidate in Britain. From 1967 to 1970 he was Conservative candidate for the safe seat of Thirsk from which he resigned a few weeks before the General Election because his Official Secrets Act case was still incomplete.

Officially Secret

—=○=—

Jonathan Aitken

Weidenfeld and Nicolson
5 Winsley Street London W1

ISBN 0 297 00373 9

Printed in Great Britain by
Willmer Brothers Limited, Birkenhead

for Hugh and Antonia

Contents

Acknowledgments

I would like to express my thanks to the many people who have helped me when I was writing this book.

In particular, for invaluable assistance over documentary research, I am grateful to Mr John King and Mr E. J. S. Brisland of the *Daily Express* Library, to Jean Stead of the *Evening Standard* Library, to Henrietta Lawrence of Sotheby's and to the staff of the British Museum Reading Room.

I am also grateful to several journalists and authors for relating to me their experiences of incidents connected with the Official Secrets Act, especially Mr John Alexander-Sinclair, Mr James Evans, Mr Anthony Howard, Mr Ronald Hyde, Mr Derek Marks, Mr Chapman Pincher, Professor Hugh Thomas, Mr Andrew Wilson, and many others who prefer to remain anonymous.

This cloak of anonymity is obligatory, as long as Section 2 of the 1911 Act remains in its present state, for all those past and present civil servants who talked to me about the practical workings of the law in Whitehall. Nevertheless I would like to record my gratitude and appreciation to these discrete informants.

For information about Official Secrets legislation and its operation in other countries, I would like to thank Mr Tom Hughes QC, Attorney-General of Australia, 1969–71, Mr Lawrence N. Strenger of Debevoise, Lyons, Plimpton and Gates, New York, and to the French and Swedish Embassies in London.

No full-length book on the Official Secrets Act has ever before been published, but I am glad to acknowledge my great reliance on those chapters of Professor David Williams' *Not in the Public*

A*

Interest (London 1965) which relate to Official Secrecy, and am grateful to the author for permission to quote from his book.

As for those chapters of this book which deal with my own trials and tribulations under the Official Secrets Act, I would like to say a very special word of thanks to Mr Jeffrey Maunsell of Goodman Derrick and Company, my solicitors. He assembled a mass of essential documents for me, and with his able assistant, Mrs Diana Rawstrom, kept meticulous verbatim notes of all the public proceedings on which I relied heavily in this account.

During the preparation of the manuscript, the heavy burden of secretarial work was shared between Mrs Sally Corfield and Mrs Evelyn Hicks, whose patience, encouragement and industry made this book possible. I would particularly like to thank Mrs Hicks for indexing the entire book with such speed and efficiency.

Finally my warmest thanks are due to Mr Hugh Fraser MP, and to Mr Anthony Godwin, Deputy-Chairman of Weidenfeld and Nicolson. Both read and re-read my manuscript several times, and made many invaluable suggestions for improvements.

Grateful as I am to all those who helped in any way during the preparation of this book, the final responsibility for all facts, opinions, or errors is of course my own.

47 Phillimore Gardens,
London W8

Foreword

Earlier this year I stood in the dock of the Central Criminal Court accused of two offences under the Official Secrets Act. The charges related to a newspaper article published in the *Sunday Telegraph* on 11 January 1970 which had quoted extracts from a British diplomat's report on the Nigerian Civil War.

The other defendants in the case were Colonel Douglas Cairns, a former member of the International Military Observer team to the Nigerian war; Mr Brian Roberts, the Editor of the *Sunday Telegraph*; and the Sunday Telegraph Ltd. All of us were indicted with charges of 'communicating' and or 'receiving' a confidential report by Colonel R. E. Scott in contravention of Section 2 of the Official Secrets Act 1911.

The trial which lasted for three and a half weeks, made legal and political history. It ended with the acquittal of the accused on all counts followed by the almost unprecedented (for a full length Old Bailey case) direction of the judge that the defendants' costs should be paid out of public funds. In his widely acclaimed summing-up, Mr Justice Caulfield suggested that parts of the existing law 'should be pensioned off' in the interests of freedom of speech. The Conservative Government (which had inherited this state prosecution from its Labour predecessors) swiftly accepted this judicial advice and announced that it would review the Official Secrets Acts with the object of introducing amending legislation.

The military, political, journalistic and legal aspects of the *cause célèbre* which led to this dénouement were so extraordinary that their story has seemed worth telling in full. The bulk of this

1

book is therefore given over to the first complete account of what became popularly known either as 'The Fleet Street Secrets Case' or 'The Scott Report Affair'.

I first decided to write this account during the summer of 1970. That was a particularly unoccupied moment in personal terms, for as a result of the criminal charges outstanding against me I suddenly found myself without the constituency I had expected to represent in Parliament, without the television interviewing work I had been doing for the previous two years, and with only a limited behind-the-scenes role in journalism. Yet although the preparation of this book began partly as private therapy, it has I hope resulted in a work of some public usefulness. For during the eleven months between the first announcement of the charges in March 1970, and the final judgment at the Old Bailey in February 1971, I started to research into the full history and operation of Britain's laws of Official Secrecy. From these researches it soon became apparent that the Scott Report prosecutions were not just an isolated aberration on the part of a misguided government. Instead one could see clearly that the Official Secrets Act had over a long period increasingly been used as a means of controlling the flow of information about the executive government.

What had begun in the 1880s as a simple legislative move to combat espionage had by the 1960s developed into complex power frequently operated for the suppression of non-secret information whose disclosure might prove merely embarrassing to ministers and civil servants. By the end of the latter decade Whitehall was making increasing use of the Official Secrets Act as the drawbridge for the fortress of closed government, while Fleet Street was becoming increasingly resentful of managed news, D-notices, restricted information facilities and all the paraphernalia of quasi-censorship which the Official Secrets Act had come to represent. In this historical perspective, the Scott Report Affair could be seen as the inevitable collision between the communications media and the Civil Service establishment.

For this reason I decided, win or lose the Scott Report battle in the courts, to write a book which would further the chances of reforming the Official Secrets Act. To this end, this book is written in three parts. Part One contains six chapters tracing the development of the Official Secrets Acts up to the moment when the Attorney-General decided to instigate prosecutions over the publication of the Scott Report. Part Two is the detailed account of my own case from its first beginnings through to the final verdict and historic judgment by Mr Justice Caulfield at the Old Bailey. Part Three is a brief plea for the kind of legislative amendments which are necessary if Parliament is now to enact a meaningful reform of the Official Secrets Act.

Part One

How the Act Began

The first Official Secrets Act was conceived in farce and born in pique. It had its origins in a comic political imbroglio during the forty-second year of Queen Victoria's reign when a leak to the Press was alleged to have caused immense diplomatic embarrassment to the Prime Minister, Benjamin Disraeli, and the Foreign Secretary, the Marquess of Salisbury.

The individual responsible for this indiscretion was a twenty-six-year-old clerk named Charles Marvin, who in 1878 was working as a temporary copyist in the Foreign Office.

Before taking up this lowly employment, Charles Marvin had enjoyed an exotic and peripatetic youth. Leaving school at fifteen he worked for a few months as a clerk in the City, until travelling to St Petersburg to accept a position with a shipbuilding company. While in Russia he became friendly with the son of Colonel Volykoff, a senior officer in the Emperor's bodyguard. The Colonel took such a liking to the young Englishman that Marvin became in effect an adopted member of the Volykoff family and appears to have accompanied them on journeys all over Europe. During these peregrinations a photographic memory and a flair for languages enabled Marvin to become fluent in French, Italian, German, Dutch, Spanish and Russian. He also acquired a useful understanding of European politics which enabled him to become the regular St Petersburg correspondent for the *London Globe*. But after seven agreeable years away from England, an attack of ophthalmia* forced Marvin to leave his Imperial surroundings and come home for treatment. Back in London, his talents did

*Inflammation of the eye, especially of the conjunctiva of the eye. O.E.D.

not receive the recognition he thought they deserved, and finding it impossible to earn an adequate living as a journalist and author, he reluctantly signed on at the Government secretariat in Cannon Row as a temporary clerk in the Civil Service. In this role he worked for short spells at the Customs, the Inland Revenue and at the Post Office, earning the meagre sum of tenpence an hour for his pains. Although he was able to supplement these slender earnings by freelance journalism, Marvin always resented what he called the 'Bumbles, Barnacles and Boobies' of the Civil Service, his particular grievance being that 'the temporary tenpennies' were never allowed to rise above the status of mere menials, while permanent clerks enjoyed the benefits of a well-paid promotion system.

In 1877 Marvin left the Civil Service and attempted to start an institute of language teaching in Regent Street, whose prospectus (five thousand copies of which were printed) provided an insight into the character of the putative founder – 'Marvin : Master of Mastery'.

> Lectures on the Science of Linguistry delivered at Public Institutions in London or in the Provinces. The Mastery Metabolical apparatus used by Mr Marvin to illustrate his lectures and to explain to his pupils the working of the couplet system shows how thousands of sentences may be manufactured by interlacing two or more common sentences without any possibility of grammatical error. Froebel's method of teaching by objects applied to linguistry, rendering the matter of languages a matter of mirth and amusement.

Perhaps Charles Marvin had subsequent doubts about 'the Mastery Metabolical apparatus', for he never distributed his prospectus. Instead, an unexpected letter from the Cannon Row secretariat offering him a special vacancy at the Foreign Office proved more alluring, for after lengthy self-musings on the course of life's destiny, Marvin accepted a job in the Treaty department, evidently believing that a great career might be in store for him. Unfortunately, his frustrations were as acute as ever when it became clear that he had no hope of ever being anything other than a Foreign Office temporary. He continued to be paid the regulation tenpence per hour plus a bonus fourpence halfpenny per folio for copying in foreign languages, yet did the same work

8

as permanent Foreign Office staff earning six hundred pounds a year. Marvin's salary, with bonuses, amounted to ninety pounds per annum, considerably less than the pay of cleaners and messengers. As he himself wrote in his autobiography:

I compared my ninety pounds a year with the one hundred and fifty which the messenger who waited upon me was receiving and I was indignant that someone who knew languages and was a gentleman should be valued at half the pay of a flunkey, and that at the Foreign Office the broom and the duster should be held in higher esteem than the tongue and the brain. I was so disgusted with the Foreign Office for sucking the best years from my life for the miserable sum of ninety pounds that I resolved from that moment to place upon the market every piece of information that chance threw into my way. I made a reservation only when I was asked to maintain silence as in the case of the Somali Coast treaty or when I saw that a disclosure would be attended with evil results.[1]

This questionable conduct does not seem to have raised many eyebrows in the Treaty department, although the Foreign Office was notorious for its indiscretions[2] at this time, for as Marvin claimed : 'I made no secret of my connection with the *Globe*. It was my first and only newspaper, and I was vain of my connection with it.'[3]

The connection proved lucrative but harmless until May 1878 when Marvin was asked to help with the copying of an Anglo-Russian memorandum. At the time, the Chancelleries of Europe were struggling to find a solution to the vexatious 'Eastern Question', and to this end a top level summit meeting or Congress had been arranged to take place in Berlin. As a prelude to the Congress, the British Foreign Secretary, Lord Salisbury, and the Russian Ambassador, Count Shouvaloff, concluded a secret agreement on the negotiating positions of their respective governments. It was this agreement, set down in the form of a treaty, that the Foreign Office had been instructed to copy. Charles Marvin's personal knowledge of Russia, his distrust of Count Shouvaloff[4] and his disapproval of the extent of the British concessions, provided him with a political motive for disclosing Salisbury's terms to the Press. An added spur to indiscretion was a condescending remark by the head of the Treaty department, Mr

George March, who told the indignant Marvin: 'Considering your position here you should think it a great honour to be permitted to help in such important work.'[5] A final excuse for the leak came when an assistant in the Treaty department, Mr Francis Irving, said that the details of the treaty would be revealed to the House of Commons and published in *The Times* on the following day. This information led Marvin to the ingenuous conclusion: 'If the Government has the right to give a state document to *The Times* tomorrow, I have a right to give a summary to the *Globe* overnight.'[6] Accordingly, before punctiliously returning the document to his superiors, he memorised the salient points of the Anglo-Russian memorandum and then went down to the offices of the *Globe* to tell all he knew.

The editor was so excited by Marvin's disclosures that he laid on an extra shift of printers and ran a special edition on 30 May, proclaiming in banner headlines:

THE BERLIN CONGRESS DECIDED UPON!
TERMS OF AGREEMENT BETWEEN BRITAIN AND RUSSIA
We have good reason to believe that the question of the assembling of the Congress is now definitely settled and that the following are the points on which the Governments of England and Russia have arrived at an understanding.

There then followed a lengthy summary of the agreement, set out in a wealth of embarrassingly accurate detail. These revelations caused consternation at the Foreign Office. Queen Victoria was not amused at reading the treaty in the *Globe* before she had been told of it by her ministers,[7] and almost every foreign representative in London (particularly those whose governments were about to participate in the Congress of Berlin) demanded an explanation for this apparent perfidy.

'All the rest of the afternoon the quadrangle resounded with the rolling of carriages. Every ambassador and minister called on the Foreign Secretary, and the Foreign Secretary, I imagine, had a very awkward time of it'[8] recounted Marvin, who was perturbed to discover that neither *The Times* nor the House of Commons had been told of the treaty. However, the heat was taken off the Foreign Office after Lord Salisbury had been questioned on 3 June 1878 in Parliament over the *Globe*'s revelations and had given some highly deceptive answers. The exchange in the House of Lords went as follows:

Earl Grey : I wish to ask whether there is any truth or not in the statement in the *Globe* last Friday as to the terms agreed upon between this country and Russia.

The Marquess The statement to which the noble Earl refers
of Salisbury : and the other statements that I have seen are wholly unauthentic and are not deserving of the confidence of your Lordship's House.

Earl Grey : I should not have supposed that what was said with regard to the retrocession of Bessarabia was correct. It appeared too monstrous to be believed that Her Majesty's Government could have made such a stipulation as was alleged.[9]

Lord Grey's instant acceptance of the Foreign Secretary's disavowal appeared to put an end to the matter. The *Globe*'s reputation 'suffered cruelly'[10] for publishing false information, and it may be supposed that Charles Marvin's reputation with the editor must have undergone a certain devaluation. Vexed by this situation, and furious with Lord Salisbury for his diplomatic mendacity, Marvin decided on a more dramatic course of action.

To me it appeared there was only one way of dealing with the matter and that was to divulge the full text of the agreement . . . had the Marquess of Salisbury admitted the truth of the summary, the full text would never have been divulged. There would have been no need for it. It was the course adopted by the Foreign Secretary that impelled me to heroic measures.[11]

Marvin's 'heroic measures' first took the form of writing letters marked 'Private and Confidential' to several newspaper editors declaring that as a Foreign Office clerk he knew the *Globe*'s disclosures of the Anglo-Russian agreement to be accurate. When these epistles failed to produce results, Marvin again got access to the Treaty document in the Foreign Office, and in a phenomenal feat of memory learnt every word of it off by heart. He then returned to the offices of the *Globe* and wrote out the full text for the editor.

On 13 June 1878 the Congress of Berlin assembled under the

11

august presidency of Prince von Bismarck to settle the Eastern Question. Disraeli 'The Lion of the Congress'[12] and Salisbury represented Britain, while the Russian plenipotentiaries were Prince Gorchakov and Count Shouvaloff. Other delegations present included France, Austria-Hungary, Holland and Bulgaria. With all the diplomatic world on tenterhooks to know the outcome of these delicate negotiations, the *Globe* caused acute embarrassment by publishing verbatim the eleven clauses of the Anglo-Russian Treaty on its front page on 14 June. This leak (now beyond hope of denial) could have provoked serious international tensions, as it showed that Britain and Russia had gone to the Congress with an already agreed settlement, while other nations thought the Congress existed for consultations about a settlement.

However, despite furious questions to other ministers in both Houses of Parliament, no damage seems to have been done to British interests at the Congress, for the resulting Treaty of Berlin was hailed as a triumph for Disraeli. Returning to London, the Prime Minister was greeted by cheering crowds and was offered a dukedome, the Garter, and a peerage for his brother or nephew by his grateful Sovereign. He declined everything except the Garter and only accepted this on condition that Salisbury should receive the same honour.[13] In spite of the Garter and the success of the Congress, Salisbury remained enraged over the *Globe's* disclosures and telephoned instructions from Berlin that the culprits should be brought to justice.

The Foreign Office called in Scotland Yard, who carried out a thorough investigation headed by Sir Howard Vincent. Cleaners, messengers and clerical staff were interrogated. Marvin's letters were intercepted, detectives eavesdropped at the keyhole of his office, even his blotting paper was scrutinised with microscopes and at one point his movements were watched by a police officer with a telescope from the roof of the adjacent India Office.

Marvin attempted to put Scotland Yard off the scent by writing letters to personal friends protesting his innocence, and leaving these on his desk where he knew they would be discovered and read by the detectives. But he was trapped when the editor of the *Morning Advertiser*, a Captain Hamber, gave the police one of the 'Private and Confidential' letters Marvin had written when trying to convince the Press that the *Globe's* first disclosures were authentic. Another key piece of evidence was the discovery that the *Globe* had paid forty guineas into Marvin's bank account on 16 June. These items of information led to the arrest of Marvin, who had the effrontery to tell the police: 'Of course you know that as well as being employed by the Foreign Office I write for the Press.'

After an uncomfortable night in the cells of King Street police station, Charles Marvin appeared at Bow Street Magistrates' Court on 27 June 1878 charged under the Larceny Acts[14] with the theft of a document from the Foreign Office and also with the theft of the paper on which he had copied the treaty for the *Globe*.

The Treasury Counsel, Mr Poland, who led for the prosecution argued that to abstract Foreign Office documents and give copies to a newspaper was an offence at common law. The defence submitted that since neither the original nor the copy had been removed from the Foreign Office there could have been no theft. Once the head of the Treaty department had said under cross-examination that 'no actual rule forbade members of the Foreign Office to write for the newspapers'[15] and the publisher of the *Globe* had confirmed that the paper had relied for its information on Marvin's memory and not on any actual document, the prosecution's case was in the throes of collapse. After another member of the Treaty department admitted that a 'high authority' in the Foreign Office (he would not say whom on the grounds that the authority was too high) had declared that the agreement would be published in the next day's papers, even the moral stigmas against the accused began to fade. At this point Mr Vaughan, the chief magistrate at Bow Street, stopped the case without waiting to hear defence and commented:

I fail to see that either of the charges have been established. It has been clearly shown that it was only an effort of memory that the defendant was able to supply the articles which were printed . . . Since as now appears the defendant had good reason to believe that the information would be circulated to the Press the next morning, it was not unnatural that he should have endeavoured to secure priority for a journal with which he himself was connected.[16]

Although the chief magistrate made some less kind remarks

about the ethics of newspapers who published such documents, the *Globe* was unabashed and reprinted the full text of the Anglo-Russian Treaty the day after Marvin's acquittal. In a leading article entitled THE GOVERNMENT AND THE PRESS the *Globe* impudently proclaimed :

> This ignominious collapse of the prosecution of Mr Marvin affords just cause for congratulation so far as the freedom of the Press is concerned. A more ill-advised step than this was scarcely ever undertaken in that connection by an English government . . . the petty revenge of exposure was zealously striven for not in the interests of truth and justice but to appease the ire of sensitive officialism.[17]

While the unrepentant disclosers of the Russian treaty leak made good publicity for themselves out of the affair,* officialism remained sensitive. Lord Salisbury in particular pressed for law reforms to prevent any such future indiscretions, and it may fairly be ascribed to his influence as the newly installed Prime Minister that eleven years later the necessary legislation was introduced.

Mr A. J. Balfour, who had attended the Congress of Berlin as Lord Salisbury's Parliamentary Secretary, later described the new addition to the criminal law in his memoirs *Chapters of Autobiography* :

> After his [Marvin's] corrupt transaction with the *Globe* an attempt was made to bring him to justice. It failed not because there was any doubt of what he had done but because what he had done was no crime in the eyes of the law. The law was then changed and Mr Marvin might justly have asserted, that if not the author of an important legal reform he had at least been its occasion.[18]

The important legal reform in question was the Official Secrets Act of 1889.

---

*Charles Marvin became something of a journalistic celebrity after his acquittal and wrote several books, two of them attacks on the Civil Service. He died suddenly while on a reporting assignment in St Petersburg, aged thirty-six.

The Passing of the Acts

No part of Britain's criminal law ever reached the Statute Book with such a marked absence of discussion and deliberation as did the first two Official Secrets Acts. Reading the Parliamentary debates on the Official Secrets Bills of 1889 and 1911 the contemporary student cannot fail to be struck first by the atmosphere of casual unawareness about the significance of the proposed legislation, and secondly by how little consideration was given to the possible erosions of individual freedom resulting from these statutes. Not until the third Official Secrets Act of 1920 was there serious Parliamentary criticism of the executive's demands for radical new powers to protect government information, but by this time the opposition was too little and too late. The principle of preserving Civil Service secrecy by criminal penalties had come to stay, yet even so it is doubtful whether the legislators who passed the three Official Secrets Acts intended in practice to sanction a law with the scope and severity it encompasses today.

The first Official Secrets Act was introduced in 1888 soon after the arrival of Lord Salisbury at Number 10 Downing Street. Moving its second reading in the House of Commons on 28 March 1889, the Attorney-General, Sir Richard Webster, thought it necessary to give only a sixty-seven word explanation:

> I wish to say just a word or two with regard to this Bill. It has been prepared under the direction of the Secretary of State for War and the First Lord of the Admiralty in order to punish the offence of obtaining information and communicating it against the interests of the State. The Bill is an exceedingly simple one and I beg to move its second reading.[1]

There was only one member who objected to the brevity of the Attorney-General's introduction of the bill, which was there and then given its second reading after a discussion filling less than half a column of Hansard.[3] On the third reading which was broken up over four days because of irrelevant adjournments proposed by Irish members, the bill held the House's attention for a mere seven columns of debate and received only minor amendments. But there was one exception when an opposition MP moved that in a clause covering the communication of secrets 'contrary to the interests of the State or of any Department of the Government' the words 'or of any Department of the Government' should be struck out.

The Attorney-General, who was evidently under pressure from backbenchers, gave way on this saying:

> There may be cases where the divulging of official secrets may be injurious to a Department without quite coming under the description of being detrimental to the State . . . I only desire to say in answer to the honourable gentleman's criticism that the words were not inserted to prevent proper information being given. From a drafting point of view I do not care about the words and as the Secretary of State for War and the First Lord of the Admiralty think that substantially sufficient protection will be given without them, I consent to the amendment.[3]

The significance of this concession was that the original Official Secrets Act legislators appreciated the difference between State secrets and Civil Service departmental secrets. It is a distinction which does not seem to have been acknowledged by more recent enforcers of the Official Secrets Act, as later chapters of this book will show.

In any case, the whole emphasis of the 1889 Act was on espionage and treason. When the bill went through the Upper House on 11 July 1889, (their Lordships giving it a scant one-and-a-half columns of discussion), the Lord Chancellor Lord Halsbury made no reference to any potential offenders under the new law other than spies or government servants who communicate secrets 'to those who may become the Queen's Enemies'.[4]

Receiving the Royal Assent on 26 August 1889, the Official Secrets Act was operated for the next twenty-two years with exemplary moderation. Only a handful of prosecutions were brought under it, all save one dealing with military and naval secrets. Even that exception[5] concerned a clerk in the Supply Reserve Depot at Woolwich Dockyard who tried to sell information on the estimates of certain government contractors, and his sentence for these commercial indiscretions was merely to be bound over to be of future good behaviour. But despite such judicial restraint, there were stirrings within the executive government to have the Official Secrets Acts strengthened. On 26 June 1896, the Attorney-General, Sir Richard Webster brought in a new bill to amend certain defects in the original legislation. Claiming that 'cases had arisen in which there was no moral or practical doubt of the guilt and yet conviction had failed because of the impossibility of obtaining evidence'[6] the Attorney-General argued that the revised bill was needed to put the onus of proof on the accused when it came to showing that information had been obtained innocently, rather than for the illegal purpose of communicating it to a foreign government. This startling legal innovation proved abortive when the entire bill was withdrawn a few weeks later.

A second unsuccessful attempt to revise the law was made in 1908 when the Lord Chancellor Lord Loreburn introduced a new Official Secrets Bill on 16 March. By this time there appeared to be a considerable measure of agreement among politicians that the old Act was proving inadequate, largely on account of public criticism of the 1892 case of *R. v. Holden.*

Edward Holden, a former quartermaster in the Royal Engineers, had attempted to persuade a lance corporal stationed in Gibraltar to supply him with details of artillery positions and fortifications in Malta and Gibraltar. It was alleged by the prosecution that the accused was in contact with a mysterious secret agent in Paris who signed his letters with a hieroglyph and that the information Holden had been attempting to procure would have been invaluable to an enemy government. Although there was no doubt either of Holden's guilt or of the serious nature of his activities, he was sentenced to only twelve months' imprisonment. The Lord Chief Justice, Lord Coleridge, who took the trial at Liverpool Assizes in April 1889, publicly expressed his regret that he was unable to impose a heavier term of penal servitude on such a dangerous offender and criticised the prosecution for failing to charge the accused with a felony under the 1889 Official Secrets Act.

17

The reason why such charges had not been laid was that the government's legal advisers felt Holden might escape under a technicality on that offence, as there was no definite evidence that he intended communicating the information to a foreign power. Commenting on the case on 7 May 1908, the military correspondent of *The Times* wrote that it had been an occasion in which 'the inadequacy of the law was made painfully manifest', and went on to support Lord Loreburn's proposed new Official Secrets Act. However, the rest of the newspaper world disagreed with *The Times*, for a deputation of editors called on the Lord Chancellor to express their anxieties about the bill's threats to press freedom, and conducted a vigorous campaign in their columns against the new law. After much journalistic criticism had been voiced it appeared that the Prime Minister, Mr H. H. Asquith, was not entirely enthusiastic about the proposed legislation,[7] and despite Lord Loreburn's assurance that 'anyone in the Press conducting his duties honourably would be quite safe'[8] the bill was withdrawn on 23 June 1908.

Around this time, Britain began developing the symptoms of spy-fever. From 1908 to 1910 the Member of Parliament for Epping, Colonel Lockwood, made numerous interventions in the House of Commons claiming to have discovered evidence of foreign espionage activities. His allegations included charges that military men from a foreign nation had been 'getting up to no good' in his constituency since 1906; that the German High Command had organised a staff ride through England in 1908; and that enemy agents were taking naval soundings off Holyhead in 1910. Similar stories were frequently reported in the press, and spy rumours abounded.

In Whitehall a new department in charge of counter-espionage was set up in 1909, which later became known as MI5. Its founder, Captain Vernon Kell, sent voluminous memoranda to Sir Henry Wilson, the Director of Military Operations at the War Office, urging more vigorous legislation against spies.[9] Kell's crusade was accelerated in 1910 when a German infantry officer Lieutenant Siegfried Helm was arrested and charged under the Official Secrets Act of 1889 with unlawfully sketching naval fortresses and fortifications in Portsmouth. This was the first prosecution of a foreign spy under the Act, and the Attorney-General, Sir Rufus Isaacs, came down to Winchester Assizes to lead for the

Crown. The defendant pleaded guilty, and a surprisingly lenient judge, Mr Justice Bankes, sentenced him only to be bound over. No such leniency was extended to a similar case in 1911, involving Ober-Leutnant Max Schultz of the German Hussars. Schultz was arrested in July, making his first appearance at Plymouth Magistrates' court on 19 August. By posing as a representative of a German News Agency he had encouraged residents of Plymouth to supply him with information on Naval movements and equipment. Schultz was later sentenced to twenty-one months' imprisonment at Exeter Assizes, the first and last major conviction under the 1889 Official Secrets Act.

In the summer months of 1911, international tension between Britain and Germany had been building up. The chief cause of the friction was the arrival of the German gunboat 'Panther' in Agadir harbour on the coast of Morocco. On 1 July the German Emperor announced that this warship had been despatched 'to protect German interests'. These were thought to be threatened by a French colonising expedition which had recently occupied the nearby town of Fez. The Franco-German dispute over Morocco caused tremors throughout the chancelleries of Europe. In London the Foreign Secretary, Sir Edward Grey, warned the German Ambassador that Britain would support France if hostilities occurred. The Fleet was put on the alert, Whitehall began compiling a 'War Book' of emergency orders, and on 21 July the Chancellor of the Exchequer, Mr David Lloyd George, publicly warned of the possibility of war in a speech at the Mansion House.

Winston Churchill in the first volume of *The World Crisis* wrote that during the summer 'the atmosphere in England became constantly more charged as one hot day followed another'.[10] He catches the spirit of the times in a description of a political garden party which took place on 27 July 1911, just ten days after a new Official Secrets Bill had been introduced in the House of Lords. Churchill was then Home Secretary and at the party he met the Chief Commissioner of Police, Sir Edward Henry:

> We talked about the European situation . . . he then remarked that by an odd arrangement the Home Office was responsible through the Metropolitan Police for guarding the magazines at Chattendon and Lodgehill in which all the reserves of naval cordite were stored. For many years these magazines had been

19

protected without misadventure by a few constables. I asked what would happen if twenty determined Germans in two or three motor cars arrived well armed upon the scene one night. He said they would be able to do what they liked. I quitted the garden party. A few minutes later I was telephoning from my room in the Home Office . . . I rang up the War Office. Haldane* was there. I told him that I was reinforcing and arming the police that night and asked for a company of infantry for each magazine in addition. In a few minutes the orders were given, in a few hours the troops had moved. By the next day the cordite reserves of the Navy were safe.[11]

Against this background of war scare and spy mania, a new Official Secrets Bill was introduced in the House of Lords on 17 July 1911. Moving the second reading the Secretary of State for War, Viscount Haldane said that the legislation had been drafted after consultation with military and naval authorities 'to strengthen the law with regard to official secrets and espionage generally . . . its purpose is not to enact any large body of new restrictions but to make more effective the law as it was intended to be made by the Official Secrets Act of 1889.'[12] Viscount Middleton said the bill was 'urgently needed in the interests of the country'[13] and in a reference to the Helm case Lord Ellenborough claimed that 'a recent occurrence near Portsmouth has shown that it is quite clear that our law needs strengthening'.[14] After only five columns of debate, the bill was given a second reading, formally read a third time in the Lords on 3 August, and introduced in the House of Commons on 17 August. The following morning it passed through all its stages after a debate lasting approximately thirty-five minutes.† The Minister piloting the bill was Colonel Seeley, the Under-Secretary of State for War, who stressed the urgency of getting the legislation swiftly enacted. Although one MP declared the bill 'upsets Magna Carta altogether'[15] and several members criticised the rushed procedure,

---

*The Secretary of State for War.

†For a Bill as important as the Official Secrets Act of 1911 to pass through all its stages in the House of Commons in one day is a situation without precedent in the annals of Parliamentary history. Even in the nineteenth century important bills took several days of debates over the report and committee stages. In 1971 the Industrial Relations Bills took nearly six months' worth of intermittent debates before it became law.

the few legalistic doubts raised were disposed of by reassurances from Colonel Seeley who said:

> It is undoubtedly in the public interest that this Bill should be passed at once . . . the change in the law is slight and it is perfectly true to say that none of His Majesty's loyal subjects run the least risk whatever of having their liberties infringed in any degree or particular whatever.

Although Labour MPs half-heartedly forced a division on the motion to report the bill without amendment (they were defeated by a hundred and seven votes to ten), the Under-Secretary's verbal bromides seemed acceptable to most members at this time of national war panic, and the bill was given its first, second and third readings before lunch on Friday 18 August, receiving the Royal Assent four days later.[16] It is still the basic law of Official Secrets today.

It now seems difficult to reconcile certain provisions of the Act with Colonel Seeley's claim that individual liberties were not being infringed. Section 1 is a widely drafted attempt to cover all forms of spying. It prohibits the making of any sketch, plan, model, article or note which could be useful to an enemy; the obtaining or communicating to any person of any sketch, plan, model, article, document or information which could be useful to an enemy, and the approach to or entry into 'any prohibited place' within the definitions laid down by later sections of the Act. In all these cases, the accused must have been acting 'for any purpose prejudicial to the safety or interests of the State'. But, in the ensuing sub-section of the Act it is stated that for a prosecution to succeed it is not necessary to prove the accused's actions were prejudicial to the interests and safety of the State. The onus of proof is placed on the accused for showing that he was acting innocently.

Apart from the much more clearly defined offence of receiving stolen goods, there is no other comparable instance in English criminal law where an accused is presumed guilty unless he can prove himself innocent. Only in a mood of war hysteria could the House of Commons have swallowed the statement that this was a necessary innovation for catching spies and did not amount to an infringement of liberty.

Section 2 of the Official Secrets Act contains some provisions which are even more draconian than the crucial clauses in Section 1, for the first part of the Act at least confines itself to activities which must be *prima facie* useful to an enemy and prejudicial to the interests of the State. The terms of Section 2 on the other hand have nothing to do with spying and are so widely drawn that they make it an absolute offence for anyone holding office under the Crown to communicate *any* information to *any* unauthorised person. This blanket provision, which must be broken daily by hundreds of thousands of civil servants who tell their wives what they have been doing in the office, appears to have been inserted into the Act to ensure that no-one could escape by a legal quibble. But by phrasing Section 2 in such an all-encompassing form, the parliamentary draughtsmen of the day made it impossible for there to be any defence of innocent intention to a charge under this section. This makes the Official Secrets Act almost the only major criminal statute under which the basic doctrine of *mens rea* (a guilty act cannot be committed unless there is a guilty mind) does not necessarily apply.*

A sub-section of Section 2 makes it an offence for a person to receive any official information, knowing or having reasonable ground to believe that the information is communicated in contravention of the Act. Again the vagueness of the wording makes it possible for the offence of receiving to be committed by a far wider range of persons than spies. Journalists, politicians, and all those who specialise in public affairs are particularly vulnerable to this open-ended charge.

Offences under Section 2 carry a maximum of two years imprisonment but may be punishable by a fine, while offences under Section 1 are punishable exclusively by imprisonment of up to seven years.

The remaining eleven sections of the Act are less important and deal with such issues as the repeal of the 1889 Act, powers of search and arrest, and penalties for harbouring spies. One significant clause headed 'Restriction on Prosecution', states that prosecutions

*It is still by no means clear whether *mens rea* is an essential ingredient of certain offences under the Official Secrets Act of 1911. Some judges have clearly ruled that offences under Section 2 are absolute (notably Mr Justice Hawke in the Compton Mackenzie case of 1932 – see p. 55). But in the most recent Section 2 case, *R. v. Cairns, Aitken* & *Roberts,* the Crown accepted from the outset that they would have to prove *mens rea* to secure convictions.

under the Act can only be brought with the consent of the Attorney-General.

In view of the all-embracing scope of earlier sections, it is clear that this requirement in Section 8 was intended to restrict prosecutions to serious offences, for if the Act was zealously enforced, the authorities would need several new prisons to accommodate the innumerable journalists, civil servants, authors, and politicians who regularly and frequently transgress Section 2.

At first the new law was applied only to serious cases, for the first prosecutions under the 1911 Act were all concerned with German espionage, and were brought under Section 1. In the immediate pre-war years spy fever was again rampant in Britain, this time with more justification, for during the period 1911–14 at least six German agents were given substantial prison sentences.

One case[17] during this period, which provided the first authoritative rulings by the Court of Criminal Appeal on the Official Secrets Act, concerned a Petty Officer in the Royal Navy who was charged in January 1913 with feloniously communicating to an unknown person at Ostend unspecified information about naval armaments which could be useful to an enemy. The accused was sentenced to four years' imprisonment, but on appeal the defence counsel strenuously argued that his client had been convicted only on suspicion. The Court of Appeal confirmed that the onus of proof was on the accused to show that the information had been communicated for some purpose that was not prejudcial to the interests of the State, and it was also held that the word 'enemy' in Section 1 of the Act did not pre-suppose a state of war between Britain and a foreign power, for as Mr Justice Phillimore put it, the term 'could cover a potential enemy with whom we might some day be at war'.

As soon as Britain did have real rather than potential enemies, the executive government swiftly provided themselves with drastic emergency powers for eliminating spies and traitors. Although the Official Secrets Act was still used for minor breaches of the law, serious espionage offenders were dealt with by the antique machinery of High Treason, while suspected spies were interned under the Aliens Restrictions Act of 1913.

After the war, the Official Secrets Act was fully re-activated and in 1919 there came an important prosecution under Section 2 which showed for the first time how far the Act could be extended into areas having no relevance to national security. In *R. v. Crisp and Homewood* (1919), a War Office clerk, for commercial purposes, passed on to a firm of tailors details of War Office contracts for the supply of officers' uniforms. When the preliminary hearings took place at Westminster Police Court, the magistrate accepted the argument that the Official Secrets Act was inapplicable as this was merely a departmental offence. However, the Attorney-General insisted on taking the case before a judge at the Old Bailey. Mr Justice Avory there held that Section 2 ranged far beyond espionage and said it could be applied to *any* information and not exclusively to information which might be classified as secret.

With a precedent like this, the executive government appeared to have no need of further powers to protect official secrets. But this view did not prevail among members of a Whitehall committee which had been set up following a series of leaks from Lloyd George's cabinet meetings to the Press.[18]

The committee, whose members included representatives from the War Office, the Home Office and the Admiralty, were given the task of recommending whether any of the wartime emergency security regulations needed to be kept on as a permanent legislation in peace time. Against a background of insurrection and threatened civil war in Ireland, the committee recommended that the Official Secrets Act should be extended. Accordingly the Government introduced the Official Secrets Act 1920, designed to strengthen and amend (but not to repeal or replace) the Act of 1911. Its passage through the House of Commons was exceedingly stormy, partly because the main debate took place on 3 December 1920, only thirteen days after the notorious 'Bloody Sunday' in Dublin when IRA terrorists assassinated some fifteen intelligence officers of the Black and Tans.

Piloting the bill through its second reading, the Attorney-General, Sir Gordon Hewart explained that a new law was necessary because of the ever-increasing ingenuity of spies. This was accepted, but there followed a hotly disputed argument as to whether or not this legislation would place limits on press freedom.

Already in the Lords, fears had been expressed about the position newspapers would be placed in by the proposed law, Viscount Burnham going so far as to say: 'I do not believe any editor would be safe if the Bill were passed in its present form.'[19]

Such statements were strongly denied in the Commons by the Attorney-General, Sir Gordon Hewart, who said in his opening speech:

> It is said this Bill deals with the Press. That seems to me to be an astonishing statement and it is very strange that persons connected with the Press should say that this Bill deals with them. How can it possibly be said that it is the function of a journalist to retain for some purpose prejudicial to the safety or interests of the state an official document that he has no right to retain or which it is contrary to his duty to retain.[20]

But several members disagreed, none more passionately than Sir Donald Maclean who declared:

> If this Bill is passed in anything like its present form their [journalists'] position as public servants in and through the Press would be completely hampered ... the position in which the Press would be put is one I think which would very much militate against the public service which from time to time they render. The Rt. Hon. Gentleman asked what reputable journalist would desire to hold in his possession any information which might be prejudicial to the interests of the State. But who is going to decide that?[21]

At this moment, the Attorney-General interjected, 'The courts', whereupon Sir Donald Maclean pointed out the grave threat to freedom of speech that future prosecutions of newspapermen would constitute, and added:

> I find it difficult to confine my language in regard to this Bill within the range of Parliamentary propriety. It is another attempt to clamp the powers of war on to the liberties of the citizen in peace.[22]

Maclean's indignation was shared by several other members including Mr Spencer who quoted from Burke, Emerson and the New Testament to show that the real purpose of the bill was not to deal with spies but to stifle the opinion of individuals.[23] The threat to press freedom was reiterated by Commander Bellairs who said of the Attorney-General:

> He does not realise what sensitive men publicists often are. They

25

are men who bear an unblemished character and would flinch from having a charge like this made against them which puts them in the same category as spies and people working against the State.[24]

But in the heated atmosphere following the Irish insurgencies, most MPs were inclined to support the Government's request for extra powers. Refuting Sir Donald Maclean's argument that war-time measures were being imposed in peace, a Tory member, Captain Thorpe, demanded:

> Where is peace? Is it peace to go into the Lobbies of the House and see oneself protected by Scotland Yard detectives and double police patrols? Is it peace to walk along Downing Street and find that even a Member of this House is not entitled to pass through the Horse Guards because he may be a dangerous person ...? In my view the State is in great danger and no power which would tend to protect it should be withheld from the Government.[25]

Further indications of inflamed feelings came when one Labour Member suggested that some of the bill's supporters were using un-democratic methods to rush the legislation through. 'Never mind democracy. I won't be shouted down by Bolshies!' yelled a government backbencher, Mr Stanton.[26] After many more angry words about plots and international conspiracies, the bill was given a second reading by a hundred and forty-three votes to forty-four, receiving the Royal Assent on 23 December 1920.

The Official Secrets Act 1920 created several new offences committed for a purpose prejudicial to the interests of the State. These include the unauthorised wearing of official uniforms, forging passports and official passes or stamps, and the retention of official documents. Section 3 makes it a crime to 'interfere with or impede' any police officer at a 'prohibited place', a provision which was the basis for prosecutions against demonstrators at US air bases in the 1950s. Section 6 makes it a crime for anyone to refuse to give the police information relating to an alleged Official Secrets Act offence, an innovation of the criminal law which conflicted sharply with the journalistic commandment 'never disclose your sources'.

Another innovation is found in Section 7 of the new law which makes it a crime to do *any* act preparatory to a breach of the Official Secrets Acts. This is a remarkable extension of the normal doctrines of criminal law whereby proof of an attempt to commit a crime depends on the accused's having committed a preparatory act *immediately* connected with the main offence.

These new amendments, together with the Act of 1911 remain to this day the fundamental British law of official secrets. They make up the widest, vaguest, and most far-reaching criminal statutes ever enacted in this country. Although there have been several attempts by parliamentarians to repeal substantial parts of both Acts, only one met with any success. This involved the abolition of Section 6 of the 1920 Act, following an outcry by the Press in 1938 after journalists had been convicted for failing to disclose their sources. The events leading up to this alteration are described more fully in the following chapter. With this one exception, the 1911 and 1920 Official Secrets Acts still stand. One was passed at the height of German war and spy mania, the other at the zenith of tensions over Irish assassinations and rebellions. They are products of a bygone age when cloak and dagger espionage was still a reality, when Britain as a world power still had numerous secrets worthy of protection, and when government activities extended over a much narrower front than they do today.

3

The Press and Official Secrets

'If we are to have legislation on the Press, let it not be mixed up with penal provisions aimed at spies and revolutionaries.' So thundered *The Times* in a leading article published a few days before the Official Secrets Act of 1920 passed through the House of Commons on 16 December.

Such sentiments were ridiculed by the ministers of the day, who protested that there was not the slightest intention on the part of the Executive Government to encroach on the cherished liberty of the Press. These disavowals have not stood the test of time. A study of the public prosecutions and private pressures applied to newspapers under the Official Secrets Acts during the last fifty years shows all too clearly that this law has often been used to restrict free expression and investigation on the activities of Government. These restrictions have steadily increased over the years, due to an apparent extension of Parkinson's law, which might be stated as 'The influence of the Official Secrets Act grows in inverse proportion to the number of secrets to be guarded.' Indeed the Civil Service's obsession with secrecy has grown to such an extent that the legitimate operations of journalists are today much hindered by the Official Secrets Acts than are the illegal machinations of spies.

The first clash between the Press and the Government over Official Secrets came in 1930 when the Viceroy of India Lord Irwin, consulted the Home Government as to whether he should order the arrest of Mahatma Ghandi on charges of provoking civil disturbances. At a Cabinet Meeting on 30 April a decision was taken to authorise the arrest. Three London newspapers disclosed this fact the following day, greatly to the annoyance of the India Office, which feared that the apprehending of Ghandi might be frustrated by the premature publicity. As events turned out, no such difficulties arose; nevertheless the Government decided to use its Official Secrets Act powers to trace the Cabinet leak. At the instigation of the Attorney-General Sir William Jowitt, three editors and one reporter were interviewed by Scotland Yard detectives. The reporter was subjected to two interrogations, one of ninety minutes, the other of two hours. In the end, no further action was taken and Parliament was solemnly told that the journalist concerned* had merely used his faculty of 'intelligent anticipation'.[1]

The incident caused a storm of protest both inside and outside Parliament. The Prime Minister was compelled to receive an angry deputation from the Newspaper Proprietors' Association, the Newspaper Society, the National Union of Journalists, the Institute of Journalists and other interested parties, while the Attorney-General soothed Parliament by guaranteeing that such actions would only in future be authorised in really serious cases. Even so, demands for immediate law reform were not stilled for more than a year. The cause of this somewhat over-inflated controversy was that the questioning of the journalist had been carried out under Section 6 of the 1920 Act, a clause which a previous Attorney-General gave assurances would only be invoked in cases of spying.[2] It was the use of Section 6 which provoked the entire Press into condemning the Government's action, one of the more moderate comments coming from *The Times,* which declared in a leading article of 15 May 1930: 'The main conclusion of the matter seems to be not that the Act is tyrannical or a menace to the freedom of the Press, but that it was stupidly, impulsively, clumsily and unnecessarily invoked.'

The same set of pejorative adverbs could well have been applied to the next newspaper case involving Official Secrets, when in

*The journalist concerned was Mr W. J. Foss, the lobby correspondent of the *Daily Telegraph.* At the time the proprietor of the *Daily Telegraph,* Lord Burnham, made enquiries as to how Foss had picked up the news of Ghandi's imminent arrest and received the startling reply that the information had come from Mr J. R. Clynes, the then Home Secretary. As Lord Burnham later wrote in his history of the *Daily Telegraph, 'Peterborough Court',* p. 131, 'We then decided that through unofficial channels we should indicate to the Home Secretary, Clynes, that he had better call off his sleuths and we heard no more of the matter.'

1932 the *Daily Mail* published the wills of three celebrities – Mr Leo Maxse, Sir William Pryke, and Sir John Rutherford – a few hours before the time when they were scheduled to be officially released by Somerset House. The breach of the embargo was traced to a Somerset House clerk who had accepted a small gratuity from the *Mail* reporter in return for the disclosure. For this crime, the unfortunate clerk was dismissed from his three pounds a week job and prosecuted under Section 2 of the Official Secrets Act 1911. Although sixty years old and chronically sick he was sentenced to six weeks' imprisonment by the Bow Street Magistrate who described the case as 'a serious breach of confidence'. Shortly afterwards the *Daily Mail* journalist was charged under Section 2 with receiving these momentous Official Secrets about wills, and was gaoled by the same magistrate for two months. Sir William Jowitt KC appeared for the reporter and appealed on his behalf to the London Sessions, arguing that no great public mischief could have been done by the disclosure, and that the defendant could hardly have had the Official Secrets Act in mind when he acquired the information. But the Attorney-General of the day, Sir Thomas Inskip, evidently feeling that the national interest was at stake, appeared in person to contend for the Crown that the accused had 'carried on this tampering with the official sources of information to the prejudice of trade competition and the corruption of civil servants'. The sentence of imprisonment was confirmed.

Public indignation over the Somerset House case was equalled five years later by the furore when a crime reporter on the *Manchester Daily Dispatch* was prosecuted under Section 6 of the 1920 Act. The case involved a circular sent out by the Chief Constable of Southport to all police forces in Lancashire and Cheshire. The document, which was not marked confidential, described a man wanted for fraud, and gave details of his methods.

A few days later an article appeared in the *Daily Dispatch* which was clearly based on the circular. Anxious to trace the police officer responsible for the leak, the Chief Constable authorised an interrogation of the newspaper's editor which revealed that the journalist who had written the story was a Mr E. D. G. Lewis. When Lewis was questioned he refused to disclose the source of his information, was charged under Section 6, and fined five pounds. His appeal to the Divisional Court of the King's Bench

Division was rejected as being 'too plain for argument',[3] by Lord Chief Justice Hewart, the very man who as Attorney-General in 1920 had promised the House of Commons that Section 6 of the Act would be confined to espionage cases.

Given such conclusive proof that both the Hewart assurances of 1920 and the Jowitt assurances of 1930 were worthless, the Press began a major agitation for law reform. In November 1937 the National Union of Journalists and the National Council for Civil Liberties held a conference to demand changes in the Official Secrets Acts. The chairman was Major Gwilym Lloyd George (later a Conservative Home Secretary) and the principal speakers were Mr E. D. G. Lewis, Mr Compton Mackenzie and Mr Dingle Foot (later a Labour Solicitor-General). Mr Foot claimed the Official Secrets Acts were a 'sort of statutory monstrosity' and could easily become 'an efficient instrument of despotism'. He carried his battle into the House of Commons in May 1938, introducing a Private Member's Bill to Section 6, condemning the offending clause with the words 'Nothing quite like it exists anywhere else in the whole range of our criminal laws'. Unfortunately all this sound and fury signified nothing in legislative terms. The Home Secretary of the day Sir Samuel Hoare made a lengthy statement summing up the arguments for and against both sides of the controversy but rejected any amendments to the law by saying:

> The difficulty in the way of limiting the application of the Official Secrets Act to naval or military secrets is that there are other secrets the disclosure of which might be equally prejudicial to the national interest and it is impracticable to define by statute in which the use of the special powers is warranted.[4]

Soon after this rejection there came a ministerial volte-face which brought about the reforms which the Press had been demanding. The cause of the change in attitude was a major parliamentary row between Mr Duncan Sandys the MP for Norwood and the Attorney-General Sir Donald Somervell. The 'Sandys storm' is recounted in detail in another chapter of this book, but the crux of the matter was an alleged attempt by the Attorney-General to use the powers under Section 6 of the 1920 Act to compel Mr Sandys to disclose the source of the information on which he was basing a potential Parliamentary Question. In the course of the debates on this episode it became clear that Members of Parliament regarded their sources of information in just as sacrosanct a light as journalists did theirs. For this reason pressmen and parliamentarians joined forces in again demanding an immediate amendment to Section 6 of the 1920 Act. This time the Government bowed to the pressure and brought in the Official Secrets Act 1939, which briefly ordained that the powers of interrogation in Section 6 should henceforth apply only to offences or suspected offences under Section 1 of the 1911 Act. It is quite clear from the debates in both Houses of Parliament at this time that the 1939 legislators thought both these sections would deal exclusively with espionage offences.

The 1939 Act did no more than amend one clause of Official Secrets legislation. It made no attempt to alter Section 2 of the 1911 Act, which prohibits the unauthorised communication and receipt of official information. Many observers expected that this opaque and omnipotent Section 2 – which journalists are apt to regard as the negation of free investigation and expression – would be repealed after the war. Instead, Section 2 has become the holy writ on which the entire post-war expansion of executive secrecy is based.

It is inevitable in any democracy that there should be a conflict between the desire of the Press for unfettered rights to disclose information, and the inclination of the Civil Service towards departmental discretion and the prevention of leaks. There would be little cause for concern over this conflict if the authorities restrained themselves from obstructive or punitive action against the Press except in those exceedingly rare cases where a newspaper's disclosures genuinely jeopardised national security. Unfortunately the gargantuan scope of Section 2 of the Official Secrets Act has given the government machine restrictive powers which go far beyond the protection of state secrets. There are three main ways in which those powers are today being abused to restrict press freedom – by prosecutions or threats of prosecution against newspapermen; by extensions of the D-notice system; and by unreasonable pressures on civil servants to maintain unnecessary secrecy.

The first of these abuses occurs when journalists are prosecuted or directly threatened with prosecutions under the Official Secrets Act on matters that do not involve national security. In

fact, the actual arrests or summonses of newspaper men are mercifully rare. Apart from the Scott Report case of 1970 and the
Isis case of 1958 there have been no more than two or three press
prosecutions since the war, all of them of negligible importance.
Even so, one was the subject of a House of Commons debate in
1948, after a Yorkshire journalist had been fined ten pounds by
Driffield magistrates for receiving tip-offs about local police activity from a GPO telephone operator. Raising the matter in a motion
on the adjournment on 24 June 1948, Mr Tom Driberg MP
claimed that the Official Secrets Acts 'were not intended originally
or ever for use in this kind of case and that it is stretching them
beyond the bounds of assurances given by successive Governments
so to use them'.[5]

He ended his speech with a quotation from an editorial on the
case in the *Manchester Guardian* of 1 June 1938: 'The Attorney-
General should not let it happen again. It is not necessary to kill
a field-mouse with a field gun.'

Replying to the adjournment debate, the Attorney-General Sir
Hartley Shawcross refused to intervene in the case and added 'I
cannot for a moment lend myself to the view that the Official
Secrets Acts are limited or restricted in some way to cases of spying'.

This was the first time in sixty years of Parliamentary discussion
of Official Secrets that a Law Officer had made it clear that the
Acts could be used against journalists or other members of the
public in cases quite unconnected with espionage.

Although instances of journalists being hauled before the courts
are infrequent, the same cannot be said for threats of Official
Secrets Act prosecutions against the Press. That doyen of
contemporary Defence Correspondents, Mr Chapman Pincher
of the *Daily Express,* can recall numerous occasions when veiled
hints of action were made to him or his editors in order to get
embarrassing information suppressed. Some of these examples are
worth relating.

In 1950, Chapman Pincher discovered that huge sums of the
taxpayers' money had been wasted during the construction of the
big atomic reactors at Windscale. A mistake had been made in the
specifications for the concrete with the result that the main walls
were porous to radioactivity, and had to be completely rebuilt.
When the *Daily Express* asked for Whitehall's reaction to the

story, the chief civil servant in the ministry involved contacted the then editor and warned him that publication would lead to a prosecution under the Official Secrets Act. The *Daily Express* did not publish. A year later after the walls had been repaired at enormous cost, the ban on the story was reluctantly removed. The civil servant concerned subsequently told Chapman Pincher with considerable amusement that Official Secrets Act charges could never have been laid and that he was astonished how easily the *Daily Express* had given in.[6]

In 1958 another major *Express* scoop was held up by Official Secrets Act pressures when Chapman Pincher learned that a swing-wing aeroplane developed by Dr Barnes Wallis had been scrapped following the cancellation of the contract by the Ministry of Defence. High level attempts to prevent publication of the news were made, accompanied by dark hints of prosecution. After some delay, the *Express* printed the story, Pincher having successfully argued that the aircraft could hardly be secret when it had been abandoned. There was no prosecution.[7]

Aircraft stories seem particularly vulnerable to bizarre applications of the Official Secrets Act. Specialist aviation journalists have often complained that information which is still classified in Britain is freely published in technical journals abroad, and there is considerable resentment at the way in which 'Top Secrets' about civil and military aeroplanes are suddenly made public at each annual Farnborough Air Show.

One unusual suppression of an aircraft story occurred in September 1956 when, at the height of the Cold War, a Russian Air Force General, Alexei Blagoveschensky, made an official visit to Britain. During the course of his tour he was invited to fly the RAF's 'top secret' Hawker Hunter Mark 7 powered by the even more secret Rolls Royce Avon 122 jet engine. Although this high-ranking member of the Soviet defence establishment was allowed to handle the Hawker Hunter's controls in flight and ask questions about its performance, all details of the aircraft remained classified to British aviation journalists for another two years.[8]

An attempt by a newspaper to challenge Farnborough 'secrets' was thwarted in 1957 just two weeks before the show began. A British invention known as 'the Flying Bedstead' was practising its vertical take-off and landing trials in preparation for Farnborough when an acute *Daily Sketch* photographer used his telescopic lens to get a picture of the device. Publication of these pictures was stopped by the Ministry of Aviation under threat of prosecution on Official Secrets Act charges. The *Sketch* withheld its scoop. A fortnight later the Minister of Aviation, Mr Duncan Sandys, got full publicity from his air-show speech revealing the Flying Bedstead, pictures of which were issued to all the newspapers. Mr Sandys has subsequently said that the *Daily Sketch* would probably not have been prosecuted had they gone ahead with their scoop because no actual damage would have been done by the premature publication.[9]

During the 1950s application of the Official Secrets Acts with regard to the Press was generally confined to matters relating to defence and national security, even though a good many of the applications were straining the definition of those terms to absurdity. The 1960s, however, saw a considerable extension of the Official Secrets Act's use to suppress information which was merely embarrassing.

In 1965 Mr Chapman Pincher was personally threatened with charges under the Official Secrets Act by Mr George Wigg, then the Labour Government's Minister responsible for Security. The incident concerned some Cabinet papers which had been carelessly left on a table at Prunier's Restaurant in London by the Housing Minister, Mr Richard Crossman. After these papers had been brought to the *Daily Express* by a member of the public, Chapman Pincher telephoned Wigg, who first urged the *Express* to drop the story on grounds of 'charity'. When this ruse failed, Wigg mentioned the possibility of a prosecution under the Official Secrets Act if the contents of the documents were reported. The *Express* ran a story on the loss of the papers but only made an oblique reference to their subject matter. The documents in fact referred to nothing more secret than discussions about housing but the reason for Mr Wigg's sensitivity was probably the disclosure in the text that there had been a major disagreement between Crossman and the Home Secretary Mr Roy Jenkins over the question of housing coloured immigrants.[10] This attempt by Mr George Wigg to silence Mr Chapman Pincher was by no means the only one of its kind during the six years of Harold Wilson's government. Although previous Conservative administrations have also used the Official Secrets Act to coerce journalists into stifling inconvenient information, it is generally agreed in Fleet

Street that there was a substantial increase during the Labour years of Official Secrets Act pressures being used against newspapers and television companies.

One major example of this trend occurred in 1965 when the *Sunday Times* appointed Mr Anthony Howard, the former political columnist of the *New Statesman,* to be their 'Whitehall Correspondent'. In a leading article announcing the appointment the *Sunday Times* boldly declared 'National security alone excepted, it is the job of newspapers to publish the secret matters of politics, whether the secrets are the secrets of the Cabinet, of Parliament, or of the Civil Service'. The leader went on to claim that a journalistic innovation of this kind was necessary because power had shifted away from ministers and towards the hitherto unreported Civil Service machine. It suggested that Mr Howard's column would prove to be 'a major departure, and one which if it is successful will change British newspaper practice in an important way'.

Mr Howard got off to a flying start in his new role as the divulger of Whitehall's secrets, for on 21 February 1965 his first article, headlined A CLASH HAS BEEN ARRANGED, revealed that there were major differences of opinion on economic policy between two powerful civil servants, Sir Richard Clarke of the Treasury and Mr Douglas Allen of the newly created Department of Economic Affairs. Although the disclosures in this admirably researched story were doubtless embarrassing to the named civil servants and their ministers, nothing that was published could conceivably have affected 'the national interest' let alone 'national security'. All that had happened was that the *Sunday Times* had given its readers an extremely interesting insight into the friction between two government officials and their respective departments.

Unfortunately, the Labour Government did not look favourably upon this journalistic development. The *Sunday Times* appointment of a Whitehall correspondent was discussed in Cabinet. Soon afterwards, the Civil Service department despatched a circular to all Government offices which laid down the rule that no officials were to speak to Mr Howard. A similar rubric was sent round to all ministers and junior ministers, which in addition to banning interviews with Mr Howard, ordained that members of the government were not to see journalists except in the presence of a Ministry Press Officer. This Press Officer was to send a record of what was said at such meetings to Colonel George Wigg, the Minister responsible for Security.

In the face of these draconian measures, Mr Anthony Howard's attempts to become a probing 'Whitehall Correspondent' bore forth the most disappointing of journalistic fruits. Less than a year after the launching of its 'major departure' the *Sunday Times* terminated their experiment of having a 'Whitehall Correspondent' and Mr Howard switched to the *Observer,* as head of their Washington office. The power of the Press had been skilfully defeated by the power of the Whitehall suppress.

From the mid-1960s onwards, there were several occasions when the Official Secrets Act was used to stifle journalistic enquiries on subjects infinitely more trivial than those which the ill-fated Whitehall correspondent of the *Sunday Times* was trying to cover. Here are one or two examples:

In 1964, after an Aberdeen typhoid epidemic had caused £670,000 worth of tins of corned beef to be withdrawn from circulation, newspapers wanted to know where these tins had been stock-piled. The information was classified as 'secret' by the Ministry of Health and journalists had their enquiries thwarted by mentions of the Official Secrets Acts.[11]

The same obstructive technique was applied in December 1965 when reporters tried to discover facts about the membership and the activity of the Winter Emergency Committee. This had been sent up by the Prime Minister, Mr Harold Wilson, in the previous month with a fanfare of publicity, and given the job of preventing the breakdown of gas and electricity supplies during cold spells. Requests for information on its work were blocked by references to the Official Secrets Acts.[12]

In December 1966 a girl journalist from the *London Evening News* was trying to find out what use the Ministry of Defence made of land at Kidbrooke, which the Greater London Council wanted to use for a big housing scheme. Her inquiries were halted when a Ministry Official warned her that she might be committing an offence under the Official Secrets Acts.[13]

Later that month, Miss Anne Sharpley, a feature writer on the *Evening Standard,* asked the Ministry of Defence if she could borrow a copy of the Services' Manual for Survival. She was about to appear on a radio programme 'Desert Island Discs' and wished to make some informed comments about life as a castaway. The

Ministry refused her request on the grounds that the manual was classified and that quoting from it would constitute an offence under the Official Secrets Acts. The resourceful Miss Sharpley obtained a similar survival manual from the US Department of Defense, and quoted from that instead.[14]

One of the last recorded cases of the Official Secrets Acts being used to harass journalistic enquiries occurred on 5 March 1970, just twelve days before the Scott Report prosecutions were announced. The incident arose out of an advertisement in the columns of the pacifist newsletter *Peace News* which said the editors were seeking information on 'all aspects of Britain's military complex . . . to range from ex-CD shelters, research contracts and arms dumps'.[15] The request was published in hopes of obtaining additional material for a pamphlet *Peace News* was intending to produce giving a comprehensive list of military and military research establishments in Britain. Since this information is in any case freely available, it is difficult to understand what *Peace News* was trying to achieve by this somewhat naive appeal to its readers. As a quest for new information it was certainly a failure, since the paper received no worthwhile replies on the subject. However, the security services evidently took the matter seriously, for two Scotland Yard detectives from the Special Branch called on the editors of *Peace News*, informed them that the advertisement violated the Official Secrets Acts, and asked for an undertaking that it would not be published again. The editors spiritedly declined to give any such undertaking whereupon the senior police officer, Detective Inspector Dixon, gave a 'friendly warning' that 'if you continue then consideration may be given to taking proceedings against you'.[16] Needless to say, no proceedings were, or ever could have been taken.

Absurdities like some of those quoted above are doubtless due to nothing more sinister than excessive zeal on the part of security advisers or excessive caution on the part of Ministry public relations officials, but the blame should not be put entirely on their shoulders since the whole system of government information leans towards over-secrecy. The few examples of Official Secrets Act obstruction given in this chapter are but the tip of the iceberg which so often leaves information-seeking journalists out in the cold. The disagreeable truth is that the entire government machine uses the Official Secrets Acts as a law of administrative convenience to conceal from the public harmless facts whose disclosure might conceivably result in unfavourable publicity for the Whitehall establishment. Even ministers, whose political upbringings should cause them to be more enlightened on such matters, have been known to use the Official Secrets Act for their own purposes – as when Mr George Brown, then the Minister in charge of the Department of Economic Affairs, threatened the *Sunday Telegraph* in August 1965 with the Official Secrets Acts when it was about to publish advance details of the National Economic Plan.[17]

Mr Brown made another personal plea with the law in February 1968 when as Foreign Secretary he warned the Chairman of Granada Television, Mr Sidney Bernstein, that direct contact with the defected Foreign Office diplomat Harold Philby in Moscow on the subject of espionage might amount to an offence under the Official Secrets Acts.[18]

Mention of the Philby affair brings this account to the second major abuse of the Official Secrets Act in regard to the Press, namely the present-day operation of the D-notice system. This used to be a voluntary censorship scheme by which the Press could be forewarned against disclosing information which damaged national security. The organization which originally administered the system was set up in 1912 and was known as the Admiralty, War Office and Press Committee. Sending out letters of guidance to newspapers whenever sensitive security secrets needed to be protected, this body worked well for some thirty-seven years until the outbreak of the Second World War when a more formal system of mandatory censorship was needed. When peace returned, Rear Admiral Sir George Thompson followed up his successful wartime role of Chief Press Censor by becoming Secretary of a reconstituted Services, Press and Broadcasting Committee. Its method of operation was to issue D- or Defence-notices which warned editors against publishing security-breaking stories which would contravene the Official Secrets Acts. The system worked well for the first fifteen years of the Committee's existence, because Sir George Thompson operated it in a strictly impartial way. From an independent office in Belgrave Square he steered a fair course between the needs of national security and the demands of the Press to publish as much information as possible. But by the 1960s the

D-notice system began to break down, its demise being marked by a series of illustrative incidents.

In May 1961, just before the trial of the Russian KGB spy George Blake, a D-notice was sent round urging the Press to withhold several details of the case. This was duly done, but foreign newspapers were far less co-operative and published stories revealing that Blake had been a double agent responsible for the betrayal of several British agents abroad. A few days later a second D-notice was issued requesting British newspapers not to reproduce what was in those foreign journals, even though many of them were openly on sale in Britain. This was an obvious attempt to prevent domestic embarrassment, for Britain's enemies must have been able to buy the foreign press and so there could have been no question of national security being jeopardised by British publication. The row over the issue of the D-notices in this case led to several questions in Parliament, and seriously damaged the reputation of the system. Further harm was done in July 1961 by the issue of a D-notice headed 'Classified Weapons and Equipment', which attempted to prevent the Press from disclosing details about any military equipment, news of which had not been officially released. After widespread protests, the matter was referred to the Radcliffe Committee on Security Procedure, which agreed that this particular D-notice had been very badly worded and ordered suitable modifications. There were a succession of minor frictions over D-notices throughout the early 1960s, among them an impassioned complaint by the editor of the magazine *Aeronautics* over alleged censorship in 1962, and in 1964 a row over a D-notice banning the publication of the names of the heads of MI5 and MI6. This was made to apply even after the names of Sir Dick White and Sir Roger Holles had been printed in a best-selling American book, and serialised in magazines around the world. When one of these intelligence chiefs retired, the *Daily Express* sought permission to take a photograph of the back of his head receding into oblivion, proposing to publish it with a caption about the departure of this anonymous man leaving with a load of secrets he could never tell. The D-notice on the non-identification of the security services was even extended to prevent this innocuous journalistic coup.

Such developments of D-notices inevitably tempt minor officials to try and use censorship for their own convenience. One absurd but indicative example of this came in 1966 after some trees in Greenwich Park had been blown down in a gale. A reporter from the *South East London Mercury* asked the parks superintendent about the incident. 'I cannot give you any information' replied the superintendent, 'because it would contravene D-notices and the Official Secrets Act'. As John Gordon wittily put it in his *Sunday Express* column a few days later: 'Obviously Tree-notices have now been added to D-notices.'[19]

After a succession of similar, if less comic, incidents it came as no surprise that one respected peer, Lord Balfour of Inchrye, should tell the House of Lords that he did not believe there was a minister in the Government who could put his hand on his heart and say he did not know of instances where D-notices 'have been used to cloak individual or departmental failures'.[20]

This comment was re-echoed in 1965 when a joint working party of newspaper representatives and members of the law reform organisation 'Justice', under the Chairmanship of Lord Shawcross, claimed that D-notices were sometimes used 'to protect a department rather than national security'.[21]

The worst example of D-notices being used as devices to conceal failure came in 1967 over the Philby affair. Just before the *Sunday Times* and the *Observer* published their detailed reports on the activities of the defected Foreign Office diplomat Harold Philby, the D-notice committee issued two major notices which virtually prohibited the publication of information about Philby, Burgess, Maclean or any other traitors living abroad unless official clearance had first been given. Since the Russians were only too well aware of the exact roles of these defectors, the attempts to muzzle publication could only have been made to cover up from British newspaper readers the magnitude of the Foreign Office's security blunders. Fortunately the editors of the *Sunday Times* and the *Observer* took a robust approach to the attempted suppression, and both papers went ahead and published their stories with only minor excisions. They were not prosecuted under the Official Secrets Act.

Shortly before the abortive Philby censorship there had been a national uproar over D-notices and a *Daily Express* scoop on cable vetting. This saga can be said to have amounted to the most bizarre abuse of security procedures ever attempted against the

Press by any British government, and it marked the beginning of the end of the D-notice system.

The story began on 16 February 1967 when a former employee of Commercial Cables and Western Union called on Mr Chapman Pincher in the *Daily Express* offices. This informant, a Mr Robert Lawson, claimed that copies of all overseas cables were collected daily by van from the cable companies' offices and taken to the Ministry of Defence. They were returned forty-eight hours later. Mr Lawson thought that the operation had been routine practice for at least two years. On attempting to check the story, Chapman Pincher received substantial confirmation as to its authenticity from a GPO spokesman. Pincher's next move was to telephone the Secretary of the D-notice committee Colonel Leslie G. Lohan to ask whether D-notices would apply to a story on GPO telegrams being collected and sent to the Ministry of Defence. The answer was that D-notices would not apply. When the Ministry of Defence learned that the *Daily Express* was considering publishing a story on cable interception, various Whitehall officials conferred together at the Foreign Office and decided that every effort must be made to prevent such a leak. Colonel Lohan was not invited to this conference, but instead was given somewhat confusing instructions on the telephone by Security Service and Foreign Office officials about the need to get the story suppressed. As a result of these instructions Lohan and Pincher, who were long-standing acquaintances, lunched together on Monday 20 February at *L'Ecu de France* in Jermyn Street. During the meal Lohan produced two D-notices from his pocket but agreed that one of them did not apply and the other was 'so bloody marginal we can put it away'. However, Lohan did make a definite personal request for Pincher to ask the editor of the *Daily Express* on behalf of the Government not to print the story for reasons of security.

Mr Derek Marks, the editor of the *Express*, was told of Lohan's plea but decided that the official pressures to get the story suppressed were attempts to avoid political embarrassment. Assured that D-notices were not involved, Marks took the decision to publish.

On 21 February the *Express* ran the story as its front page lead, headlined: CABLE VETTING SENSATION – SECURITY CHECK ON PRIVATE MESSAGES OUT OF BRITAIN. Chapman Pincher's account referred to the vetting process as 'The Big Brother intrusion into privacy' and said that its purpose was 'to provide intelligence for the security, military, and criminal investigation departments. A regular check on cables may reveal the activities of persons or organisations suspected of operating against the national interest'. The story continued : 'But while the cables are being vetted there is nothing to prevent information being passed to the Exchequer, the Board of Trade, or any other interested department.'

In the House of Commons on the same afternoon that the *Express* story appeared, the Prime Minister Mr Harold Wilson described the story as 'sensationalised and inaccurate' and added 'What I am concerned with today is a clear breach of two D-notices despite the fact that the newspaper concerned was repeatedly warned that it would be contravening the notice'.

This prime ministerial accusation was resoundingly refuted by the *Daily Express* the following morning in a story giving details of the conversations between Lohan and Pincher. The Leader of the Opposition, Mr Edward Heath, took up the case and pressed for an enquiry. Mr Wilson then changed his original charge of 'a clear breach of two D-notices' to 'a breach of the long standing D-notice convention' and later to 'a breach of the whole D-notice procedure'. He suggested that the D-notice Committee should be convened to a special meeting to discuss the dispute between the Government and the *Daily Express*. This recommendation provoked Mr Lee Howard the editor of the *Daily Mirror,* into resigning from his position as the national newspapers' representative on the committee. Describing the plan as 'a gross abuse of the D-notice Committee', he wrote : 'I know of no D-notice which would have any direct bearing on the story published by Mr Chapman Pincher in the *Daily Express*. If no such notice exists, as I believe, I cannot see what possible function the committee can fulfil in considering this dispute between a most reputable journalist and a disapproving Government.' This resignation resulted in the Prime Minister setting up a Privy Councillors' committee of enquiry consisting of Lord Radcliffe, a former Lord Justice of Appeal, the Right Hon. Emmanuel Shinwell MP and the Right Hon. Selwyn Lloyd MP. After hearing a mass of evidence, the Radcliffe Report gave its verdict clearing the *Daily Express* of all the Prime Minister's charges. Specifically the report said Pincher's story was 'not inaccurate', that 'it would not be right to say that the article amounted to a breach of the D-notices' and that there was 'no evidence to indicate that the decision to publish was taken with a deliberate intention of evading or defying the D-notice procedure'.

Instead of accepting the umpires' decision, the Government issued a White Paper repudiating the Radcliffe Report. This White Paper again said that the *Express* story had been 'sensationalised and inaccurate' and that the case 'fell within the ambit of D-notices'. The document also claimed that the effect of the disclosures had been 'to cause damage, potentially grave, the consequences of which cannot even now be fully assessed'. Both the White Paper and the Radcliffe Report were published on 13 June, and on that afternoon in Parliament Mr Wilson refused to retract his earlier allegations against the *Express* and stood by the conclusions in his White Paper.

The next day virtually every newspaper condemned the Prime Minister for refusing to accept Radcliffe's findings, and an emergency debate on the affair was scheduled for 22 June. This acrimonious and inconclusive debate ended with a solid party majority for the Prime Minister but not before Mr Wilson had made an attack on the integrity of Colonel Lohan, referring to the Secretary's 'over-close association with journalists especially with Mr Chapman Pincher'. The Prime Minister finally announced that Colonel Lohan had never been given full positive vetting and was resigning from his post. On this astonishing note of character assassination, which was largely repudiated by a subsequent Civil Service enquiry, Mr Wilson sat down. The whole affair had been an outrageous example of the desperate lengths to which Government is prepared to stretch official secrecy in order to get its own way on an embarrassing issue.

After the dismissal of Colonel Lohan in June 1967, the new Secretary appointed to the Press, Services, and Broadcasting Committee was Vice-Admiral Sir Norman Denning. Arriving at a difficult time to a job which demands the highest standards of impartiality in deciding between the interests of the press and the interests of government departments Denning has so far done little to win the confidence of journalists. One of his first public comments was that 'other countries are very envious of our D-notice system', which may well be true of foreign governments but is certainly not true of a single foreign newspaper in the free world. It is also unfortunate that he should have accepted an office and a staff inside the Ministry of Defence, a sharp contrast with his predecessor's insistence on an administrative base which was physically and psychologically independent of both Whitehall and Fleet Street. Finally there has been considerable criticism of some of Denning's rulings, of which perhaps the most controversial was his guidance to the *Sunday Telegraph* in the Scott Report case (see Chapter 8).

It is however, a matter only of academic interest whether the disrepute into which D-notices have fallen is due to any short-comings of the Secretary, the bad atmosphere left by the cable-vetting affair, the increased censorship pressures from Whitehall or the submissive concessions to those pressures by members of the committee. All that really matters is that confidence in the original voluntary system has broken down. Today D-notices are a com-pulsory extension of the Official Secrets Acts, and all available evidence suggests that they are used just as unfairly as the Act itself in suppressing non-secret information which may prove embar-rassing to the Government of the day.

With the Official Secrets Acts providing the foundation for D-notices, hints of prosecution, obstructions to reporters' en-quiries, and actual prosecutions of newspapers, it can be seen that the Press is finding it increasingly difficult to co-exist with this much misused legislation.

But although direct official action always causes the loudest journalistic protests, ironically it is the indirect action of the law on officials which does most damage to Press freedom. Under modern conditions in the Civil Service, the Official Secrets Acts successfully dry up all potential sources of government information except for the authorised handout. By making all government ser-vants sign an Official Secrets Acts declaration form (which quotes Section 2 of the 1911 Act) and by constantly reminding them of the strictures of the law in circulars and directives, a Trappist-like vow of silence is effectively imposed throughout Whitehall. This vow is made to extend beyond retirement, beyond all matters bearing the slightest relevance to national security, and beyond common sense. The overall effect of having the Official Secrets Acts dangling like a sword of Damocles above the head of every minor bureaucrat is that Britain today has the most closed government in the free world, a situation which seriously hinders the legitimate activities of a free press.

It is interesting to trace the application of the law that has brought about this state of affairs. The first prosecution of an official or ex-official for communicating information to the Press took place in December 1926 when a retired Governor of Pentonville Prison, Major F. W. Blake, was charged under Section 2 in connection with some articles in the *London Evening News*.

Under the headline WHAT BYWATERS SAID TO ME, Blake had written a story of the last-minute confession alleged to have been made to him as Governor by the condemned murderer Bywaters a few minutes before the execution. The prosecution said these revelations were in 'execrably bad taste', and should not have been made without authority. The defence argued that Official Secrets Act legislation only covered disclosures prejudicial to the safety and interests of the state. These latter arguments did not convince the court, and Major Blake was found guilty and fined two hundred and fifty pounds.

During the next quarter of a century there were several minor cases involving officials or ex-officials who had leaked stories to the press. Of these the most important was the *Isis* case of 1958. This *cause célèbre* arose out of an article headlined FRONTIER INCIDENTS EXPOSURE which was published in the Oxford University undergraduate magazine *Isis* on 26 February 1958. Its authors were twenty-two-year-old Paul Thompson of Corpus Christi College and twenty-four-year-old William Miller of Lincoln College, both of whom had done National Service in the Royal Navy between 1953 and 1955. Their *Isis* story claimed that British forces on the Russian frontiers sometimes went to 'extraordinary lengths of deception' in provoking Soviet ships and aircraft in order to tape-record the Russian commands during these incidents. The article stated that monitoring stations all along the frontier were recording 'the least squeak from Russian transmitters – ships, tanks, aeroplanes, troops and control stations' and added that 'British embassies usually contain monitoring spies'. Apart from a description of how a Royal Navy patrol boat had on one occasion provoked the Russian fleet by sailing too close, there were no other significant disclosures in the text. However, it was clear even from these modest indiscretions that the authors could only have acquired their knowledge as a result of their National Service duties.

The article created no particular interest when *Isis* was first published in Oxford, but a few days later it was taken up by the national press* and followed up by questions in the House of Commons. Amidst mounting excitement, Special Branch detectives carried out an investigation in Oxford and questioned a number of undergraduates. Following these enquiries Thompson and Miller were summonsed under a variety of Official Secrets Act charges and in due course appeared at the Old Bailey before Lord Chief Justice Goddard. At the request of the Solicitor-General who prosecuted, most of the trial was heard in camera, the proceedings ending when the undergraduates pleaded guilty to one of the charges under the ubiquitous Section 2 in return for the dropping of all other charges. Passing judgment, Lord Goddard described the undergraduates' action as 'youthful folly', but nevertheless sentenced each of them to three months' imprisonment. Perhaps the most pertinent comment on the affair came from the *Observer*, which said in an editorial of 23 March 1958 'To invoke the Official Secrets Acts in such a case is surely the perfect example of crushing a butterfly upon a wheel'.

Despite the occasional drama like the *Isis* case, actual prosecutions of officials or ex-officials are almost as rare as prosecutions against journalists. In both categories the true obstacle to the dissemination of information is the deterrent rather than the active effect of the Official Secrets Acts.

Civil servants are made so acutely aware of the Act from the day they join the Government payroll that specific threats of its use would hardly seem necessary. Yet sharp reminders of Section 2 are not infrequently issued in Whitehall by establishment circulars and directives, particularly if leaks have been appearing in the Press. In the event of a highly embarrassing indiscretion, a department puts into operation 'the leak procedure'. This is a process whereby inter-departmental security officials visit all the civil servants who had access to the material leaked and after citing the Official Secrets Acts ask them whether they had been in recent contact with any journalists from the newspaper which published the offending story. Needless to say the culprits do not give them-

*Ironically the only reason why the story was noticed by the national press at all was because William Miller visited the offices of the *News Chronicle* to be interviewed for a job and personally showed the editor the *Isis* article which he had just published.

selves away in the purely formal interviews, so the exercise is normally one of future protection rather than present detection, but the overall effect is to increase the already excessive emphasis on office secrecy. In recent years the leak procedure has been operated in such unlikely places as the Ministries of Agriculture, Public Building and Works, and Transport; locations which in themselves give further indications of the way in which the Official Secrets Acts are now stretched to cover matters totally unconnected with national security.

Once in a while, internal threats of Official Secrets Acts prosecutions against Civil Servants become public knowledge. There was a major controversy over one such threat in 1938 when the General Secretary of the Civil Service Clerical Association Mr W. J. Brown publicly claimed that a government department had tried to use the Official Secrets Act to prevent the Association from tendering relevant evidence on a case affecting the working conditions of Civil Servants. Mr Brown raised the issue in an emergency debate at the Association's conference in Margate on 10 May 1938, saying:

It is common knowledge that government departments have recently threatened journalists with the use of the Official Secrets Act in order to prevent them from publishing facts which the Government wanted to suppress. It is not commonly known, and I make it public for the first time, that at least one department of the Civil Service has sought to use the Official Secrets Act to prevent us tendering relevant evidence on a case affecting the conditions of Civil Servants whom we are representing. We received the letter threatening us with the invocation of the Official Secrets Act. We replied to that threatening letter that unless the letter were withdrawn and burnt immediately we should publish it to the world and challenge the department concerned publicly to put us in the dock. I will not give you the name of the department because the matter has been settled by the burning of the correspondence. But it is significant of the growth of this repressive tendency of Government that any department could ever have contemplated the sending of such a letter. I have warned them privately that next time they will be given no opportunity of withdrawal or the burning of the letter. It will be published as soon as received, and we shall insist on being prosecuted if for no other reason than to mobilize the public conscience on this sort of thing.[22]

Despite this bold exposure in 1938, evidence suggests that attempted suppressions of internal Civil Service freedom by means of the Official Secrets Acts still occur today.

Customs officers at their 1966 annual conference protested that they had been threatened with prosecution under the Official Secrets Act if they described their work conditions to journalists[23]; prison officers who in 1968 talked to the Press about the poor quality of their accommodation were warned of possible action against them[24]; and a member of the Highlands and Islands Development Board was sacked and warned of Official Secrets Acts action against him after he had written to *The Times* criticising a £150 million industrial project for the Moray Firth.[25] There appears to be only one recently recorded case of an ex-Civil Servant who called the authorities bluff on the Official Secrets Act. He was Mr Robin Page, a twenty-six-year-old special investigator working for the Supplementary Benefits Commission who in 1969 wrote a series of pseudonymous articles for the *Spectator* in which he disclosed extensive Welfare State frauds. Although clearly in breach of his terms of employment, Mr Page appeared to have done the State some service by his revelations as the Department of Social Security increased its staff of special investigators by one hundred inspectors soon after the articles appeared. Nevertheless Mr Page was dismissed from his job, a punishment whose immediate effect was to bring him considerable publicity and a flood of invitations to write more articles about dishonest Welfare State scrounging. At this point an official from the Department of Social Security pointedly sent Mr Page by registered post a copy of the Official Secrets Act declaration form which he had signed in 1964. Mr Page retorted with a sharp letter to Mr Richard Crossman, the Minister responsible for the Supplementary Benefits Commission, which said:

I have received another letter from your department and am perturbed by its contents. It is a reminder of the Official Secrets Act and seems to be another attempt to intimidate me in an effort to suppress the sorry state of your department. It does however illustrate yet again how the Official Secrets Act and staff rules can be used against the interests of State and public.[26]

Soon after despatching this communication, Mr Page wrote a further series of articles on Social Security frauds under his own name for the *News of the World*. He was not prosecuted under the Official Secrets Act, although some of his disclosures clearly amounted to a technical breach of Section 2.

Unfortunately, Whitehall Hampdens like Mr Robin Page are all too rare. Most British civil servants have a pathological fear of discussing their work with journalists, and refuse to answer any direct enquiries other than those filtered through the Ministry Press Office. This clam-like silence even extends to outside government contractors. The standard Ministry of Transport business contracts contain clauses prohibiting any discussion of the work involved with unauthorised persons, and emphasise that only the Minister may make disclosure of such parts of the contract as he thinks fit. These sort of regulations, together with the enforcement of the Official Secrets Act itself, are in sharp contrast with the rules governing press enquiries in other democracies. In the USA for example, the Freedom of Information Act (1967) entitles anyone to see government files subject only to nine specific exceptions covering such things as defence, foreign policy, trade secrets and personal privacy. Sweden has similar legislation permitting citizens to inspect official records. No other country in the free world makes routine civil service information as inaccessible as does Britain. The dangers of this situation from the point of view of the Press have been admirably pointed out by Mr Edward Heath. In a speech of 8 January 1969, when he was still Leader of the Opposition, he said:

> The result of unnecessary secrecy is that it exalts 'the informed circle', the off-the-record comment, and the leak. The manipulation of news takes the place of news gathering. Such methods can only bring the present law on Official Secrets into disrepute. So we must review the Official Secrets Acts.[27]

These encouraging words from the present Prime Minister highlight the present sorry state of investigative political reporting by the British Press. 'News gathering' about the inner workings of government is a rare and almost unknown art in Fleet Street.

Anyone who doubts this should read the columns of prominent Washington journalists such as Mr Stewart Alsop, Mr Joseph Alsop, Mr Jack Anderson, Mr Tom Wicker, Mr Nicholas von Hoffman – and until recently Mr Drew Pearson and Mr Walter Lippmann. These reporters regularly dig out fascinating exclusive scoops about events and decisions at the heart of the US Government. They publish their revelations, however embarrassing to officialdom, without fear of reprisals. In this respect the American Press is a far better watchdog for the public interest than the British Press. When one compares the skills of transatlantic political correspondents in getting access to and printing detailed inside information about government affairs, with the similar skills of their British counterparts, one is forced to award Fleet Street's efforts with a most unfavourable rating. This may be partly due to the British 'lobby system', an arrangement whereby a carefully screened group of Westminster reporters are given regular off-the-record briefings by senior ministers and officials. Members of the lobby are under an obligation to keep secret the fact that such briefings are held and to avoid revealing the sources of their information. Since the information is usually given out on a collective basis, exclusive stories are unusual. The criticism most frequently made of this system is that the Lobby is spoon-fed with managed news of the sort which the Government wants to see publicised. As Mr Anthony Lewis, the London bureau chief of the *New York Times* percipiently wrote in 1967 :

> I think the central mechanism of political reporting in your newspapers has gone wrong. I refer to the Lobby system. That a selected group of trusted correspondents should have access to the leaders of the Government on a confidential basis sounds wise, but all too often the result is only to make captives of the reporters.

Whatever the virtues and vices of the Lobby system, it would not need to exist at all but for the iron curtain of official secrecy which separates Whitehall from Fleet Street. Political correspondents should not have to hang round the ante-rooms of government, gratefully awaiting a mass briefing at which they will be tossed a few scraps of (possibly doctored) information. This makes them, as Anthony Howard once put it 'the messenger-boys of British democracy'. Good reporters should instead be the detectives of democracy, issued with warrants to sleuth around for any information of bona fide public interest which is not prejudicial to national security, personal privacy, or budgetary secrecy. Such a concept of good reporting on public affairs is and may well remain a pipe dream. At present, the octopus of the Official Secrets Act and its attendant tentacles of D-notices, leak procedures, lobby rules and all the other information-suppressing devices combine to throttle investigative journalism. Whitehall remains closed and Fleet Street remains submissive. Only a major reform of the Official Secrets Act can lift the legal and psychological barriers which at present prevent the press from reporting on anything more than the tip of the iceberg of contemporary British government.

4

Historians and the Acts

In July 1935 Messrs Sotheby and Company offered for sale some letters written between 1800 and 1815 by the Duke of Wellington and Admiral Lord Nelson. The correspondence came from the original collection of Lord Stuart de Rothesay, who was British Ambassador in Paris during this period, and some of the letters gave details of the British espionage system in France just before Waterloo.

Although one hundred and twenty years had elapsed since the defeat of Napoleon, two days before the sale took place the Foreign Office announced that anyone who purchased the letters was liable to have them confiscated and to be prosecuted under the Official Secrets Acts. As a result of this warning the sale was stopped and the documents were possessed by the Foreign Office.

After considerable protests had been made, the Foreign Office explained in a statement that all documents giving details of British intelligence such as the names of spies and their operations were normally placed under seal and withheld from students 'even if all the persons concerned have been dead a century or more'.[1]

There can be few more eccentric uses of the Official Secrets Acts than its application to historical papers more than one hundred years old, yet even today the law is used to thwart bona fide authors in their desire to research and publish material which could do no possible harm to any living person or institution. Historians wishing to write about past events of this century are normally hindered by the thirty year rule (until 1966 it was the fifty year rule) which prohibits research in government records within thirty years of the present day. However, this arbitrary period may be extended in the case of 'sensitive' official documents, for example many papers relating to the Irish troubles around 1915 are still embargoed. When the *Observer Colour Magazine* recently commissioned an historian to write an article commemorating the fiftieth anniversary of "Bloody Sunday" (22 November 1920, the day on which IRA terrorists executed fifteen British officers in Dublin) permission was sought for the writer to study the Home Office records covering the episode. Although the events fell comfortably outside the thirty year epoch of censorship the reply came back: 'In special cases the Government reserves the right to withhold the documents for a longer period. In the case of Bloody Sunday it could be one hundred years.'[2]*

The only legal justification for such obstructions to historical research is that the information in the documents concerned is still covered by the Official Secrets Acts. Such an attitude contrasts sharply with the practice of the US Government, which conceals little from the contemporary historian. President Kennedy gave clear instructions on the open approach of America's public archives in a directive to the State Department on 6 December 1961 which said:

It is the policy of this administration to unfold the historical record as fast and as fully as is consistent with national security and with friendly relations with foreign nations. Accordingly I herewith request all departments, agencies, and libraries of the Government to collaborate actively with the Department of State in its efforts to prepare and publish the record of our diplomacy. In my view any official should have a clear and precise case involving the national interest before seeking to withhold from publication documents or papers fifteen or more years old.

If such a spirit prevailed on this side of the Atlantic, a great many living historians would have published their books in a more complete and accurate form, and there would never have been prosecutions of bona fide authors for disclosing antiquated official secrets in their historical accounts.

*Another 'special case' which has resulted in Government documents being withheld for one hundred years is the abdication of King Edward VIII. In January 1971 the Prime Minister, Mr Edward Heath, told the House of Commons that Cabinet papers relating to this episode would not be available to historians until the year 2036.

Like journalists, authors are rarely prosecuted but often intimidated by the Official Secrets Act. Indeed there have been only two occasions in which Official Secrets charges have resulted from books although instances when writers are obstructed by the law are legion.

The first prosecution of an author occurred in 1932 when Mr (now Sir) Compton Mackenzie was charged under Section 2 of the 1911 Act in connection with passages in his book *Greek Memories*. He was accused of 'having in his possession information he had obtained owing to his position as an officer in the Royal Marines during the 1914–18 war and wrongfully communicating that information to his publishers, Cassell & Company'. The charges centred on Mackenzie's revelations of the names of British Secret Service officers in Greece and his quotation of some Foreign Office telegrams. At the Magistrates' Court a considerable element of farce crept into the proceedings when it transpired that of the Secret Service officers whose names had been revealed one, by this time Consul-General in Alexandria, had recorded his period of Secret Service work in *Who's Who*; one was Deputy Keeper of the Victoria and Albert Museum; one had never been in the Secret Service at all; and one was dead. This information was extracted from a Crown witness, Major X of the Secret Service, who began his testimony by claiming that the future safety of Secret Service agents had been jeopardised by the book's publication. In the interval following the exposure of this claim, the Clerk of the Court remarked to Mr Compton Mackenzie that the nineteenth-century Guildhall courtroom in which the case was being heard had been used by Charles Dickens as the setting for his description of the fictional case of *Bardell v. Pickwick*. 'Bardell and Pickwick, eh?' replied the accused. 'Well I suppose this case must be the most ludicrous heard in it since.'[3]

However, the joke turned sour when Compton Mackenzie was advised by his lawyers to enter into a plea bargain with the Crown, a move which resulted in a fine of a hundred pounds, and an order to pay a hundred pounds towards the costs of the prosecution. Before passing sentence on 12 June 1933 at the Old Bailey, Mr Justice Hawke confirmed the inescapable rigours of Section 2 when he said to the defendant:

I cannot possibly conceive how your counsel can have given you any other advice than to plead guilty. The section is absolute in its terms and if a person offends against those terms, it matters not in what, it is against the laws of the country.[4]

The Mackenzie case had a number of disturbing features in addition to the absoluteness of the offence for it transpired that the Director of Intelligence from 1919–21, Sir Basil Thompson, had himself published a book, *The Allied Secret Service in Greece,* in 1931 which divulged material very similar to Mackenzie's *Greek Memories.* Indeed parts of Mackenzie's book completely contradicted Thompson's account of the same events, thus making the former Director of Intelligence look somewhat ridiculous. Because the actual harm done by Mackenzie's disclosures was non-existent, it is difficult to disagree with the widely held opinions at the time that the prosecution had been brought either for the settlement of scores, or to warn off more eminent Crown servants from making unauthorised disclosures about their wartime activities.

Although the Compton Mackenzie case was the most serious of its kind, there have been several incidents during the last twenty years involving authors in conflict with the Official Secrets Act.

One of these occurred in 1951 when Major Clayton Hutton, a former head of a War Office department specialising in inventing escape gadgets and methods wrote a book about his wartime experiences entitled *An Escape has been arranged.* The text dealt mainly with descriptions of ingenious escape devices such as fly-button compasses, handkerchief maps, and false boot-heels containing pen-knives. Some weeks before the book appeared Hutton's publishers were notified by a joint service security office that Official Secrets Act charges might be brought against them after publication. The author pointed out the absurdity of this threat saying 'practically every trick and gadget has been already publicised in one way or another. Many of the gadgets were sold after the war as Service surplus'.[5]

Nevertheless, the book was held up for nine years, during which the manuscript was subjected to prolonged scrutiny by both the War Office and the Air Ministry. Hutton was eventually asked to hand over various documents in his possession, including his draft manuscripts. He refused and a summons was issued against him for failing to return certain sketches, models, articles and documents to which, as a person holding office under the Crown, he had access. The summonses were later withdrawn because the documents concerned were returned, and Hutton's book appeared in a somewhat emasculated form in 1960.

Another military author who ran into trouble with the Official Secrets Act was Lieutenant-Colonel Alexander Scotland, a seventy-three-year-old ex-intelligence officer who in 1954 wrote *The London Cage,* a book of autobiographical experiences including mentions of his duties in command of a unit concerned with German prisoners. He delivered his manuscript to the War Office for vetting, and was refused leave to publish. No reasons for the refusal were given. The author expressed anger at this treatment, claiming that his book disclosed nothing which had not already come out in the evidence he had given at the trials of German war criminals.

In February 1955 Special Branch detectives swooped on Colonel Scotland's home in London, and armed with a search warrant issued under the Official Secrets Act, took away certain documents. After some stormy Parliamentary questions had been asked of the Home Secretary, Colonel Scotland was eventually given leave to publish, and the book appeared in 1957. However, the War Office insisted on the insertion of a notice in the book saying that the views and facts therein were entirely the authors' own responsibility and in no sense whatsoever those of the War Office.

Such harassment of authors seems to have become more muted during the 1960s, but there have certainly been occasional instances when the Official Secrets Acts were used to prevent former civil servants from contributing to historical records. One retired Foreign Office official, Mr John Alexander-Sinclair, has had the misfortune to be silenced on two occasions. In both cases his clash with the Official Secrets Act arose from his studies of the Stationery Office's publication *Documents on British Foreign Policy 1919–39.* On the first occasion the official history omitted an important incident in diplomatic negotiations about the future of Germany's Jews in 1938. Mr Alexander-Sinclair had himself played a minor but crucial role in the discussions on this subject with Rudolf Hess' Chief of Staff, Herr von Pfeffer. From his personal knowledge of the negotiations, Mr Alexander-Sinclair noticed 'an important gap' 'in the Foreign Office's authorised version. He wrote an article pointing out the omission in a reply to a review of the book by the *Economist*. The *Economist* accepted the article, but the Foreign Office warned him off its publication, citing the Official Secrets Act.

A similar warning came again to Mr Alexander-Sinclair a year later, in connection with another volume of *Documents on British Foreign Policy*. In Volume 9 of this opus Mr Alexander-Sinclair read about the siege of Tientsin by the Japanese in 1939 and was aware from his own experiences of the episode that the official account contained certain inaccuracies and omissions. Having been private secretary to the British Ambassador in Peking at this time, he wished to add to the pages in question a footnote which he said was 'vital to the understanding of the dénounement of the case'.[7] When he formally applied to the appropriate department of the Foreign Office for permission to write an article on this, he was advised by double negative that the authorities could not state such disclosure would not result in a prosecution under the Official Secrets Act.

In addition to specialised cases of suppression like those of Mr John Alexander-Sinclair, there is a steady flow of complaints from writers thwarted by the operation of the thirty or fifty year rule. Mr Anthony Heckstall-Smith, the author of *Tobruk, the Story of a Siege* and other Second World War histories, summed up the general frustration among contemporary historians in a letter on the thirty year rule to the *Daily Telegraph* of 7 May 1966 in which he said 'So long as it [the Official Secrets Act] exists in its present form, reputable historians can be severely restricted in their terms of reference and their work made the subject for acrimony, while the public is left wondering what to believe or what not to believe'.

Such complaints are frequently re-echoed, especially by authors who are asked to submit their work to the Cabinet Office for 'security clearance'.

One of these was Mr Edward Cookridge who in 1966 published *Inside SOE,* an official history of the wartime Special Operations Executive. During his research, the author received excellent co-operation from the American, French, Dutch, Danish, Norwegian and even German authorities, but was obstructed by the Official Secrets Act from seeing a considerable amount of British material, including identical records already made available to him by foreign governments. As Mr Cockridge himself put it in his book, 'the authorities still believe that twenty-five-year-old secrets of

SOE must be kept from the British public although any potential enemy can seek them out, for what they are worth, in official archives abroad'.

Strangely enough, the official historian of SOE, Mr M. R. D. Foot, seems to have come into just as much conflict with the Official Secrets Act as his unofficial rival. Mr Foot was commissioned by the Foreign Office to write an authorised account of SOE, and his book was published by the Government Stationery Office.* Yet despite the establishments blessing, the author was refused permission to interview certain 'sensitive' survivors of SOE and was denied access to many documents. At times these prohibitions were ludicrous, as when a manual of sabotage techniques was witheld in a triple locked strongroom in a guard building. Yet thousands of copies of this same manual had been parachuted into Europe during the war, and its text had been published, complete with illustrations, in the memoirs of a French Resistance hero in 1947. No wonder Mr Foot later wrote of his book 'Nothing secret can come out in these recollections for the author was trussed up in the Official Secrets Act before he was allowed near any secret archives.'†

A different annoyance which rubs salt into authors' wounds is the unevenness and sometimes downright unfairness with which the Official Secrets Act is applied to books.

In 1962 Mr Montgomery Hyde published *The Quiet Canadian*; an account of the work of Sir William Stephenson in British Intelligence. It contained a considerable amount of hitherto unrevealed information on espionage and counter-espionage and was described in the House of Commons as containing 'flagrant breaches of the Official Secrets Act'.[8] Dame Irene Ward, the Conservative MP for Tynemouth, asked the Prime Minister :

Is my right honourable friend aware that the whole of the Official Secrets Act is in the most appalling mess? Will he explain how it is that Mr Montgomery Hyde has an access to papers – presumably Foreign Office papers – how it is that Sir William Stephenson has been able to give all his experiences, while other people have their books refused? Why do some people feel that they must adhere to the Official Secrets Act and

SOE in France by M. R. D. Foot (HMSO) London 1966.
† *The Author*, Vol LXXXI No. 2, 1970.

others that they need not do so? It is a most terrible muddle and I think that everybody concerned would welcome a proper definition.[9]

The Prime Minister, Mr Harold Macmillan, declined to clarify the situation, but later explained that publication of *The Quiet Canadian* did not in fact prejudice current security in any way'.[10]

Another more political instance of uneven application of the Official Secrets Act was raised in the columns of the *Sunday Telegraph* on 29 October 1961, when the paper compared the treatment given by the authorities to two recently published biographies. One was Mr Iain Macleod's portrait of Neville Chamberlain in which the author, according to the story, 'had clearly been given a very free hand'. The other was a study of Lord Cherwell, *The Prof in Two Worlds* by the Earl of Birkenhead. In this book the chapter dealing with Mr R. A. Butler's attempt to introduce convertibility of the pound in 1952 had clearly been censored to prevent the disclosure of positions taken by ministers and civil servants in the controversy. Apart from a mention that Mr Butler had been Chancellor of the Exchequer at the time, no names were given to the figures who took up positions in the argument that raged throughout the upper levels of the Government on this issue. Mr Macleod's book on the other hand named numerous politicians and civil servants who had taken up positions on the question of Chamberlain's policy of Appeasement. The *Sunday Telegraph* commented 'The rules on historians are not being fairly applied. There is a feeling in some circles that the Official Secrets Acts are used to prevent publication of material not on security grounds, but because it might be embarrassing to ministers'.

This complaint, which could be made in a great many similar cases, brings this study to the delicate subject of politicians and the application of the Official Secrets Act.

5

The Privileged Politicians

All men are theoretically equal under the criminal law of this country, but under the law of Official Secrets, politicians are more equal than others.

This unspoken axiom of British public life has been built up over the years by a series of precedent-setting cases, rulings, and incidents. Taken as a whole they show clearly that the operation of the Official Secrets Act is governed by a highly favourable leniency towards ministers and Members of Parliament.

The double standard appears to date from 1916 when the Prime Minister Mr H. H. Asquith told the House of Commons that the Official Secrets Act definitely applied to Ministers of the Crown. This authoritative Prime Ministerial ruling was in reality a splendid piece of hypocrisy, for at the time Mr Asquith was writing daily letters to his mistress Miss Venetia Stanley packed with unauthorised disclosures about the most sensitive of Cabinet problems. However, the absurdity of this situation did not become apparent until the publication of the Stanley letters by Mr Roy Jenkins in his 1964 biography of Asquith, so it may be true to say that one of the first people to appreciate that there was one law for politicians and another for ordinary mortals was Mr Compton Mackenzie in 1932.

During his own Official Secrets prosecution for remarkably trivial disclosures about events during the First World War, Mackenzie's solicitor, Sir Reginald Lane Poole told him : 'You are taking this too lightly. It's very serious. I understand the Government intend to make an example of you in order to warn Lloyd George and Winston Churchill that they can go too far in using information they could only have acquired in office.'[1]

The following year there was another prosecution apparently designed to frighten indiscreet ex-ministers without taking action against them. It concerned no less a person than the then Leader of the Labour Opposition, Mr George Lansbury, who in 1934 was indirectly involved in a case about his own biography. The book in question was written by the Labour Leader's son Mr Edgar Lansbury and was entitled *George Lansbury, My Father*. It contained about four pages of quotations from a memorandum which Mr George Lansbury had placed before the Cabinet in May 1930 when he was First Commissioner of Works. These quotations consisted largely of Lansbury's own opinions on subjects such as unemployment, raising the school leaving age, special taxation for high incomes and the general policy of the Labour Government. Although the extracts were personal views there was no doubt that they had been directly quoted from a Cabinet paper which had been clearly stamped 'Property of His Britannic Majesty's Government'.

The author, Mr Edgar Lansbury, was prosecuted under Section 2 of the 1911 Act for receiving the memorandum. Although the Attorney-General Sir Thomas Inskip conceded that there was no suggestion that anything had been done with the intention of harming the interests of the state, the defendant was found guilty and fined ten pounds.

The strangest aspect of the affair was the failure to prosecute Mr George Lansbury himself, since only the ex-minister could have been responsible for the rather more culpable offence of 'communicating' the offending document to his filial biographer. The inference drawn from this curious omission was that ministerial leaks are given a high degree of immunity from Official Secrets Act prosecutions.

This bizarre doctrine of Official Secrecy was strengthened two years later in 1936 after the Colonial Secretary in the National Government Mr J. H. Thomas made an unauthorised disclosure of Budget secrets to a financier Alfred Bates. This had led to premature speculation on the Stock Exchange, and a special Tribunal of Inquiry under Mr Justice Porter found that Thomas had been responsible for the leak. Although Thomas resigned both from the Government and from the House of Commons, suggestions that Official Secrets Act prosecutions should be undertaken came from the Opposition and from Sir Alfred Butt, an MP criticised in the Tribunal's report.

Defending his decision not to prosecute Thomas, the Attorney-General Sir Donald Somervell explained: 'There cannot be an offence of receiving information under Section 2(2) unless an offence of an unauthorised communication under Section 2(1) is first proved. That unauthorised communication must in my opinion be deliberate.' In response to Opposition questions the Attorney-General pointed to the lack of evidence as to whether Thomas' disclosures had been deliberate and went on to say that it would not be an offence to receive secret information from a drunk civil servant: 'A communication might easily get out in circumstances which would not create an offence under Section 2(1) as the Act stands', commented Sir Donald. 'A person might get the information and make improper use of it, and as the Act stands it would not, I think, be an offence.'[2]

This unusual interpretation of Section 2 of the Official Secrets Act 1911 brought considerable criticism. The Labour leader, Mr Clement Attlee, said that the Attorney-General's statement 'opens a very, very wide door in the Official Secrets Act', and several MPs asked for a judicial ruling to clear up the doubts surrounding the case. Nevertheless neither Mr J. H. Thomas, nor the immediate beneficiaries of his indiscretion Messrs Butt and Bates, were ever charged.

In 1938 there occurred an episode known as 'The Sandys Storm' which clarified still further the privileged position of Members of Parliament under the Official Secrets Act. The central figure was Mr Duncan Sandys, then a thirty-year-old back-bench MP whose extra-parliamentary activities included being a Territorial Army Lieutenant in a regiment responsible for London's anti-aircraft defences. In the course of his military duties Mr Sandys became anxious about the inadequacies of these defences and decided he must speak to the Secretary of State for War about the shortage of 3.7 guns and the need for improved aiming techniques. The adjutant of the regiment, Captain Hogan, was in complete sympathy with Mr Sandys' anxieties and provided the young MP with precise details of the numbers and types of existing guns being used to protect London. Mr Sandys had a talk with the Secretary of State for War Mr Hore-Belisha during which the latter denied that there were any gaps in London's anti-aircraft defences. Angered by this ministerial whitewash, Mr Sandys sent the War Office a copy of a Parliamentary Question he was thinking of tabling on the subject. The text of this question revealed many of the figures and details which had been provided by Captain Hogan.

Mr Sandys' avowed purpose in making this move was simply to stir Hore-Belisha into action, for he claimed he had no intention of publicising the secrets in Parliament and was merely threatening to table a question in order to get more anti-aircraft guns. Unfortunately the Secretary of State for War did not see the matter in this light, and after being informed by his military advisers that highly secret information had been disclosed, he consulted the Attorney-General about a possible Official Secrets Act prosecution against Mr Sandys. The Attorney-General, Sir Donald Somervell, saw Mr Sandys, who claimed that during the interview he was threatened with a prosecution and told that he would be compelled to disclose the sources of his information by the powers of the Official Secrets Act. 'When I inquired what would be the consequences were I to refuse to comply with the request,' Mr Sandys later told Parliament, 'he [the Attorney-General] read me the text of Section 6 of the Official Secrets Act and pointed out that I might render myself liable to a term of imprisonment not exceeding two years'.[3] After Mr Sandys had revealed the details of his confrontation with the Attorney-General to the House of Commons, a parliamentary furore ensued. After some heated discussion the affair was referred to a Select Committee of the House, and this body was instructed to report on the immediate and wider aspects of the dispute.

The first Select Committee report, published in December 1938, enquired into the facts of the episode and concluded that the matter had been greatly exaggerated. Although all the principal participants in the dispute came in for a certain amount of evenly apportioned criticism, most members accepted the comment of the Prime Minister Mr Neville Chamberlain that the trouble had been due to 'a most extraordinary catalogue of misunderstandings.'[4] The Second Select Committee report published in June 1939 dealt with the more general topic of the application of the Official Secrets Act to Members of Parliament. The Committee thought it would be inadvisable to attempt to define with precision the immunity of prosecution under the Official Secrets Act to which Members of Parliament ought to be entitled. But it was concluded that: 'disclosures by Members of Parliament, during debates or proceedings in Parliament cannot be made the subject of proceedings under the Official Secrets Act' and that 'disclosures made between members directly relating to House of Commons business even though it did not take place in the House should be similarly protected'.[5] The committee urged that considerable flexibility should be given to the extension of parliamentary privileges to make them adaptable to varying conditions and new or unusual circumstances.

One significant piece of evidence given to this Select Committee came from Sir Gilbert Campion, the Clerk of the House of Commons, who put forward a new doctrine of parliamentary immunity under the Official Secrets Act when he said in his evidence on 15 March 1938:

A person who communicates official information to a person to whom he is not authorised to communicate it, commits no offence if the person to whom he discloses it is a person to whom it is his duty in the interests of the State to communicate it. It could be absurd to say that there would be a duty to give official information to any Member of Parliament, but I could imagine circumstances in which it would, in the interests of the State, be the duty of a person having information to communicate it to an MP although he was not authorised to do so.

This concept of the application of the Official Secrets Act to politicians was certainly allowed to give some immunity to Winston Churchill, who as a backbencher during the late 1930s received from official sources a great deal of confidential information which he used to alert Parliament to the dangers of Britain's unpreparedness for war. One of Churchill's sources was Mr Ralph Wigram, head of the Central Department of the Foreign Office. 'Like other officials of high rank, he spoke to me with complete confidence'.[6] Churchill later wrote of Wigram, a statement which at face value indicates that the future Prime Minister was in those days persistently flouting the Official Secrets Act.

Winston Churchill also showed a cavalier disregard for the Official Secrets Act during the preparation of his war memoirs. Immediately after the first volume of *The World Crisis* was published in 1923, questions were asked in Parliament about the unauthorised disclosures of Cabinet documents in the book. One backbencher, Captain O'Grady, went so far as to ask whether the Law Officers were going to be instructed to institute legal proceedings against persons using State secrets. The Prime Minister Mr Bonar Law, curtly replied: 'The remedy proposed does not appear to be practicable'.[7]

There was further controversy about possible breaches of the Official Secrets Act after Churchill began publishing his Second World War memoirs, but the position was clarified in a statement to Parliament by the Leader of the House, Mr Herbert Morrison, on 1 August 1946. After explaining that any former Crown Servants wishing to publish information which they had obtained in office were under an obligation to apply to the Secretary of the Cabinet, Mr Morrison explained that in considering such applications the Government would 'distinguish between the position of a former minister who has been responsible to Parliament and subject to public criticism and other former Crown servants who have not had a minister's responsibilities'.[8] Comparing the free hand given to books by Churchill to the restrictive measures taken against books by less celebrated Crown servants such as Colonel Scotland and Major Clayton Hutton,* it seems that Morrison's distinction between politicians and the rest of the public results in highly favourable treatment for the former.

Mr Herbert Morrison's ruling was again quoted in the House of Commons on 25 February 1960 when Mr Emmanuel Shinwell complained that extracts from Cabinet minutes, Foreign Office telegrams and other Government documents had appeared in *The Times'* serialised extracts of Sir Anthony Eden's memoirs. The Prime Minister. Mr Harold Macmillan replied that he had not recognised direct quotations from Cabinet minutes or Cabinet memoranda although the Eden memoirs did contain 'general references to the subject matter of Cabinet discussions' and 'extracts from other official documents'. Explaining that for actual quotations of state papers authority had to be given by the Queen on the advice of her Prime Minister, Mr Macmillan added: 'Sir Anthony Eden submitted the text of his book to me through the Secretary of the Cabinet. I did not regard the publication of these references and extracts as open to objection.'[9]

With the publication of the Eden memoirs the rules about ministerial discretion seem to have become substantially relaxed from

*See Chapter 4.

the days of the Lansbury case. Another clear breach of the Official Secrets Act during the 1960s concerned a contemporary political chronicle *The Fight for the Tory Leadership* by Randolph S. Churchill. In this book Mr Churchill referred to a memorandum dictated for Mr R. A. Butler on 14 October 1963 by Mr Harold Macmillan about the methods for choosing a new Prime Minister.[10] Of this memorandum the author wrote: 'It was of a magisterial character, but since officially it is a Cabinet paper it cannot be quoted here.' Nevertheless Mr Churchill went on to give a detailed summary of the document, and another part of his account made it clear that the paper had been shown to him by Mr Harold Macmillan. Needless to say, neither the author nor his eminent source were prosecuted under the Official Secrets Act.

One extraordinary interpretation of the rule about ex-ministers having to refer their books to the Cabinet Office for clearance occurred in 1967 when the Right Hon. Anthony Nutting, a former Minister of State in the Foreign Office, wrote his account of the Suez crisis entitled *No End of a Lesson*. Mr Nutting did not ask for access to official documents in preparing his book; instead he wrote from personal notes taken at the time of the crisis. At first he did not submit his manuscript to the Secretary of the Cabinet, but eventually did so under pressure when the book was in page proof form. The text contained several technical breaches of the Official Secrets Act including accounts of Cabinet meetings, conversations between the author and the Foreign Secretary and mentions of Foreign Office telegrams. The Cabinet Office censored the book but only to the extent of removing the names of the civil servants involved and obscuring the author's description of meetings so that it was not clear whether the discussions had taken place in Cabinet or at ministerial committees. All disclosures regarding the author's conversations with ministers were allowed to stand, and as a result particularly embarrassing material relating to privileged discussions with the Foreign Secretary Mr Selwyn Lloyd and the Prime Minister Sir Anthony Eden was freely published. Nevertheless no action was taken against Mr Anthony Nutting. As Professor Hugh Thomas has written of the episode: 'Therefore it can be said that the acts are not made to apply to politicians provided they accept the strictures of the Civil Service by the channel of the Cabinet Office.'[11]

With the advent of a new Labour Government in 1964 the possibility of extensive ministerial transgressions of the Official Secrets Act increased substantially, if only because at least five members of Mr Wilson's Cabinet declared their intention of writing books about their time in office. This threat of literary indiscretion worried some members of the Government so much that a special Cabinet committee was set up to discuss whether some mandatory form of censorship could be imposed on ex-ministers. But the discussions came to nothing and as a result the same agreeably loose Cabinet Office vetting procedures still apply today.

One Labour minister who kept a tape-recorded diary throughout his years as a minister was Mr Richard Crossman, now the editor of the *New Statesman*. He is currently working on his memoirs, which should make riveting reading if they are anything like as indiscreet as his weekly editorials. Mr Crossman's attitude to the Official Secrets Act can be summed up by the reports of an incident which took place at the *New Statesman*'s offices in September 1970. Apparently disturbed by the steady flow of Cabinet secrets which kept appearing in the *New Statesman*'s columns two Law Officers in the previous Labour Government, Sir Elwyn Jones and Sir Dingle Foot, formally called on Mr Crossman and asked if he was going to continue to breach the Official Secrets Act. Mr Crossman assured them that he would continue to do so at the rate of one secret per week, adding for good measure, 'You buy the paper and see.'

After the astonished lawyers had departed, Mr Crossman remarked, 'I know lawyers. My father was one. Their job is to suppress things. Mine is to reveal them.'[12]

Mr Crossman's attitude to the Official Secrets Act is today not regarded as outrageous. Politicians tend to be an indiscreet species, and once they are out of power they rarely endeavour to remain silent about anything other than those secrets which genuinely affect national security. Since the Labour Government left office in June 1970 we have seen a spate of ministerial indiscretions in newspaper articles and no doubt juicier revelations will follow when the more weighty Cabinet chroniclers produce their memoirs. There can be few objections to this practice since the 'secrets' these ex-ministers are disclosing are largely irrelevant to the safety or interests of the State. But is it too much to hope that the same generous interpretation of the Official Secrets Act for politicians will soon be applied to other members of the public?

6

A Law in Disrepute

One of the most damning indictments of the Official Secrets Act is to be found in the Civil Service's authoritative definition of an official secret. This first appeared in a directive headed 'Disclosure of Official Information'* which was circularised to all Government offices on 10 September 1957 by the then Secretary of the Cabinet, Sir Norman Brook. Paragraph 1 of this document stated that the procedures for preventing the unauthorised disclosure of official information had proved unsatisfactory and were being revised along new lines set out in the circular.

Paragraph 2 continued:

> The aim of these procedures, and your objective in adopting them, is to ensure that Crown Servants and former Crown Servants and in some cases persons outside the government service are aware that the publication of *any* official information which has not already officially been made public renders them liable to prosecution under the Official Secrets Acts.

After setting out the methods by which formal permission to release authorised government information might be obtained, Paragraph 3 stated: 'These arrangements apply to all information officially acquired and not only to secret information.'

This directive, which has been re-issued with minor amendments on several subsequent occasions, would surely make the original legislators of the Official Secrets Acts turn in their graves. A criminal statute intended to prohibit spying has now been manipulated by successive governments to the point where it pro-

*Establishment Circular No. 40/57.

hibits the disclosure of 'any official information which has not already been made public'. 'What further need have we of witnesses!' a critic of the law might justifiably exclaim after reading the circulars sent out by Sir Norman Brook and his successors.

But apologists for the Official Secrets Acts argue that the safeguard which prevents the law from falling into ridicule and contempt is Section 8 of the 1911 Act, which ordains that : 'A prosecution for an offence under this Act shall not be instituted except by or with the consent of the Attorney-General.' This consent is formal and is given in the shape of an official fiat, but it is given without reasons and depends entirely on the discretion of the Attorney-General of the day.

All Attorney-Generals no doubt endeavour to carry out impartially their quasi-judicial duties in giving or refusing their fiats for Official Secrets Acts prosecutions. But impartiality, like justice, must not only be done, it must be seen to be done. No outside observer will ever believe the pained protests of those members of the establishment* who claim that Law Officers scrupulously separate their political and judicial functions. The trouble with Attorney-Generals is that they are practising politicians, and as such they are always vulnerable to internal pressures from the Governments in which they serve. These pressures may come in the form of nods and winks from other ministers or much more likely in the shape of direct requests for prosecutions from the civil service departments which feel their secrets have been jeopardised. This places the Attorney-General in a most invidious position, for the very fact of a department declaring that some disclosure has prejudiced the public interest almost amounts to a *prima facie* case against the disclosers.

A study of Attorney-Generals' attitudes to Official Secrecy indicates that no hard and fast rules have ever applied, and that decision-making on prosecutions has been largely a matter of erratic administrative whim. At least five incumbents of the office never authorised any prosecutions at all, while Sir Donald Somervell, Sir Reginald Manningham-Buller and Sir Elwyn Jones between them brought more than a quarter of the prosecutions in the entire sixty-year history of the present Acts. Even when one examines the records of these last three prolific prosecutors, ano-

*Sir Hartley Shawcross and Sir Dingle Foot (both former law officers) are currently the most prominent propagators of this doubtful argument.

malies become quickly apparent. Sir Donald Somervell refused to institute proceedings against Mr J. H. Thomas MP and others over the budget leak of 1936; threatened Mr Duncan Sandys MP with prosecution over his Parliamentary questions on anti-aircraft defences in 1938; and the same year prosecuted the journalist Mr E. D. G. Lewis on the minor matter of the Cheshire police circular.

Sir Reginald Manningham-Buller initiated a major new development of the law of official secrets when he brought charges under Section 1 of the 1911 Act against six members of the Committee of One Hundred (a nuclear disarmament protest group) who had held a demonstration at Wethersfield Air Force base. These prosecutions were fiercely criticised by some elements in the legal profession on the grounds that Section 1 of the Official Secrets Act 1911 had always been limited to espionage on account of the assurances given to Parliament by previous Attorney-Generals. However, the courts found otherwise and sentenced the defendants to terms of imprisonment ranging from twelve months to eighteen months. In justifying his decision to approve these prosecutions Sir Reginald Manningham-Buller said in Parliament: 'In considering whether or not to prosecute I must direct my mind to the language and spirit of the Acts and not to what my predecessors said about them many years ago in an entirely different context.' Yet eighteen months later 'the language and spirit of the Acts' appeared to be violated in a far more serious way with the publication of the 'Spies for Peace' nuclear disarmament pamphlet entitled 'RSG 6'. This gave details of the system of government planned for Britain in the aftermath of a nuclear attack, pinpointing the locations of the 'Regional Seats of Government' which had been built as the headquarters for civil defence and military operations. Although the Government of the day at first took the matter seriously, launching a major investigation by the security services and slapping a D-notice on the national press to prevent any of the information in 'RSG 6' from receiving further publicity, nevertheless no prosecutions for breaches of the Official Secrets Acts ever ensued and the Prime Minister later told Parliament that the disclosures in 'RSG 6' were 'not seriously damaging to the national interest'.

As for the prosecutions launched by Sir Elwyn Jones, more later, but they too highlight the fact that each Attorney-General appears

71

to authorise or not authorise Official Secrets prosecutions on a highly subjective and selective basis.

The outside observer struggling to comprehend the judicial basis for the way this law is enforced must sooner or later conclude that individual judgment alone decides on prosecutions and that in studying the individual judgments of Attorney-Generals during the last half century, there is far more evidence of prejudice than of principle. This point was well made by the authoritiative legal magazine *New Law Journal* which said in an editorial of 14 May 1970:

> Prosecution under the Official Secrets Acts depends entirely on the length of an Attorney-General's foot: the Government's claims (in Information and the Public Interest, Cmnd 4089 of 1969) that the Attorney-General's fiat provides a very real safeguard and that the Acts are invoked only 'in the public interest' are both disingenuous and question-begging . . . a major review of the whole subject of official information is long overdue.

The above comments about the idiosyncrasies of Attorney-Generals do not apply to cases of foreign espionage. In these matters the fiats authorising Official Secrets Acts prosecutions have been issued with unerring consistency. Since the law was originally created specifically to combat spies, there can be no complaints about this strict enforcement, yet even in this uncontroversial area of Official Secrecy certain doubts have arisen on account of the uneven sentencing policies of the courts.

The first-ever prosecution of a foreign spy under the Official Secrets Act, that of Siegfried Helm in 1910, resulted in the accused merely being bound over to keep the peace. Since then, penalties for spying have rightly escalated. In the aftermath of the Second World War serious traitors such as Dr Allen Nunn May – who was sentenced to ten years' imprisonment in 1946 – and Dr Klaus Fuchs – who was given a fourteen-year sentence in 1950, received or came close to receiving the maximum punishment of fourteen years laid down in Section 1 of the 1911 Act. But in the 1960s these maximum sentences were massively increased by the courts after the Lord Chief Justice, Lord Parker, made use of the device of causing the penalties on each count to run consecutively. Thus in the 1961 Naval Secrets case, centring on the Underwater Detection Establishment in Portland, the principal defendants,

Peter and Helen Kröger and Gordon Lonsdale, (all of whom were Russian agents) received sentences averaging twenty years each. A few months later John Vassall, an Admiralty clerk who was blackmailed by the Russians into selling documents from his office was sentenced to a total of eighteen years' imprisonment. The harshest penalty of all went to George Blake who until his arrest in 1961 had worked for nine years as a double agent for the Russian and British secret services. The Lord Chief Justice gave Blake the maximum fourteen-year sentence on three counts and ordered that the terms of imprisonment should be served consecutively, thus imposing a total sentence of forty-two years. An appeal against this sentence was lodged on the grounds that it amounted to an evasion of the 1911 Act's maximum penalties. Blake's counsel argued that there was no record of a punishment of over twenty years ever having been imposed on any convicted criminal during the twentieth century, save for the sentence given to Gordon Lonsdale, also by Lord Chief Justice Parker. Urging the Court of Criminal Appeal to mitigate the 'inordinate, unprecedented and manifestly excessive' penalty, Blake's QC described the sentence as 'so unhuman as to be alien to the principles of punishment in a civilised country'. But this plea fell on deaf ears, and the term of forty-two years in jail was upheld.

One should not perhaps waste too much sympathy on the receivers of these marathon sentences. In the first place the defendants were all dangerous traitors, and secondly it has become apparent that heavy sentences are now an essential ingredient in the international game of spy-swapping. Of the five spies who received the above-mentioned penalties during the 1960s, only Vassall is still in prison. Blake mysteriously escaped, while Lonsdale and the Krögers were exchanged for alleged British agents held in Russian prisons. Such deals follow a global pattern. The only point of mentioning them is to show up the absurdity of a criminal statute which seeks to cover both minor leaks of embarrassing government information to the Press and serious espionage activities meriting forty-two years prison sentences. Here again it is perhaps appropriate to re-echo the prescient comment of *The Times* in 1920: 'If we are to have legislation on the Press, let it not be mixed up with penal provisions aimed at spies and revolutionaries.'

On the subject of heavy sentences, mention must be made of the case of Miss Barbara Fell, a senior civil servant who in 1962 pleaded guilty to communicating government reports marked confidential to her lover, Mr Smilijan Pecjak who was the Press Counsellor at the Yugoslav Embassy. Miss Fell had access to these reports by virtue of her £3,800 a year position as Acting Controller of the Overseas division of the Central Office of Information, a department which exists to disseminate British Government information to the domestic and foreign press. In these circumstances, any material which found its way to Miss Fell's office would almost inevitably have been destined to be passed on to the outside world in some form or other. No doubt it was indiscreet to disclose such material before it had been emasculated into the appropriate form of a Central Office of Information press handout, but Miss Fell's indiscretion bore the mitigating signs of a *crime passionelle,* for it was conceded on all sides that her motives had nothing whatever to do with espionage. Nevertheless, when it came to penalties, Miss Fell received the maximum sentence permissible under Section 2 of the 1911 Act, and was sent down for a term of two years' imprisonment. Not unnaturally there was an outcry at the severity of this punishment, but both the protests and an appeal against sentence failed. The authorities' decision to hound Miss Barbara Fell with a heavy criminal penalty instead of dealing with the matter by way of dismissal and loss of pension rights came as an indication of the excessive importance the Civil Service was by this time applying to the protection of what Sir Norman Brook's circular had called 'any official information which has not already officially been made public'.

Another indication of this trend came from a diverting House of Commons statement on the destruction of officially secret papers. On 28 February 1967, the Financial Secretary to the Treasury, Mr Niall MacDermot, told Parliament that some three hundred and fifty tons of Whitehall's classified waste paper was carefully destroyed each year in selected incinerators belonging to local authorities. However, because some unimportant secrets had recently fallen off a lorry near Chiselhurst Common en route for an incinerator, Whitehall's destruction procedures were being urgently reviewed. Complete destruction, Mr MacDermot said solemnly, could be ensured only if the responsible Government department cleaned out the incinerators itself. This was what would happen in future whenever outside incinerators had to be used. The Government was also considering installing its own incinerators and other suitable secrets-destroying apparatus in Whitehall departments.

After the House of Commons had finished rolling in the aisles at the imagined spectacle of civil servants raking out their own secret ashes, MPs had several pertinent suggestions to make, among them demands for a massive reduction in the number of secrets; a review of the Official Secrets Acts; and an onslaught on the growing tendency for civil servants to over-classify unimportant material. So far as is known, none of these recommendations was ever implemented.

Thus by the end of the 1960s officialdom's passion for excessive secrecy was at its zenith, for by skilful use of an outdated Act of Parliament, Britain's Civil Service had developed the most enclosed system of governmental communication in the free world. This situation was particularly resented by the Press, whose journalists knew better than anyone how the Official Secrets Acts were being manipulated to thwart or stifle legitimate disclosures, and to control the flow of government information.

When it came to the enforcement of the law, successive Attorney-Generals found themselves placed in an impossible position by having to exercise a personal discretion in the dubious danger zone between prosecutions in the public interest and prosecutions in the bureaucracy's interest. Too often proceedings were instituted because the two types of interest were held to be the same, to such an extent that the Attorney-General's fiat seemed to have become the Whitehall establishment's poodle.

On a different front there were widespread anxieties about the uneven application of the law. In particular, thoughtful Parliamentarians were disturbed by the apparent immunity of politicians from Section 2 of the Official Secrets Act 1911. Above all, everyone who studied the problem of official secrecy in a democracy appreciated that the operation of Britain's law had gone too far for it was being used to prohibit activities which the original legislation had never intended to control at all.

On a ridiculous level, it could justifiably be argued that civil servants who came home to their wives and discussed what they had eaten for lunch in the office canteen were technically committing the offence of communicating official information. Another absurdity was that those sections of the 1920 Act which prohibited the 'wearing of military uniforms' were sometimes being technically infringed by teenagers buying martial finery from London boutiques such as 'I was Lord Kitchener's Valet' and wearing them (as some do and did) on political demonstrations. On a more serious level, some civil servants and politicians were certainly manipulating the law to cloak their own failures.

Mr Edward Heath summed the situation up with percipience when he said in a speech in January 1969:

> What was once a law specifically framed to counter espionage has in too many cases been used to hide facts and figures which may be inconvenient or embarrassing to the Government of the day, but which strictly speaking are not secrets at all . . . There is a case for a most stringent Official Secrets Act to prevent the secrets of our country being passed on to those who would make use of them to the detriment of our country. There is no case for an Act more honoured in the breach than the observance.

Yet despite such manifestations of increasing concern about the Official Secrets Acts of 1911 and 1920, there seemed little prospect of meaningful law reform in this field, for as Professor David Williams percipiently wrote in 1965: 'The irony is that while there are many people who deplore the two statutes, there are few who would repeal them.'[1]

This seemed to be the status quo until the beginning of 1970, when there occurred an episode which was to shatter the foundations of Britain's laws on official secrecy. It was a saga which highlighted all the main grievances about the operation of the Official Secrets Acts. The threat of the law to press freedom; the inequitable abuse of the Attorney-General's discretion; the privilege of politicians; and the control of non-secret information by the Civil Service machine, all these emotive ingredients were found in abundance in the *cause célèbre* that came to be known as 'The Scott Report Affair'.

Part Two

7

Background to the Scott Report Affair

The Scott Report Affair had its origins in the Nigerian civil war of 1967–70, or more specifically in the foreign policy of Harold Wilson's Labour Government towards that struggle. At the time, the slow crushing of the secessionist state of Biafra by the Federal Military Government of Nigeria during thirty-one months of fighting and blockade had made a searing impression on the conscience of the Western World. Nowhere did feelings run higher than in Britain, largely on account of the Government's controversial policy of sending substantial arms shipments to the Federal Military Government of Nigeria.

At the outset of the conflict there had been very little outcry over these arms supplies, for most people in Britain seemed tacitly prepared to tolerate 'a short surgical police action'[1] as General Gowon, the Nigerian leader in 1967, described his military manoeuvres against Biafra. Yet as the months and then the years rolled by with Biafra bloody but unbowed, it gradually became clear that the policy of 'the quick kill' (as one MP infelicitously called it) was being supplanted by a policy of the slow starve. By the time the war had dragged on for over twenty months with the death toll nearing two million, a vocal minority of MPs, journalists and public commentators began demanding an end to British military and political support for Nigeria.

The Foreign Office opposed this vocal minority by justifying British policy with the arguments that it was in Britain's interests to preserve the unity of Nigeria; that we were not increasing traditional arms shipments but merely continuing a pattern of pre-war supplies which amounted to less than fifteen per cent of Nigeria's requirements; and that the Biafra rebellion would be swiftly and humanely ended by a Federal victory in a matter of months. Whatever the original merits of this case, they looked less meritorious after the conflict had been raging for nearly two years with steadily increasing military activity and steadily decreasing prospects for a solution.

In September 1969 I had an opportunity to assess the Nigerian situation at first hand when the *London Evening Standard* sent me to both sides of the war lines in order to write a series of feature articles. One of the hardest parts of the assignment was getting permission to travel at all for both Nigerian and Biafran officials were deeply suspicious of admitting a journalist who might favour the other combatant. The Biafrans took enormous pains to check that I did not hold any preconceived opinions prejudicial to their cause, while the Nigerians delayed giving me a visa until after I had been to the British Foreign Office and had a long and presumably satisfactory conversation with Mr Donald Tebbitt, a senior official in the West Africa department. There were also considerable logistical problems in moving from Biafra to Nigeria, as this unusual route involved stop-overs in three separate West African states. But after long delays all these difficulties were ironed out, and on 25 September 1969 I flew via Paris to Libreville, Gabon, from where I got a lift on a Joint Church Aid food relief aircraft into Biafra. Within moments of my 2 a.m. arrival at Uli airstrip, the serious nature of the conflict became uncomfortably apparent when I was unceremoniously shoved face downwards into a ditch while a Nigerian air raid took place.

As the offending Ilyushin bomber rumbled temporarily out of earshot having missed the unloading relief aircraft by just a few hundred feet, a voice from the ditch pealed with jolly African laughter and said warmly: 'Welcome to the Independent Republic of Biafra.'

I had expected to find the independent republic of Biafra in a demoralised and devastated condition. Certainly the starvation situation was desperate, particularly among the children, yet my strongest impression from a week in Biafra was the astonishing intensity of the people's nationalistic morale. Amidst all the sorrow, bitterness and misery, I could detect few signs of a weakening in militancy, and still fewer signs of opposition to the Ojukwu govern-

80

ment. Even the Biafran leadership's stubborn refusal to let daylight relief flights land at Uli airstrip was popular with the starving masses owing to irrational fears that a clause in the agreement saying the flights should be 'without prejudice to military operations' could lead to a 'Trojan horse' type of Nigerian invasion.

During my visit, after I had met and talked with a very varied cross-section of people, it became clear that a passionate dedication to the cause of independence surged throughout all classes and communities of Biafrans, making them proud to face any hardship, including even a painful death by famine or fire-power. Because of their pathological and unjustified terror of a repeat of the 1966 pogrom in which some thirty thousand Eastern Nigerians had been slaughtered by Northerners, the Biafrans' cause of self-determination had become something akin to a religious faith whose main tenet was that it would be better to be dead rather than to be subjected again to the yoke of a Federal Nigeria dominated by the hated Hausa and Yoruba tribes.

Such primaeval fears were undoubtedly the major forces in building a genuine spirit of nationhood in Biafra. But there were positive factors as well, of which the most important was the remarkable character of the Ibo people (who accounted for over eighty-five per cent of Biafra's population). The Ibos have been called 'The Jews of Africa', a soubriquet which seemed singularly appropriate. During the war, Biafra drew obvious comparisons with Israel by virtue of its role as a persecuted state fighting for survival with great courage and military resourcefulness against overwhelming odds. But long before the war there were similarities to the Jewish people, for the Ibos have for many years been both respected and resented throughout Africa on account of their exceptional intelligence, their high level of education, their skills as administrators and bureaucrats, their success at trade and all financial affairs, and their somewhat pedantic arrogance. These qualities, when channelled into the building of a new nation, produced a reasonably efficient civil service dedicated to duty in triplicate : a new and viable currency arrangement; a legal system whose bewigged judges dispensed justice at roadside courts between air-raids; and a propaganda machine which presented the case for Biafran independence with consummate skill both nationally and internationally. Roaming around shops, schools, government offices and townships in the diminutive seven thousand square miles enclave that Biafra had shrunk to by September 1969, I kept thinking: 'It's miraculous that the Biafrans can run things so well in these appalling conditions of war, siege and famine. If they ever do become peacefully independent, their talents will make them the best-governed state in Africa.'

Such reflections were the triumph of emotion over experience, for by this time the well fed and equipped hundred and twenty thousand strong Federal Nigerian Army had on paper an overwhelming military superiority against their thirty thousand hungry opponents. Yet even at this stage – with relief workers alleging a death rate of a thousand Biafran children a day through starvation – it looked as though the siege might continue indefinitely thanks to the deadlock produced by Nigeria's military incompetence and Biafra's moral intransigence.

Since the Federal troops had in two years launched no less than fourteen 'final' offensives against the Biafran lines and still not achieved victory, there was no good reason to believe that a fifteenth, or a fiftieth, offensive would do any better. The only factor that might break this stalemate was if Federal Nigeria's military backers, Britain and the Soviet Union, were either to increase or reduce the amount of support they were giving to the Gowon government.

The Biafrans were understandably hysterical about Britain's role in the civil war. Apart from exposure to the horrors of widespread starvation, the most personally distressing feature of my visit was listening to the repeated cris de coeur on the evils of the British arms supply policy. Hour after hour I was harangued on this by all Biafrans from General Ojukwu downwards as though I was the minister responsible for munitions exports in Harold Wilson's Government. On one occasion, when visiting the front near Owerri, I put forward the view (solemnly told me as fact by the Foreign Office) that the British Government was not actually supplying arms, but merely licensing the supply from private manufacturers. The young Biafran officers escorting me exploded with indignation, bundled me into a jeep, and drove to a dump of captured Nigerian ammunition cases clearly stamped 'UK Government Explosives – War Department/Army'.

The following day, anti-British feelings aroused by my presence almost started a riot in a market at Orodo. I was touring the stalls, writing down in my notebook the prices of the only animal proteins on sale* when my Information Ministry guide injudiciously disclosed that his charge was a British journalist. Almost at once an angry mob closed round me. Shoppers began screaming abuse, an elderly clock repairer spat at me and booed and one housewife hurled her recent purchase of a large dead white rat at my feet, shrieking 'see what the vandals' (the Nigerians) bullets from Britain make us eat.'

This painful scene lingered in my memory, getting an ironic revival several days later when I landed at Lagos airport and saw a nearby advertisement hoarding for infant food which proclaimed 'Welcome to Nigeria where babies are happy and healthy!'

By African standards, Nigeria is a superpower. Rich oil-fields, a land area as big as France, Germany and Britain put together, and a population of sixty million makes it dwarf the neighbouring West African states, all of whom are either fragmented or impoverished or both. Yet Nigeria too has been in constant danger of fragmentation, and has faced so many internal rebellions and attempts at secession that many experts believed, and still believe today, that it would be in the country's best interests to set up a much looser confederation of near-autonomous states. The Nigerian Head of State, General Gowon, was himself sympathetic to this viewpoint in 1966 when he said despairingly to *Time* Magazine 'The basis for unity is not there.'[2]

Yet the Biafran secession seemed to improve unity in the rest of Nigeria, at least in the short term. Soon after Ojukwu's declaration of independence, the monolithic north, which used to talk about secession itself, quietened down and agreed to split into six states. This ended the structural imbalance which had threatened to divide Nigeria in the past, a development which taken in conjunction with the new spirit of nationhood produced by war-

---

*These food prices were painfully exorbitant, even after allowing for currency inflation. Small lizards were fetching five shillings each, grass snakes two pounds each, cats four pounds each, rats five pounds each and snails two pounds a dozen. The main reason for these excessive rates was the chronic protein shortage. Biafra always managed to maintain an adequate, if sketchy, supply of yam and cassava—the staple vegetable diet. But without protein this diet gave rise to an epidemic of kwashiorkor, a disease which frequently proved fatal particularly to young children. By the end of the second year of the war desperate parents were prepared to pay almost any price for almost any sort of protein. More conventional animal foodstuffs (none of which were on sale at the market I visited) were reported to be fetching astronomical prices – i.e. chickens ten pounds to fifteen pounds each; goats fifty pounds each.

time emergency made 'One Nigeria' look a real possibility for the first time since colonial rule ended.

The most passionate advocates of Nigerian unity had always been the British. Ever since the nineteenth-century colonial administrators somewhat arbitrarily drew Nigeria's boundaries on the map, Britain had consistently striven to hold the artificial giant together, compulsorily amalgamating Northern and Southern Nigeria in 1914 against the will of both peoples; struggling to back up the three-state structure imposed by the Colonial Office in 1947; and continually trying to build up a central administrative structure to govern this diverse colossus. In 1966 when General Gowon was about to announce the dissolution of the Nigerian Federation, in a broadcast scheduled for 1 August, the British High Commissioner in Lagos, Sir Francis Cunningham-Bruce persuaded Gowon to change the wording and the meaning of the broadcast. Cunningham-Bruce later told certain Nigerian friends that he had saved the unity of Nigeria.[3] This mantle of saviour still appeared to be resting on the shoulders of subsequent British officials when Biafra declared her secession on 30 May 1967.

At the outset of the conflict the emphasis on Nigerian unity by British officials was defensible in terms of protecting British interests, on the grounds that a loose confederation of autonomous states with different trade policies might well have resulted in a reduction in the £170 million turnover in British trade. Even more important, Shell-BP's oil wells (increasingly vital because of the instability in the Middle East) had gone into production after complex royalty agreements with the Lagos central government, and it was feared that these arrangements might be jeopardised if the Federation was dissolved. It was largely on this basis that the British High Commission in Lagos advised the Labour Cabinet in the summer of 1967 to support General Gowon's military junta with arms supplies,[4] adding the all-important rider that the whole affair would soon be over because the trained Nigerian army could quickly suppress the disorganised Biafran rebels.

Arriving at Lagos in October 1969 I was anxious to discover how the British High Commission would now be defending its arms -to-Nigeria policy. Military supplies for an army of eight thousand soldiers carrying out 'a short surgical police action' against a handful of ill-equipped rebels can hardly be equated with the supplies needed for one hundred and twenty thousand

84

soldiers bogged down for twenty-seven months (with no end in sight) in a serious civil war against resourceful opponents discreetly equipped by the French Secret Service. Even on purely commercial grounds, Britain's action in prolonging the civil war was beginning to seem a mixed blessing. Because of guerilla attacks on oil installations, Shell-BP's oil production was down from six hundred thousand barrels per day to around a hundred and eighty thousand barrels per day, and because of Nigeria's war-economy import substitution measures some sectors of British exports – notably textiles, foodstuffs, motor cars, spirits and beer – were down by twenty-five per cent.

In short, by the autumn of 1969 Britain's justification for being the Federal Military Government's principal military supporter seemed increasingly open to question and it seemed a good moment to be asking whether our diplomats were trying any new moves such as pressing for peace negotiations or arranging an international arms embargo.

At the British High Commission I had long unattributable talks with several key officials, including the High Commissioner, Sir Leslie Glass. Although I was the only eye-witness to come out of Biafra to Lagos for several weeks, these officials assured me that many of the reports of Biafran starvation were 'greatly exaggerated' and 'largely propaganda'. One man insisted that malnutrition and kwashiorkor were endemic diseases of West African children whatever the food supplies. I recounted my story of the inflationary food prices and the rat-throwing incident at Orodo market and a very senior official retorted 'For God's sake don't be fooled by that one, the peasants here regularly eat snakes and rats as delicacies.'

Secondly, it was made clear to me that these British officials were not contemplating any solution other than outright military victory. Pointing to examples of Ojukwu's stubbornness, they argued that Nigeria had a right to be equally stubborn and that peace negotiations were out of the question. The idea of an arms embargo was brusquely dismissed with the time-honoured argument of all arms salesmen and drug pushers: 'If we don't do it, someone else will'.

On the issue of how long the war would last, several officials predicted the defeat of Biafra around Christmas time (the actual

85

surrender came on 12 January) while others were expecting up to another year of fighting.

On the commercial side, the High Commission claimed that the damage to British interests was so far 'worrying but not serious', but insisted that if we were now to press for an arms embargo, British exports would be seriously boycotted. When I pointed out that French exports to Nigeria were actually increasing even though it was an open secret that the French were supplying arms to Biafra, the reply was: 'That's different'. In any case, I was assured that the real justification for supporting Nigeria was simply that the Federal Military Government was the legitimate government and as such could expect to receive British backing whatever the rights and wrongs of the Biafran secession.

In Lagos I met two British officials who were subsequently to become significant figures in the Scott Report Official Secrets Act case. The first was Colonel Douglas Cairns, a fifty-six-year-old retired Infantry Officer holding the appointment of Senior British member of the International team of Military Observers. This team, which included Canadian, Polish, Swedish and Algerian officers, was set up by the Federal Military Government of Nigeria as a strictly neutral inspection group to make reports on allegations of genocide, atrocities and maltreatment of prisoners. The Observers, who were paid a hundred pounds a week plus expenses, made regular tours of the war zones in a fleet of Land Rovers and published reports of their findings. Because their reports invariably acquitted the Nigerian army of serious breaches of the rules of war, some doubts were expressed in pro-Biafran quarters as to the impartiality of the Observer team. These doubts magnified when one British member of the Observer team, Major I. A. Walsworth-Bell (who was Colonel Cairns' deputy from March to September 1969) publicly claimed in May 1970 that in addition to his role as an observer, he had been employed to gather intelligence for a British Foreign Office Minister and to advise the Nigerian Army on strategy.[5]

However, at the time of my visit to Lagos there were no valid grounds for doubting the bona fides of the Observer team, nor indeed have there ever been any grounds for doubting the bona fides of Colonel Cairns. He struck me as an exceptionally helpful and agreeable expert on the war, and went out of his way to provide me with much invaluable information for my articles. I had brought a letter of introduction to Cairns from a neighbour of mine in Yorkshire, Major-General Henry Alexander, who also subsequently featured prominently in the Official Secrets case.* Cairns and Alexander had served together in Ghana and in the Congo, and after Alexander had done a short spell of duty in Nigeria as the first British member of the International Observer team, he had recommended Cairns as his successor.

The last British official that I called on in Lagos was Colonel Robert Scott, the Defence Adviser to the High Commission. On the morning of 7 October 1969 I visited him in his top floor annexe to the High Commission building. Our talk started rather unsatisfactorily as Scott was anxious to discover from me the location of the jungle headquarters in Biafra where I had seen Ojukwu. Thinking such a disclosure might lead to Nigerian air-raids I pleaded vagueness about the general geography of Biafra. However, after this sticky beginning Colonel Scott gave me a very full briefing on the military situation. According to my notebook, which was later exhibited in court, Scott told me of an impending Nigerian offensive being planned at Dodan barracks; of a pincer movement by the first and second Nigerian divisions later on in October which would enable them to march on Uli airstrip; of the forthcoming delivery of two 120 mm Russian artillery batteries; of the difficulties the Nigerian mechanics were having in servicing the Air Force's fourteen MiGs, and many other interesting military details. During this briefing Scott was critical of the Nigerian army, saying that the officers were unpunctual and incompetent; that the third division was out of control; that the ammunition wastage was fantastic; and that the Nigerian soldiers were wonderful at defoliation when advancing, firing mainly at trees and rooftops instead of at the enemy. Scott also told me that Anglo-Nigerian relations were very good, but that a figure I quoted to him (given to me by another British official) saying that Britain was supplying sixty-five per cent of Nigeria's arms was too high. Colonel Scott said the figure was probably nearer thirty per cent.

When the above extracts from my notes were later put to Colonel Scott in court, he agreed that he probably had said such things to me in his briefing, and added 'As far as I am concerned it followed the pattern of a normal briefing and I have no reason to doubt that the version put to me is substantially correct.'[6]

*See Chapters 8–13.

Colonel Scott also said in court about the whole of the above conversation: 'It was an unattributable briefing which followed on a similar discussion he [Aitken] had had with the High Commissioner. It did indeed mean that he was entitled to make public the information I gave, but not to attribute it to me.'[7]

On my return to London, I wrote the most hard hitting articles of my journalistic career. It was my intention to stir up public concern over the issue of British arms supplies for after all that I had seen and heard on my visit I had developed some deep political and personal convictions on this policy. Whatever the rights and wrongs of the civil war (and it seemed to me that the Biafrans' case had a great deal of merit) I was convinced that for Britain to take sides to the extent of supplying arms to Nigeria was a morally reprehensible involvement in what should have been regarded as an exclusively local affair. For this reason I felt determined to put before the public the arguments for a change in British policy, and to this end I devoted a large part of the autumn of 1969 to making several TV and radio broadcasts, writing newspaper articles and arranging numerous speaking engagements with a Biafran motif both inside and outside the Yorkshire constituency which had adopted me as prospective Conservative parliamentary candidate. All this activity inevitably brought me into close contact with what was known as 'The Biafra Lobby'.

This nebulous but not ineffective organisation had three main elements. The first and initially the most active of these was a group of former businessmen and civil servants who had served in West Africa and believed from their local knowledge that the British Government's policy on the civil war was gravely at fault. The most influential figure in this group was Mr Peter Gatacre, the forty-three-year-old Dutch-born managing director of Madame Tussaud's waxworks. Having worked in Lagos as an executive for the United Africa Company, Gatacre had many Nigerian friends of all tribes, who in 1967 and early 1968 told him the incredible news about Britain's extensive involvement over arms supplies to the Federal Military Government. Although by no means a fervent Biafran supporter, Gatacre in 1968 began a campaign to generate concern about the Nigerian civil war among his acquaintances in British politics.

One of the first of these was the Rt. Hon. Hugh Fraser, the Conservative MP for Stafford and Stone, who had been Secretary of State for Air in the Macmillan government. Hugh Fraser had not been surprised by the first news of Biafra's secession, because during his time as a junior Minister at the Colonial Office he had read a gloomy 1962 despatch from the then British High Commissioner in Lagos, Viscount Head, in which ominous fears were expressed about the future of Nigerian unity. Early in 1968 Fraser was visited by one of his Staffordshire constituents, an Anglican priest recently returned from Biafra, who poured out a disturbing tale about Britain's involvement on the Nigerian side of the civil war. 'I immediately said the way to proceed on this is not by a public row, but by going and seeing the Foreign Office department concerned', recalls Hugh Fraser, 'so I went round to have a long interview with my old friend, Sir Leslie Monson, who was the head of the Africa department. I asked him the key question : "Can you assure me we are doing everything we can to make peace between Nigeria and Biafra?" He reassured me on this point, but as subsequent events disproved his assurance, I decided to fight the whole thing out in public.'[8]

Hugh Fraser fired his first broadside on Biafra during the August 1968 House of Commons emergency debate on the Soviet invasion of Czechoslovakia, claiming that Parliament should not be discussing events in Prague about which it could do nothing. Instead he urged an immediate reassessment of the Government's entire Nigeria policy.

From this beginning until the defeat of Biafra in 1970 Hugh Fraser waged a ceaseless political campaign against the Government's policy of sending arms to Lagos. Backed up with painstaking research work by Peter Gatacre, who became an almost daily visitor to Fraser's home in Campden Hill Square, he put down numerous parliamentary questions, moved the adjournment of the House on several occasions, conducted a correspondence campaign in *The Times* and invariably raised the issue in Foreign Affairs debates.

In addition to these public attempts to change the arms supply policy, Hugh Fraser also applied some of his efforts behind the scenes with key ministers and officials. One example of this was his correspondence with the Prime Minister in July 1969 after some information had come privately into Fraser's hands via a senior official in the US Central Intelligence Agency. On 24 July Hugh Fraser wrote to Harold Wilson saying that the CIA was disturbed by the contradictions between its own reports from Lagos and the public statements on the Nigerian Civil War put out in Washington and London by the British Government. Summarising the areas of the CIA's main concerns, Fraser passed on in his letter the CIA reports which alleged that British personnel in mufti were now working in all three Nigerian armed services; that British military aircraft, and British pilots, were being used by the Nigerians; and that there was a suspected degree of collusion in Lagos between the British Secret Services and the Russian KGB over arms supplies. On 5 August Harold Wilson replied denying all these assertions. Hugh Fraser accepted this Prime Ministerial denial and never again raised the matter, but in the light of the British Government's subsequently proved unreliability on its statements about the Nigerian civil war, the correspondence remains intriguing.

Hugh Fraser was by no means the only Parliamentarian to be publicly and privately advocating a change in the Nigerian policy. Jeremy Thorpe and Jo Grimond led the Liberals into the attack; Frank Allaun, James Griffiths and Michael Barnes were the most outspoken Labour back-benchers in criticising the Government, while in the Upper House Lords Goodman and Brockway were militant pro-Biafran campaigners. By December 1969 over one hundred and fifty MPs from all parties were determinedly opposing the sale of arms, although under considerable Foreign Office pressure both front benches maintained an uneasily united bi-partisan front.

The opposition in Parliament was fuelled by the opposition in the Press and on television. First of the pro-Biafran campaigners was the *Spectator,* which in April 1968 published a leading article entitled 'Britain stokes the Flames' written by the paper's editor, Mr Nigel Lawson, and calling for an end to arms supplies. This was followed by several similar leaders in the ensuing weeks. In July 1968 the *Spectator* sent its acerbic political correspondent, Mr Auberon Waugh, to Biafra and his impassioned despatches caused a considerable stir amongst the paper's limited but influential readership. On his return, Auberon Waugh launched into a journalistic crusade against what he called 'Michael Stewart's policy of genocide' and during the next eighteen months his polemical writings on this theme raised the art of political invective to a pitch unheard of in Britain since the days of the seventeenth-century pamphleteers. Although some observers felt that the *Spectator* might at times have been overstating its case, there is no doubt that the paper's lone stand influenced many other newspapers to investigate Britain's role in the Nigerian civil war. The night before *The Times* swung its mighty editorial artillery against Nigerian arms sales, Nigel Lawson received a telephone call from *The Times*' editor, William Rees Mogg, who said: 'We're coming out tomorrow against the Government's Nigerian policy. I'd like you to be the first to know.' It was a gracious acknowledgment to the *Spectator*'s crucial role in creating the press section of 'The Biafra Lobby'.

Nigel Lawson's first Biafra editorial had been inspired by his meeting (instigated by the indefatigable Peter Gatacre) with the Chief Justice of Biafra, Sir Louis Mbanefo. This immensely distinguished Ibo statesman, who had been Chief Justice of Nigeria until Biafra's secession, flew to London many times during the civil war to plead for a change in British policy. His visits had no effect on Whitehall, particularly as ministers refused to meet Mbanefo for nearly a year, but his first hand accounts to others certainly increased the anxiety among opponents of the official line.

As the war continued the Biafra Lobby grew in size and influence. One of the greatest stimulants to its growth was the credibility gap that arose between the Foreign Office and the informed public on the issue of Britain's involvement. To many observers it seemed clear that the facts of the Nigeria policy were being quite deliberately distorted.

Reporters such as Winston S. Churchill of *The Times,* Michael Leapman of the *Sun* and Francis Wyndham and Richard Hall of the *Sunday Times* produced accounts of events and situations in Biafra which differed sharply from the statements made by ministers and officials. Missionaries and medical teams returning from the battle and starvation zones had their stories condemned by the Foreign Office spokesmen as 'exaggerations'. Former Eastern Region civil servants who wrote letters to the newspapers criticising the validity of a 'One Nigeria' policy had their arguments contradicted by official sources. Above all, the constant trickle of evidence suggesting that Britain's arms supplies were far greater than the Foreign Office admitted evoked strong denials.

In the interests of setting the historical record straight, the contentious issue of Nigeria's arms supplies deserves to be documented in detail, for while the war was going on the truth was obscure.

Although there were constant domestic reports of big shipments of armoured cars, artillery and small arms from Britain to Nigeria, and although newspaper correspondents frequently filed stories from the war zone which showed beyond reasonable doubt that the bulk of the Federal Nigerian army's weapons came from UK sources, nevertheless the British Government concealed these transactions from the public.

Not only did Whitehall spokesmen refuse to confirm the evidence of massive arms supplies to Lagos, at first they denied them outright. In Parliament, ministerial duplicity touched new depths. Although a junior Foreign Office minister, Lord Shepherd, completely gave the government's game away on 29 January 1968 in the House of Lords when he said, under questioning from Lord Brockway: 'While we deplore the tragic and sad civil war in Nigeria, we have been supplying Nigeria with pretty well all its military equipment,'[9] nevertheless, other prominent members of the Government insisted that Britain was only sending supplies of arms that were traditional in type and quantity to Nigeria.

The Prime Minister, Mr Harold Wilson, told the House of Commons on 16 May 1968: 'We have continued the supply – not the Government; I mean that we have allowed the continuance of supply of arms by private manufacturers in this country exactly on the basis that it has been in the past, but there has been no special provision for the needs of war.'[10]

As the Federal Nigerian army had by this time expanded its troop-strength from ten thousand to a hundred and twenty thousand to fight the war, it was an astonishing claim that there had been no special provision of arms for the extra wartime manpower.

Nevertheless this remarkable fiction was preserved for more than a year, as the Foreign Secretary, Mr Michael Stewart said in the House of Commons on 19 July 1969: 'The arms which we have supplied have been broadly both in quantity and quality what we were supplying before the war began.'[11]

Four months later under considerable pressure the Foreign Secretary amended this doctrine when on 19 November 1969 he admitted that there had been 'an increase in the absolute amount of arms sent to Nigeria', but claimed that this was commensurate 'with the increase in the Nigerian army' and still remained 'about fifteen per cent of the total value of Nigeria's arms'.

This figure of fifteen per cent was repeated so often by members of the Government and apologists for the Nigeria policy that it became something of a hallowed and venerated credo. The Biafra Lobby fiercely disputed the statistic and were roundly condemned by the Foreign Secretary for their disbelief. I well remember sitting in the gallery of the House of Commons listening to a Nigeria debate on 9 December 1969 when Mr Michael Stewart said: 'There has been the suggestion that the Government have been trying to camouflage from the House what the supply [of arms] was. That is untrue. It remains, as I have informed the House, about fifteen per cent by value of the total purchases by Nigeria.'[12]

It is now possible to discover exactly who was camouflaging what on this matter, because the authoritative figures on Nigeria's arms supplies have since been published in the Nigerian Trade Summaries for 1967, 1968 and 1969. These Summaries are annual records of imports into Nigeria, compiled on a monthly basis by clerks at the country's ports of entry. They can be inspected at the Board of Trade Library, and their authenticity was not disputed when they were produced at my Old Bailey trial. What they show is that before the civil war began in mid-1967, Britain was supplying Nigeria with arms imports worth seventy thousand pounds annually. During 1969, the last year of the war, Britain shipped ten million pounds' worth of armaments to Nigeria (exact figure £10,255,089). This comprised 97.4 per cent of arms supplied from all Western sources. Although Iron Curtain exports and imports are not included in these trade summaries, it is known that Russian arms supplies could not have amounted to more than about three million pounds' worth in 1969, for during that year no Russian aircraft were delivered to Nigeria, and the only substantial items of Soviet military hardware purchased by the Federal Government were a pair of 120 mm field guns (approximate cost three hundred and fifty thousand pounds). Thus Russian arms imports in 1969 were almost entirely confined to small arms and ammunition and since the Federal troops were mainly equipped with NATO rifles which cannot use Soviet bullets, it would be amazing if Nigeria had bought more than one or two million pounds' worth of

Russian arms in the year. Stretching this total to its wildest imaginable limits by making allowances for excessive spares, extravagant orders and exorbitant prices, one is left with the conclusion that even after over-estimating Russia's contribution, Britain's share of Nigeria's total arms imports by value could not have been less than seventy per cent in 1969. In other words, the repeated claim by Mr Michael Stewart that Britain was supplying no more than fifteen per cent of Nigeria's arms was incorrect.*

Although there was no hard evidence as to the enormity of the inaccuracy until after the war, so many independent observers had come to realise that the Government's whole approach to Nigeria was based on doubtful information and conclusions that the political pressures for a change of policy were becoming formidable by the end of 1969.

Before the 9 December House of Commons Foreign Affairs debate, 151 Members of Parliament – almost a quarter of the House of Commons – signed a motion put down by Sir Edward Boyle asking 'In the name of humanity and the name of realism' that there should be a change in Government policy towards the Nigerian civil war. After opening orations by Sir Alec Douglas Home and Mr Michael Stewart (both of whom agreed there should be no change) strong attacks on the arms supply policy came from an almost unbroken succession of speakers. During six and a half hours of debate, only four back benchers spoke in support of the Government, while its most vehement critics included Parliamentary luminaries such as Mr Jo Grimond (Liberal), Mr James Griffiths, Mr Frank Allaun, Mr Colin Jackson, Mr Michael Barnes, Mr Philip Noel Baker and Mr Stanley Henig (Labour), Mrs Winifred Ewing (Scottish Nationalist), and Mr Hugh Fraser, Mr David Crouch and Lord Dalkeith (Conservative). At the end of the day Hugh Fraser unexpectedly divided the House against the wishes of his own front bench (who abstained *en masse*) and despite a half full chamber won a creditable ninety-four votes for the arms embargo cause against a Government vote

*For the fifteen per cent figure to be true, Russia would have had to be supplying Nigeria with fifty-five million pounds worth of arms in 1969. Because the Russians always insisted on cash on the nail for arms deals, and because the Federal Military Government was very short of foreign exchange, buying over fifty million pounds worth of arms would have been an economic impossibility as well as a military absurdity.

of two hundred and fifty-four (over a hundred of whom were Ministers or Junior Ministers).*

Outside Parliament the extensive television coverage being given to the horrors of Biafra, especially by the ITN's influential 'News at Ten' was making the people of Britain increasingly concerned about the rights and wrongs of sending arms to Nigeria. Further national anxiety about the Government's policy was being stirred up by press opposition, which had been considerably strengthened during the latter half of the year by stern editorial criticism from the *Daily* and *Sunday Telegraph, The Times* and all popular daily papers except the *Express.* In the wake of these manifestations of public discontent, the Conservative Opposition began reluctantly moving towards ending their bi-partisan support for the Government's Nigerian policy.†

In this December House of Commons debate even Sir Alec Douglas Home, a dedicated advocate of 'One Nigeria', had argued the case for an international arms embargo and urged the Government to consider it. He had also suggested a new international relief programme for Biafra using helicopters, and had criticised the Government for their refusal to send a British Minister to Biafra. Elsewhere in the Tory party there were clearer indications that the bi-partisan acquiescence to the Nigeria policy was coming to an end. On 7 December 1969 the *Observer* had reported:

Are the Tories about to change their policy on British arms support for Nigeria? There are several signs that the log jam has begun to break up with Ted Heath's despatch of Lord Carrington, the Opposition leader of the House of Lords, to Biafra. Miles Hudson, the Conservative Research Department

---

*When the House of Commons is unexpectedly divided by a backbencher demanding a division, it is normal for only about half of the total of six hundred and thirty MPs to be present. Most of these will be government supporters kept in or near Westminster by the Whips for just such an eventuality. For Hugh Fraser and his pro-Biafran supporters to have rounded up ninety-four of their one hundred and fifty signatories to the Boyle motion for a sudden vote was an impressive display of support.

†It has often been said that had the Labour party been in opposition when a Conservative government was supplying arms to Nigeria, there would have been outright official opposition from the start. The Conservatives, bi-partisan backing for the Stewart policy can be explained (a) by the traditional Tory reluctance to be politically partisan on Foreign Affairs issues and (b) by Sir Alec Douglas Home's own pro-Federal attitudes with which he guided the Conservatives.

man who has gone with Carrington, has argued for a change of line and Carrington himself said privately before leaving that a military solution is impossible.

Pointing out that many of the Tory MPs now advocating an end to arms supplies were 'respected undemonstrative middle-of-the-roaders like Sir Fitzroy Maclean and Sir Henry D'Avigdor-Goldsmid' the *Observer* story continued:

> Two influences seem to be at work on the Tory leadership: the strong feelings of the rank and file expressed in a movingly worded letter from the Young Conservatives to all members of the Shadow Cabinet last month, pleading for a change; and the realisation that the Government itself with Maurice Foley already in Lagos as Harold Wilson's emissary is now looking for a way of ending the war.

The *Observer* also added that if the Tory party did change its policy 'it will be a remarkable victory for a small tireless lobby which had been meeting and scheming in the drawing room of Hugh Fraser's Georgian house on Campden Hill'.

The Biafra Lobby (Campden Hill Square branch) was undoubtedly very active during the autumn of 1969. Dedicated researchers like Suzanne Cronje and Peter Gatacre brought in accurate information (often monitored from West African broadcasts and newspapers) on the state of the war. Political activists like Gerry Wade, the Young Conservative Chairman of the London area and Michael Barnes, the Labour MP for Chiswick, did their best to organise meetings, marches and motions. Powerful editors like William Rees Mogg of *The Times* and Nigel Ryan of ITN were regular contacts, while Hugh Fraser himself was in constant touch with parliamentarians, journalists, missionaries, Biafran expatriates and anyone else who could help the cause. The net result of all this activity was that Hugh Fraser was beginning to rival the Foreign Office in his ability to get hold of accurate information and disseminate it to the interested public. Yet for all the minor propaganda successes, it is easy to over-estimate the importance of a political lobby and it must be stressed that no small group could possibly have been responsible for the tremendous welling up of nation-wide concern about Biafra. Nevertheless, Hugh Fraser did play a significant role in spearheading the attack against the arms supply policy. His motivation had nothing to do with religious emotion (as one of the innumerable non-Catholics in the Biafra Lobby I never heard the issues discussed in anything but secular terms) or with political preferment (Fraser was well aware that his independent views were diminishing his chances of office in any future Heath government) or even with idealism for the State of Biafra (Fraser confined himself to opposing Britain's role in the Nigerian civil war). He originally became concerned because he saw the British Government's determination to help defeat Biafra as a policy that was morally wrong, and his concern grew into anger when he came to believe that ministers were no longer giving accurate accounts of their policy in Parliament.

In a campaign against officialdom's credibility gap, the truth is the best weapon. Hugh Fraser's crusade won a quarter of the House of Commons to its side not because of emotional outbursts (which tended to do the cause some damage) but because one hundred and fifty-one MPs no longer accepted at face value the facts and predictions Government spokesmen were making. The same scepticism lay behind the growing concern in the country as a whole. Had the Biafrans held out for a few more months, the British Government's credibility gap would have widened still further and the arms supply policy might well have been changed through public protest as a result. Certainly I believed that if journalists and politicians could continue publicising arguments and information which exposed the fallacies in the official Whitehall line, then it would be only a matter of time before the rising tide of public opinion would force the Whitehall line on Nigeria to change from a war policy to a peace policy.

8

Anatomy of a Scoop

During the autumn of 1969 when I was frequently writing and broadcasting on the Nigerian civil war, much of my information came from reliable private individuals with expert knowledge of the conflict. Of these informants, the most helpful and forthcoming was Major-General Henry Templer Alexander, who lived at the Old Rectory, Brandsby, Yorkshire, seven miles from my own cottage at Sutton-on-the-Forest.

General Alexander, who had recently retired from the army, had enjoyed a distinguished and meteoric military career. He had been a professional soldier for thirty-five years, with a war record which included active service in seven countries, two mentions in despatches and the award of the OBE and DSO. After the end of the war, he commanded the Second Cameronians (Scottish Rifles), the 26th Gurkha Brigade, and was appointed a Senior Instructor at Staff College. He became the youngest Major-General in the peacetime army, and with this rank was seconded in 1960 to the Ghanaian Army as President Nkrumah's Chief of Defence Staff. After twenty-two lively months in this job, Alexander was summarily dismissed by 'the Redeemer' who under left-wing pressure declared that because of Britain's attitudes to the Congo situation Ghana could no longer keep 'an imperialist general' at the head of its army.

Soon after General Alexander's departure from Ghana, there occurred an episode which nine years later became relevant to the Scott Report Secrets case. What happened was that after returning to the War Office in London from Accra in the autumn of 1961, General Alexander gave an interview on the Ghanaian situation to a feature writer from *Topic** Magazine. In the course of this interview, which took place at White's Club, it appeared that the General made certain disclosures of information and voiced certain opinions which caused considerable embarrassment when the interview appeared in print on 28 October 1961. General Alexander, who was of course still a serving British officer, immediately issued through the War Office a statement repudiating both the journalist and the interview. This statement, which appeared in the national press on 30 October 1961, claimed that the journalist had broken an agreement not to publish any of the interview and not to quote the General.

The statement went on: 'Not only had this understanding been entirely broken, but what is much worse the newspaper has attributed to me a number of remarks which, I never made and views, which I never expressed and which I do not hold.' About another part of the *Topic* article General Alexander said: 'This is a complete fabrication which I wish unequivocally to repudiate' and the statement ended: 'My solicitors are taking the matter up with the newspaper. In the meantime, I wish to disassociate myself completely from the remarks and opinions attributed to me in the alleged interview.'

Because of the ferocity of this repudiation statement the dispute between General Alexander and *Topic* Magazine became something of a Fleet Street *cause célèbre*. The *Topic* feature writer concerned, Mr Christopher Dobson, was a journalist of high repute and he totally denied the General's allegations of a breach of faith, producing some formidable evidence in support of his refutation. *Topic* Magazine made a full reply to General Alexander's solicitors and subsequently all threats of legal action were dropped.

This incident may possibly have had some effect on General Alexander's subsequent career. Three years afterwards, the *Observer* reported in its issue of 12 January 1964:

> When Alexander returned to England at the end of his mission in Ghana in 1961, he was generally thought to be destined for big things. But something went surprisingly wrong. Some attributed it to an unfortunate article in the short-lived *Topic* Maga-

*Topic Magazine was founded in the Autumn of 1961 by a consortium of journalists and publishers. Edited by Mr Morley Richards, it was intended to be a British equivalent of *Time* or *Newsweek*, but collapsed after only eight issues.

zine quoting Alexander in a way that made it appear he was breaking Army Regulations. For a time Alexander was given no post and finally he was put into a pretty unimportant job as Chief of Staff in Northern Command. Whatever reasons the Army Council might have had for overlooking Alexander's claims in the past three years it can hardly pass him over for the post of GOC Scottish Command which has fallen vacant. Alexander has two qualifications for the post: he served with a Scottish regiment and he is next on the seniority list. It would be odd indeed if General Alexander were passed over once again.

Despite the oddity, General Alexander was not given the job of GOC Scottish Command, nor any other army appointment after his term as Chief of Staff Northern Command ended. Instead he retired with full honours in 1965. He wrote a book on his experiences in Ghana and took up a business appointment with an oil company. In 1968 General Alexander accepted an invitation from the Foreign Office to serve as Senior British Representative on the International Military Observer team to Nigeria. He held this position for three months in the autumn of that year and subsequently made at least one return visit to Lagos. He followed the events of the civil war with close interest and wrote articles and letters for newspapers commenting on the course of the conflict. He also lectured on the war to various specialist bodies including the Royal Institute of International Affairs and the Army Staff College at Camberley.

From a journalistic point of view, I could not have found a better professional contact than General Alexander. When we met in the summer of 1969, I told him I was planning a visit to Nigeria and Biafra and asked whether I could come and ask him about the military situation. As a result of this approach, I visited him in his home on several occasions specifically to get information for my own writings on the Nigerian civil war. He showed me maps, gave me documents, and often in his presence I wrote down what he told me in a notebook. Just before my own visit to Nigeria and Biafra he gave me a detailed military briefing on the situation, and he also gave me three letters of introduction to key figures in Lagos. One was to Colonel Cairns, one was to the Nigerian Chief of Staff, Brigadier Hassan Katsina, and one was to the Permanent Secretary at the Ministry of Defence, Mr Yosoof Gobir. After my return from Nigeria, I continued seeing General Alexander. We exchanged views and information and corresponded about our differences of opinion on British policy, he being a convinced supporter of the need to help the Federal troops win the war. Despite these and other political differences, our meetings were amicable and professional. There was a clear understanding between us that I was free to make use of the information given to me in my articles, speeches and broadcasts. Apart from one article[1] in which, with his consent, I named General Alexander as holding a certain view-point on the war, I never attributed any of this information to my source. It was part of our understanding that the General's disclosures to me were for 'background information' – a phrase which, according to journalistic convention, means that the information may be published but that its source may not be revealed. Although General Alexander read many of the articles in which material gleaned from him was published, he never expressed any criticism or complaint about what I had written.

It should be stressed here that there was nothing at all improper in General Alexander giving a journalist information on the Nigerian civil war. He was by this time a private citizen holding no office under the Crown, and I believed that his main motive in briefing me was his desire to put over the pro-Federal viewpoint to someone who was speaking and writing publicly on Nigerian affairs. The information he gave me consisted largely of news titbits, observations, assessments, opinions, predictions and general military gossip connected with the civil war; in short, the sort of innocuous information which was later found in most paragraphs of the Scott Report. All this was very useful to my own understanding of the Federal Nigerian war strategy, and I was grateful to General Alexander for being such an informative journalistic contact.

Early in December 1969 Mrs Alexander telephoned to invite me to dinner on the night of Sunday, 21 December, and I accepted. In addition to General and Mrs Alexander and their son David, the guests were Colonel Geoffrey Preston, a retired military friend and neighbour of the General; his wife Mrs Daphne Preston; and two young girl-friends of David Alexander, Miss Cindy Fletcher and Miss Rosemary White. During the meal there was much general conversation which did not touch on the Nigeria-Biafra war nor on any matters connected with it.

At the end of the meal the ladies left the dining room and the four men – General Alexander, David Alexander, Colonel Preston and myself – remained behind to drink port. Most of this port-drinking session was given over to a domestic political discussion about the prospects for an election, but towards the end of the conversation General Alexander voiced the opinion that Members of Parliament were on the whole an ill-informed lot who rarely had an adequate knowledge of the subjects on which they spoke. The General supported this assertion by references to the House of Commons debate on 9 December on the Nigerian civil war. He said that he had never heard such nonsense as the speeches of the pro-Biafran MPs who claimed that the Federal Nigerian army could not win the war. As I myself had been helping with the research that went into the speech of Hugh Fraser MP (who made just this claim) I demurred, saying something like 'Your Federals are nowhere near winning this war'. General Alexander said rather curtly words to the effect of 'You're talking rubbish. I've just had a report come in from Lagos which proves the Nigerians are going to finish this war off very soon. I'll let you see it'. By the time this exchange took place we had got up from the dining room table and had walked back into the drawing room to rejoin the ladies, so there was no time for me to do anything more than indicate mild scepticism and say 'I'd like to see it, thank you'.*

At the time, this snippet of conversation seemed to be of no significance whatever. The General had given me documents about the war before, and in so far as I thought at all about the report he had just mentioned, I thought it might perhaps be a Lagos newspaper article or possibly a report by an oil company with Nigerian interests. There was certainly no reason for me to suspect that I had been put on my guard against a possible criminal breach of the Official Secrets Acts.

The dinner guests had now been joined by Mr and Mrs A. D. Cliff who lived in the nearby village of Crayke. Tony Cliff was a big local landowner, a County Alderman and a former Chairman of the constituency Conservative Association. At this particular

---

*This and many other of my recollections in this chapter were later contested in evidence given by General Alexander. For his accounts, and the accounts of the independent witnesses, see Chapters 5, 6 and 7.

time I was in daily contact with him, because our local Conservative party agent, Ian MacDonald, was bedridden with terminal cancer, and Tony Cliff had stepped in to take over all the clerical duties of constituency administration.

The assembled company stayed drinking in General Alexander's drawing room for some two hours after dinner. By about 11.30 p.m. several of the guests drifted away leaving only the two Cliffs, myself and the three Alexanders. At this time I was sitting on a sofa in one corner of the room talking to Mrs Cliff when General Alexander, who had been out of the room, came back and handed me a sheaf of papers saying that this was the report he had mentioned earlier. There was then a very brief exchange of conversation between us, largely on the subject of when I would return the document, and included the phrase 'You see it's marked confidential'. The transaction took place in a jovial and utterly casual way. Neither at this moment nor at any other time was there any request to me from the General to treat the document in strict confidence or with special discretion. It was not until I got home to my own cottage a few minutes later and read the text that I realised I had received an extremely interesting report.

The Scott Report first struck me as significant but not sensational. Its ninety-one paragraphs, formally titled 'An Appreciation of the Nigerian Conflict', contained a great deal of information which anyone following the war closely would have known. However, the sheer volume of material covered made the report an invaluable background brief on the state of the conflict, and this corroboration from an official source of findings already published in other accounts was obviously a definitive breakthrough in obtaining an accurate picture of the civil war.

The object of the Scott Report was, in its author's words, 'to examine whether either side in the Nigerian civil war can reach a successful conclusion before the end of the present dry season' – by which he meant April 1970. After sifting through a mass of evidence on manpower, troop dispositions, command structure, communications, aims and intentions, intelligence, morale, and tactics, Scott concluded that the Federals would conquer Biafra by this date, although he hedged his conclusions with so many ifs, buts and other qualifications that anyone could justifiably argue that the report proved the war might last much longer.

Perhaps the most interesting disclosures made by the report

related to Britain's arms supplies to the Federal Military Government of Nigeria.

After stressing that the Nigerian forces had expanded from ten thousand to a hundred and twenty thousand men since the war began, paragraph 6a of the Scott Report revealed that the Nigerian Army had been supplied with an unspecified number of British Ferret, Saladin, and Saracen armoured cars.

Paragraph 66 disclosed that the Nigerian Navy had been equipped with six heavily armed ex-RN Seaward Defence Boats, and that two new Corvettes were being built for the Nigerians in British shipyards.

Paragraph 70 made it clear that the bulk of the Nigerians' effective rifles and small arms ammunition came from Britain. A crucial footnote to this paragraph stated that the army had received 'over forty million rounds of 7.622 mm Small Arms Ammunition from UK sources alone in the past fifteen months'.

Contrasting these specific facts in Colonel Scott's report with certain statements to Parliament by the Foreign Secretary, Mr Michael Stewart, it was clear that I had in my hands positive proof that the House of Commons had been misled. On 10 July 1969 Mr Stewart had said 'The arms which we have supplied have been broadly both in quality and quantity what we were supplying before the war began.' On 9 December 1969 he had assured the House of Commons that British arms sales remained 'about fifteen per cent by value of the total purchases by Nigeria'. Neither these statements nor similar statements made by other ministers, including Mr Harold Wilson, corresponded with the facts given in his report by Colonel R. E. Scott, the Defence Adviser to the British High Commission in Lagos. Thus I soon realised from my brief nocturnal reading of the document that it would certainly provide the basis for a controversial newspaper article which in turn would probably cause a political storm.

Waking up next morning, I had to decide what to do with the Scott Report. It did not occur to me that I was not free to make journalistic use of it, as I had always previously published information given to me by General Alexander. Indeed one of my earliest thoughts on the matter was that the General might have handed me this report in order that I should publicise its pro-Federal conclusion that the Nigerians were about to win the war. At first I thought of filing an immediate news story on the report to the *Evening Standard,* but then I decided to get some other people's expert opinions on the arms supply points before committing myself to print.

On the morning of 22 December when these thoughts about newspaper articles on the Scott Report were passing through my mind, I kept a long-standing appointment to call in on the offices of Yorkshire Television in Leeds. I had been under contract to this company since its inauguration in 1968, first as the presenter of Yorkshire's regional news programme 'Calendar' and later as an interviewer and script-writer for the documentary department. In this last capacity I had worked closely for some time with the company's senior documentary producer, Mr Michael Deakin. We had made several network programmes together and were good friends. During the previous few weeks, Deakin and I had been having detailed discussions about filming a documentary on Biafra early in the New Year. There was some reluctance on the part of the company's senior management about this project on account of the possible risks to the safety of the film crew, but the journalistic reasons for a 1970 documentary on Biafra were so compelling that our plans for it were in preparation despite the difficulties. Knowing by this time that the Scott Report would provide invaluable material for our Biafra programme, I took the document into the Leeds studios with me and gave it to Michael Deakin. He read it, agreed with me about its usefulness, decided we would need extra copies for ourselves, the director, and the script-writers, and casually despatched a secretary to make six photo-copies. She or some helpers in the copying room pulled the existing staples out of the document to get it through the Xerox machine page by page, and when the original copy was brought back in loose leaf form Michael Deakin banged in a new and smaller clip.

At one point during my morning at Yorkshire Television, I telephoned Mr Hugh Fraser and described the Scott Report to him. He was immediately interested and asked if he could have a copy. I agreed and took two of the six photo-copies away from Yorkshire Television that afternoon for Hugh Fraser, keeping two photo-copies for myself (one for the TV programme and one for my projected newspaper article) and leaving two with Michael Deakin.

I also took away the original top copy and casually dropped it in at General Alexander's home on my way to a political engagement that same evening. The entire Alexander family were out, so I handed back the Scott Report to a member of the household staff. It is interesting to speculate what would have happened if General Alexander had been at home when I rang his doorbell on this occasion. Presumably he would have invited me in for a drink and we would have discussed the Scott Report together. I would certainly have indicated that we were using the report in preparing a Yorkshire Television documentary on Biafra. Since photo-copying of research material is a totally routine practice in a television studio, I would not have thought to mention the Xeroxing, although had the matter come up I certainly would not have concealed it. As for my newspaper article intentions, I would certainly not have concealed those either, but since General Alexander was used to seeing the information he gave me end up in print, this would presumably have come as no great surprise to him. Perhaps this is an unfair speculation, for it might well have happened that the General would have made it clear that he had never intended allowing me to make journalistic use of the Scott Report. Had this occurred, there would never have been any Official Secrets prosecution.

Anyway, we shall never know, as the General and I missed each other by about half an hour. Christmas then intervened and I forgot all about Colonel Scott's report until New Year's Eve, when I went North to spend the Hogmanay holiday with Hugh Fraser at his home in Scotland.*

Hugh Fraser was even more startled by the text of the Scott Report than I had been, for his long hours in the House of Commons listening to debates and questions on the Nigerian civil war

*Hugh Fraser's Scottish home, Eilean Aigas, Inverness-shire, must be the only house in Britain which has *twice* been the location for the preparation of literary enterprises resulting in Official Secrets Acts prosecutions. In the 1930's Sir Compton Mackenzie was the tenant of Eilean Aigas and there wrote his book *Greek Memories* which he and his publishers were prosecuted for under Section 2 of the 1911 Act (see p. 55). But the *Greek Memories* case and the Scott Report case had more in common than their origin at Eilean Aigas. Both Sir Compton Mackenzie and I claimed that we had made our respective disclosures in order to expose inaccurate statements about a war made by high government officials. The committal proceedings of both cases were heard at first instance at the Guildhall Magistrates' Court in the City of London. The full trial of the Mackenzie case began in Court No. 1 of the Old Bailey on 12 January 1933; my trial commenced in the same courtroom on 12 January 1971. Both prosecutions were widely alleged to have been brought for political reasons. A remarkable series of coincidences.

enabled him to identify several key passages in the document which were inconsistent with statements by ministers to Parliament. These inconsistencies covered three main areas in addition to the issue of British arms supplies.

First there was the matter of Nigeria's intentions to destroy Biafra's one and only airstrip at Uli. In paragraph 53 of his report Colonel Scott stressed that Uli was the Federal forces' main strategic target and in paragraph 67 he pointed out that any weakening of the blockade was due to the Nigerian Air Force's inability to destroy Uli airstrip. Yet on several occasions British ministers had given the impression to Parliament that Uli airstrip was kept open because of the humanitarian policy of the Nigerians in allowing relief flights to go in, and because of British pressure so to do.*

Secondly there was the matter of certain inconsistent statements about Nigeria's plan to conquer Biafra. The Foreign Secretary, Mr Michael Stewart, had told Parliament on 12 June 1968 that General Gowon had 'made it clear that he does not desire to invade the Biafran heartlands and that he will try to avoid that step.'[2] On 9 December 1969 Mr Stewart had said in the House of Commons that the British Government would reconsider its arms supply policy 'if it were clear that the Nigerian Government were determined on nothing but outright victory'.[3] But the sections of Colonel Scott's report headed 'Tasks' (i.e. paragraphs 136, 146 and 156) made it clear that the Nigerians were indeed determined on outright victory and were already invading the Biafran heartlands.

Thirdly there was the issue of Nigeria's arms supplies. British ministers on numerous occasions had argued that Nigeria had many sources of arms and that a British arms embargo would therefore make no difference because the UK was only 'one of many suppliers'.† But Colonel Scott in paragraph 70 of his report disclosed that Nigeria already had an ammunition shortage 'aggravated by the decision of many countries in Western Europe to place an embargo on the supply of arms to the Federal Military Government. In consequence the major suppliers of arms and ammunition are the UK, Spain and the Soviet Union'.

*See Michael Stewart to House of Commons, 7 July 1969, Hansard col. 1442. Harold Wilson to House of Commons, 2 April 1969, Hansard col. 496.

†See Lord Shepherd (Minister of State at the Foreign Office), 21 July 1969, Hansard col. 753. Michael Stewart 12 June 1968, Hansard col. 229 and *passim*.

Colonel Scott's revelations of this shortage and the limited number of suppliers thus indicated that ministers had misled the public by stressing the number of sources of arms and saying that a British embargo would be ineffective. In fact a British embargo would, if Colonel Scott's report was correct, have caused chaos in Nigeria's logistical plans for arms, and could well have brought Nigeria quickly to the negotiating table.

Finally, and most importantly of all, there was the issue of the actual totals of British arms supplied to Nigeria. Hugh Fraser was able to confirm and further document the variations I had discovered between Colonel Scott's facts and Mr Michael Stewart's statements on this point (see pp. 92–94 for details).

Hugh Fraser and I both felt a passionate indignation over this evidence that ministers of the Crown had been making misleading statements about the British Government's Nigeria policy. Over a war in which two million people had died, the apparent ministerial deceit seemed unpardonable. Moreover, it was disclosed in another part of the Scott Report (paragraph 70) that Federal Nigeria was now asking Britain for sixty million rounds of NATO 7.622 mm ammunition – a three hundred per cent increase on previous deliveries for one campaigning season. Would the Wilson government grant this request and still go on giving bland assurances about 'Britain supplies no more than fifteen per cent of Nigeria's total arms'?

Hugh Fraser and I agreed that a major press and parliamentary campaign based on the Scott Report must be launched as soon as the House of Commons re-assembled in mid-January. The only dissenting voice was that of Hugh Fraser's wife, Antonia, who thought it absolutely extraordinary that a dedicated pro-Nigerian should have given such a document to a dedicated pro-Biafran. But after I had described the exact circumstances in which I had received the document from General Alexander, the majority view was that the Scott Report was some sort of specialist brief circulated to experts in the pro-Federal lobby in the UK and that this was the reason why General Alexander was in possession of the document.*

---

*Hugh Fraser, as an ex-Defence Minister, had some previous experience of official secrets but privately decided that the Scott Report was not one of them as it had no official address, no official addressee, no distribution list, was not numbered, and was not written on official paper. This view of the unusual appearance

In considering our plans to get maximum exposure for the Scott Report's revelations, we decided that the *Sunday Telegraph* was the best newspaper to handle the document as it had taken a far more militant editorial line than any other Sunday paper in opposing the Government's sale of arms to Nigeria.

Hugh Fraser simultaneously planned to put down a series of Parliamentary questions on the Scott Report for the day the House of Commons returned, and we further intended to filter copies of the document to various other newspapers during the following week beginning with the *Daily Express* and the *Evening Standard*. Since neither Hugh Fraser nor I knew the *Sunday Telegraph's* editor, Mr Brian Roberts, we sent it to the newspaper via Mr Graham Watson of Curtis Brown Limited who normally acted as literary agent for both Hugh Fraser and myself. It was further understood from our Scottish plans that if any fees were paid through Curtis Brown these would be donated to one of the relief organisations flying food into Biafra. We also talked of television and radio programmes on which Scott's revelations could be publicised, of getting an emergency debate in the House of Commons and of forcing a change of Government policy. I realised that by using the document in this highly political way I would be going further than the pro-Federal General Alexander would have wished, for though the terms on which he normally gave me information and documents permitted journalistic use, this did not include annexing the information to fight political crusades. However, I justified my decision to use the document for political as well as journalistic purposes on the grounds that it would be morally wrong to suppress information which appeared to establish that ministers of the Crown had misled the British people on an issue involving the death of some two million African children. I still stand by that decision today.

Returning to London from Scotland on 8 January, I telephoned Mr Graham Watson of Curtis Brown to say that I had got hold of an interesting document dealing with the Nigeria–Biafra situation, and suggested that on account of its editorial sympathies for Biafra, the *Sunday Telegraph* would be the paper to handle it. I sent the report and some notes summarising its contents round to Curtis

of the document was later substantially agreed with by Lord Chalfont, a former Labour Foreign Office Minister, who gave evidence for my defence as an expert witness in the Old Bailey trial (see pp. 183–14).

Brown in a taxi, and Graham Watson sent it on to the *Telegraph,* subsequently telling the features editor that if the paper was seriously thinking of doing an article on the Scott Report they could contact me or Hugh Fraser. The next day an assistant editor of the *Sunday Telegraph,* Mr Gordon Brook-Shepherd, telephoned both of us at our homes. His principal objective was to establish the authenticity of the document. Although we had no real doubts about this, there was a remote possibility that the Scott Report (or at least its conclusions) might be a propaganda puff to strengthen the sympathies of people in the pro-Federal Lobby. Therefore to check the factual accuracy of the report, I had shown it to one or two experts in London, including one eminent Biafran. From their reactions, I was able to assure Mr Brook-Shepherd that I was convinced of the authenticity of the document and Hugh Fraser gave the same opinion. I kept up a discreet smokescreen in reply to the *Sunday Telegraph*'s request for information about my source, and beyond saying it had come through military contacts, I gave no clue as to the existence of General Alexander. I had no discussions of any sort with the *Sunday Telegraph* about the fee to be paid for the report, nor about the presentation of the story, although Mr Brook-Shepherd said several times that the *Telegraph*'s feature pages had already been set and so it would have to be confined to a news piece.

At about 6 p.m. on Friday, 9 January, I heard from Curtis Brown Limited that the *Sunday Telegraph* was definitely going to run a news story on the Scott Report. I telephoned this information to Hugh Fraser who was subsequently in touch with the *Sunday Telegraph* and gave them the text of seven Parliamentary questions he had posted to the House of Commons for tabling on Monday. These included a demand that the Scott Report should be placed in the House of Commons library 'for the House's better understanding of the military situation'; a request that the Foreign Secretary should say what action the Government would take over Nigeria's request for a further sixty million rounds of 7.622 ammunition; a tongue-in-cheek suggestion that in order to avoid wasting the money of the British taxpayer the Foreign Office should coordinate the activities of Fascist Spain, Soviet Russia and Labour Britain over Nigeria's arms supplies; and some barbed probes on the security of the British High Commissioner's office in Lagos and on the size and purpose of the new British naval training mission (referred to by Scott) in Nigeria. It required little imagination to see that these questions, backed up by supplementaries, would cause a major Parliamentary uproar.

Given this useful additional contribution to their Scott Report story, the *Sunday Telegraph* really went to town with it in their issue of 11 January. SECRET BIAFRA WAR PLAN REVEALED screamed the paper's headlines across six columns of the front page, followed by big black sub-headings MUDDLE, CORRUPTION, WASTE, BY FEDERALS; MAP OF OPERATIONS; ORDER OF BATTLE and TRIBUTE TO BIAFRANS. This lead-story, by-lined simply 'by our Diplomatic Staff' took up most of the front page and ran for three more columns on the back page. A great deal of this space was devoted to a detailed explanation of why the *Telegraph* believed the report was authentic (the paper even reproduced Colonel Scott's cyclostyled signature for this purpose) and to a speculation about General Ojukwu having received the document. Inside, two more pages were given over to an extensive verbatim reprint of much of the report, and the paper added to all of this a further Nigerian article on the leader page and an editorial comment. An early copy of this issue was sent round to Hugh Fraser by special messenger on the evening of 10 January, and as we sat reading it I remember my first reactions being those of sheer amazement at the volume of coverage. It still did not occur to me, even after seeing the newspaper's headlines, that there was the slightest possibility of any trouble under the Official Secrets Acts. This optimism was not due to my own ignorance of the law, for it was quite clear from the *Sunday Telegraph*'s account that the newspaper's security experts had taken careful steps to protect themselves against any legal repercussions by clearing the report with the D-notice Committee. The relevant paragraph of the *Sunday Telegraph*'s report ran as follows:

There was next the problem of British national security. Accordingly, earlier on Friday evening, all the section headings of the document and any requested quotations were read over the telephone to Vice-Admiral Sir Norman Denning, Secretary of the Press, Services, and Broadcasting Committee which gives official advice to newspapers on security. He confirmed to us that there was no question of British national security being affected by publication since the document in question 'exclu-

111

sively concerned the forces of a foreign power'. This verdict, coupled with the knowledge that, if only through Mr Fraser's imminent disclosures, the document was about to be revealed anyway settled any remaining reservations.

The *Sunday Telegraph* also made some knowledgeable comments about 'unorthodox features' of the document's security grading and concluded 'what we believe we have is a copy of a document written by the British Officer whose signature it bears, but not an official British Government document in the accepted sense of that term'. The relevance of these particular semantics was not apparent until several weeks later, for at the time all that seemed to matter was that the Scott Report had hit the news-stands as a major journalistic scoop.

By a cruel blow of fate this scoop was remarkably short-lived, for later that same evening all other Sunday newspapers picked up front page lead stories on Biafra which dwarfed the *Sunday Telegraph*'s triumph. From agency sources the rest of Fleet Street got the news during the late afternoon of 10 January that after thirty-one months of stubborn resistance, Biafra's troops were in head-long flight from the oncoming Federal offensive and that the total collapse of the secessionist state was imminent. In what must have been an agonising moment of decision, the *Sunday Telegraph*'s editor had to assess the value of these agency wires against his exclusive Scott Report saga. By the time the *Sunday Telegraph*'s late editions started to roll off the presses the paper was running a two-hundred-word dispatch from its Paris correspondent, Alex Macmillan, headlined BIAFRA ABOUT TO COLLAPSE. This news item was bizarrely juxtaposed on the front page alongside the un-amended six-thousand-word Scott story. It must have caused some confusion in readers' minds to read in one column that General Ojukwu had flown out of Biafra declaring 'All is finished' and in the adjacent column that Ojukwu's alleged possession of the Scott Report was 'the Nigerian equivalent of Hitler in 1944 being given the complete plan for the Allied offensive in Normandy'. But such contradictions are occasionally inevitable in journalism, and it must be remembered that with four full pages of his paper given over to Colonel Scott's document, the *Sunday Telegraph*'s editor would have found difficulty in spiking his big story for some un-corroborated agency reports. Twelve hours later, however, it was

112

confirmed that all really was finished for Biafra, and with the formal surrender on 13 January, interest in Colonel Scott's revelations became largely academic. In a broadcast on the 'World at One' programme on Sunday, 12 January, Hugh Fraser referred fairly extensively to the document, a copy of which he forwarded that day to the *Daily Express*. The following day, 13 January, I wrote a wrapping-up feature article on the civil war for the *Evening Standard* headlined THE SHAME OF THE ARMS MERCHANTS WILL RING DOWN THE CENTURIES OF HISTORY in which I quoted Colonel Scott's arms figures to show how substantial Britain's role in the crushing of Biafra had been. After this, the interest of the press and television was rightly directed entirely towards relief operations for Biafra, and so apart from being a short-lived topic of conversation in Fleet Street, the Scott Report seemed to have sunk without trace.

Unhappily for Colonel Scott, a much more serious view of the *Sunday Telegraph* leak was being taken in Nigeria. High officials in the Federal Military Government were incensed by reading Colonel Scott's rather testy criticisms of their army's 'inefficiency, corruption, muddle and waste'. One of the angriest readers was the Nigerian Chief of Staff, Brigadier Hassan Katsina, a member of the formidable Royal Dikwa family. His department had been criticised by Scott for running 'very much a 9 a.m. to 5 p.m. war – it needs a major crisis to get the staff officers to work overtime and a near disaster to bring in the civil servants after duty hours ... in these circumstances, sound planning and co-ordination is almost impossible to achieve'.[4] Katsina and other enraged Nigerian officers went so far as to express the view that Scott was a Biafran spy and demanded his immediate expulsion. Accordingly, on the night of 12 January, Colonel Scott was declared persona non grata and left from Ikeja airport shortly after lunch on 13 January. He had been Defence Adviser to the High Commission in Lagos for three years, although some weeks previously he had been notified of his forthcoming promotion to a similar post at the British Embassy in Tokyo.

Scott's departure was widely reported in Britain, but did not cause a real stir, largely because everyone interested in the Nigeria situation was by this time obsessed with the relief problems. These looked grim, particularly in view of General Gowon's decision to prohibit assistance from all the Christian relief agencies who had previously been giving food and medical supplies to Biafra. A military leader who, in the hour of victory, could heartlessly reject food for the starving with the phrase 'we do not want their blood money' might be expected to have one or two more aberrations, and Colonel Scott's abrupt expulsion was seen by many only as another example of Nigerian hypersensitivity.*

Hearing the news of Colonel Scott's fate, I was distressed that my actions should have led to such inconvenient consequences for an innocent individual, and for the first time the fear crossed my mind that some sort of Foreign Office action might be taken. However, I soon disposed of this fear on the grounds that the *Sunday Telegraph*'s D-notice clearance gave complete legal immunity, and that in any case the leak would not be traced to General Alexander or myself. Apart from listening impassively to various Biafra lobby friends who insisted on telling me all about the significance of the Scott Report, the only other action I took on the matter during the week following Biafra's surrender was to talk to Mr Graham Watson of Curtis Brown on 17 January. I thanked him for his part in getting the report published and told him that the five hundred pound fee agreed by the *Sunday Telegraph* would be donated to one of the relief organisations permitted by the Nigerians to fly food into Biafra. I asked him to send the money on direct to a charity whose name and address I would give him as soon as the relief arrangements into Biafra were clarified by Lagos. He said that in those circumstances Curtis Brown Limited would waive their commission when the *Sunday Telegraph* cheque arrived.† By 17 January there was no hint of any police investigation being directed towards the *Sunday Telegraph*, Curtis Brown, or myself, so after this conversation with Graham Watson, the Scott Report affair seemed a finished chapter. Little did I know what preparations were being made by the Special Branch of Scotland Yard.

---

*In fact, Scott's was not the only expulsion. Ten days later Colonel Eugene Dewey of the United States Army, President Nixon's special adviser on aid and relief operations, was declared persona non grata for no given reason. Many priests and nuns were also expelled.

†The cheque arrived on 25 February, five weeks after issuing these instructions. Because police enquiries and later legal proceedings were pending, I asked Curtis Brown Limited to hold the money until instructing them to forward it to the Save the Children Fund on 20 October 1970.

9

Scotland Yard Investigates

Nine days after the publication of the Scott Report by the *Sunday Telegraph*, I received a disturbing letter, dated 19 January, from General Alexander. It was a rather baffling communication beginning with several expressions of sympathy for Colonel Scott and indicating that General Alexander had been surprised to read extracts of the report in the *Sunday Telegraph* and to learn that Hugh Fraser had got hold of a copy. These sentiments were stated in a completely neutral way, and were not at all accusing or suggestive, so the first part of the letter looked as though the General had no idea whatsoever that I had played a part in forwarding a copy of his document to the *Telegraph*. However, General Alexander's letter continued with the following paragraph:

> There is going to be a full-scale enquiry. In fact I have been told that this is the case. I will have to disclose that I have a copy, but will not be saying that you have seen it because this might lead to unpleasant repercussions. I would be very grateful if you did not mention to anyone that you have seen the report. I am sure you realise the importance of this.

The two halves of this letter did not seem to fit together. In the first part the General appeared to be suggesting his total innocence from the possibility of being the original source of the leak to the Press and to Hugh Fraser. This would be a surprising claim since he had given me the document without strings attached (there was no reference in this 19 January letter to the report being entrusted in confidence) and he knew that I was a working journalist in the habit of publishing the Nigerian civil war information he had given me in the past. General Alexander also knew that I was a close friend of Hugh Fraser's, and had referred to this fact in a previous correspondence with me. Nevertheless, the General's posture of innocence might be completely genuine if some ghastly misunderstanding really had occurred about the terms on which I was given the Scott Report. Yet if this was the case, how could the paragraph quoted above be explained? I read it as a cri de coeur for silence from an alarmed accomplice.*

The news that 'a full-scale enquiry' was under way was alarming, for it indicated that the Government might be going to take reprisals against those who had caused it so much embarrassment. This conclusion was not entirely unexpected, for the day before receiving General Alexander's letter I had heard a Fleet Street rumour that action under the Official Secrets Acts was going to be pursued against the *Sunday Telegraph.* I had passed this rumour on via Curtis Brown Limited to Mr Thackeray, the features editor of the *Sunday Telegraph,* but since his reaction had been one of negative unconcern, I had dismissed the idea as idle gossip. Now with this confirmation of a full-scale enquiry from General Alexander, the rumour looked like becoming a reality.

Knowing that some sort of official investigation over the Scott Report was now in train, I inevitably recalled the affair of General Alexander and *Topic* Magazine (see pp. 98–100). This recollection, together with ambiguities in the General's letter of 19 January at once raised in my mind the spectre of being shopped by my distinguished source. For this reason I felt unable to have a candid telephone conversation with General Alexander to discuss our joint tactics in facing the forthcoming enquiry. Instead I replied to his letter with a somewhat ambiguous communication of my own.

In my reply to General Alexander, dated 20 January, my first priority was to assure a helpful contact that I would obey one of the fundamental rules of journalistic ethics and would not reveal him as my source. I therefore wrote in my reply:

> As for your having shown me a copy I will maintain a grave-like silence about this. Indeed in the very unlikely event of anyone asking me I will know nothing whatever of the existence of your copy.

*General Alexander always maintained that this paragraph in his 19 January letter in no way indicated that he knew his copy of the Scott Report had been the one leaked to the *Sunday Telegraph,* and that he had merely written it to protect Colonel Cairns.

My second priority was to protect my own subsequent contacts over the Scott Report delivery to the *Telegraph*. In order to keep all knowledge of Curtis Brown Limited, Hugh Fraser and Yorkshire Television out of reach of the possible investigations, I ended my letter to the General on an ingenuous note giving the impression that I had no idea how Hugh Fraser got his copy of the document and finished with the words:

> If I hear any Fleet Street or Biafra lobby gossip on the Scott leak I will let you know. I am most grateful to you for writing as you did about all this and can assure you that my lips are very firmly sealed – Yours ever, Jonathan.

The next move in the chain of events was a second letter to me from General Alexander dated 22 January. It was very different in its tone from the previous note and bore signs of considerable agitation. In it the General said that the police were now coming to interview him and in these circumstances he felt he must disclose that he had given me the Scott Report, though he had done this 'in strictest confidence'. He added that he had now noticed that the stapling on the document seemed to have been interfered with and hoped that this did not mean that I had photo-copied it. The letter ended with a demand that I should give him permission to reveal my name to the police.

It was at this point that I realised there was no hope of co-operating with General Alexander to thwart the official enquiry, for it seemed to me he would be maintaining that he had given me the document in the strictest confidence. Any lingering doubts I had over the General's attitude were dispelled by a telephone conversation I had with him on 25 January. In this talk General Alexander demanded to know the details of when and where the Scott Report had been reproduced and he again asked permission to pass my name to the police. I admitted to knowing about the unstapling and photo-copying of the document but added 'I can't say more because other people are involved'. The conversation ended with my reluctantly giving General Alexander my consent to being named to the authorities.

Meanwhile, a full-scale police investigation into the Scott Report leak had been launched in London and Lagos under the supervision of Detective Chief Superintendent Kenneth Pendered of Scotland Yard. These inquiries, which were conducted by Special

Branch detectives, led to an interview with General Alexander in Yorkshire on 21 January. In his police statement of that date, the General merely said that he had 'shown the report to a friend' whom he did not wish to identify without the friend's permission. A week later, having extracted this permission from me, General Alexander called in to Scotland Yard and made a new statement in which I was named as the person to whom the Scott Report had been lent 'in strictest confidence'. In the course of this visit to Scotland Yard General Alexander gave the police my letter to him of 20 January. At no stage had I been told by the General that he was contemplating handing over my correspondence to him to the Special Branch.

Scotland Yard also had some success with the Scott Report investigation from the Fleet Street end, when at about 3 p.m. on Tuesday 27 January the officers in charge of the case called on the *Sunday Telegraph*. The police were seen by the editor, Mr Brian Roberts, in the presence of the *Sunday Telegraph*'s solicitor, Mr Peter Richardson.

After some preliminary formalities, Detective Chief Superintendent Pendered cautioned Mr Roberts and began an interrogation which was taken down by Detective Sergeant Digby and later read in court. The relevant part of the questioning went as follows:

Detective Chief Superintendent Pendered : Have you still in your possession a copy of Colonel Scott's report?

Brian Roberts : I have a copy. A photograph copy of that supplied.

Pendered : May I see it?

Roberts : Yes, I don't see any objection.

Pendered : I must take possession of this.

Mr Peter Richardson : On what authority do you take it?

Pendered : It is the property of Her Majesty's Government and it is required for evidential purposes.

118

Richardson :   This copy? I am sure that if you ask Mr Roberts for it he would not mind you having it.

Pendered :   (To Mr Roberts) May I take the copy?

Roberts :   Yes.

Chief Superintendent Pendered then took possession of the document.

Pendered :   Will you tell me the circumstances in which you came into possession of a copy of the report?

Roberts :   We were offered it in the ordinary way by a literary agency of the highest repute, one with whom we deal with in this field.

Pendered :   Who gave it to you?

Roberts :   (After consulting Richardson) Yes I think so as it was an ordinary commercial transaction. We purchased it from Curtis Brown.

Mr Roberts was then asked for the address of the agency and, at his request, his secretary brought to him a *Sunday Telegraph* memorandum form on which was typed the address and telephone number of Curtis Brown Limited. Chief Superintendent Pendered took this piece of paper away with him.

The disclosures from this interview, added to the disclosures made by General Alexander, gave the police two vital pieces of evidence. First, by making scientific comparisons between the photo-copy given them by Mr Roberts and the original copy given them by General Alexander, the detectives had definite proof that the General's document was the one which leaked to the *Telegraph*. This was by no means a foregone conclusion, as Colonel Scott had distributed some fifty copies of his report. Secondly, the revelation of the *Sunday Telegraph*'s immediate source narrowed the probable suspects down to a slender category of persons who were both clients of Curtis Brown and acquaintances of General Alexander.

As a result of the *Sunday Telegraph*'s disclosing who gave them the document, the Special Branch immediately called on Mr Graham Watson of Curtis Brown, arriving at the agency's offices at about 5 p.m. on 27 January. Mr Watson confirmed that his agency had forwarded the report from one of his clients to the features editor of the *Sunday Telegraph* but declined to reveal the client's identity. Although he was under no obligation to maintain this discretion, and although there is no convention saying that literary agents should not reveal their sources, Graham Watson honourably refused to disclose my name to the police until after the charges had been laid against me. Nevertheless, under questioning from Chief Superintendent Pendered on the afternoon of 27 January, Graham Watson was compelled to admit that I was one of his agency's clients (a fact which is in any case published on a Curtis Brown publicity pamphlet) and he could not give a denial to the police's suggestion that the document had reached the agency from me. After I heard about the questions asked by the detectives at Curtis Brown, I knew it would only be a matter of time before they were round on my doorstep.

At about 6.30 p.m. on 27 January, Graham Watson telephoned me and Hugh Fraser to let us know that he had been questioned by Scotland Yard detectives about the Scott Report. Around 7 p.m. Chief Superintendent Pendered telephoned Hugh Fraser and asked to come and interview him. Hugh Fraser agreed to this request and arranged an appointment for the police to see him at his own home two days ahead. There was no mention of the Official Secrets Act in this telephone conversation.

Dining with me on the evening of 27 January, Hugh Fraser suggested that the time had come for us both to seek professional legal advice. An appointment was duly made for us to call on Lord Goodman, Hugh Fraser's own solicitor, before breakfast the following day. It would of course have been completely understandable if Hugh Fraser had at this stage indicated that he and I should go our separate ways over the whole affair. After all, I had been the prime mover in obtaining the Scott Report and forwarding it to the *Sunday Telegraph,* while he had been only an adviser and encourager. But Hugh Fraser would not hear of such a suggestion, and insisted that we should stand or fall together. He never deviated from this generous line of joint responsibility throughout the saga.

After dinner I returned to my flat in Phillimore Gardens at

about 11.45 p.m. Within two minutes of my arrival the doorbell rang and Detective Chief Superintendent Pendered announced himself. He explained that he and his Detective Sergeant wished to interrogate me there and then about the disclosure of the Scott Report which he claimed had been published 'in contravention of the Official Secrets Act'. I declined to answer questions at this late hour and politely but firmly turned the detectives away with the promise of a mid-morning appointment. In doing so, it was a matter of some consolation to know that I had an even earlier assignation with one of Britain's most eminent lawyers.

At 8 a.m. in his Portland Place flat the next morning Lord Goodman heard my story, accepted the case and immediately rearranged my appointment for two days later with the police in order to obtain Counsel's opinion from Mr Basil Wigoder QC and Mr John Lloyd Eley QC. This opinion was set out in an encouraging document, for it argued that any prosecutions under Sections 2 (1) or 2 (2) of the Official Secrets Act were unlikely to succeed against me or Hugh Fraser. The two counsel advised that if the police were conducting their enquiries under Section 1 of the 1911 Act (which deals with espionage cases 'prejudicial to the safety or interests of the State') and had the written permission of the Home Secretary to interrogate suspects, then of course the Special Branch's questions would have to be answered for it is an offence to refuse to assist the police in such circumstances. But the opinion continued 'if the police have not got such permission, then we advise Mr Aitken and Mr Fraser on legal advice to answer no questions and to make no statement of any sort whatsoever'.

Confronting Chief Superintendent Pendered and Detective Sergeant Digby with me on 29 January, Lord Goodman extracted the crucial information that the police enquiries were not being carried out under Section 1 of the Official Secrets Act and then declared 'In those circumstances, after taking Counsel's opinion, it is my duty to advise my client not to answer any questions'. After a formal consultation with Basil Wigoder QC in the Temple the same evening, Hugh Fraser followed exactly the same formula when the police saw him in Lord Goodman's presence on 30 January. The basic reason for this uncompromising silence was that both the lawyers and the participants were convinced from the start that any attempt to bring prosecutions under the Official Secrets Act over the Scott Report leak would amount to a blatant abuse of the criminal law for political purposes. We all agreed, as a matter of principle, that we would not co-operate in this travesty of a criminal investigation.

During the next few days Hugh Fraser and I talked to several advisers, legal, journalistic and political, about the outcome of Scotland Yard's enquiries. Although it was clear that a technical case could probably be made out against both of us under Section 2 of the Official Secrets Act, everyone to whom we spoke thought the chances of a prosecution were remote. The consensus view went something like this: 'Well, you may or may not have cut a few corners in the way you handled this document, but your disclosures had no relevance to national security, were not leaked to you by a government official, and in any case the secretary of the D-notice Committee cleared the Scott Report for publication by the *Sunday Telegraph*. Although you may have caused embarrassment to some ministers and officials, the Nigerian civil war is over now and the sooner it is all forgotten about the better. Since you can't be prosecuted except by the decision of the Attorney-General, it is extremely unlikely that his fiat would be given to proceed against journalists and politicians doing their job in a case as unimportant as this one is in official secrets terms.'

There was no substantial deviation from this kind of opinion, and some people went much further, saying 'Wilson would never risk another Vassall-type row with the Press,* especially in an election year.' I was heartened by such comments, and even more so by the fact that there appeared to be no further attempts by the police to question people connected with the case.

Because of the deafening silence from Scotland Yard from 30 January onwards, I took the view that there was little likelihood of anything more being heard about Official Secrets Acts prosecutions over the Scott Report. Accordingly I flew off on 7 February to India and Australia for a month of previously arranged overseas reporting assignments. On about 26 February, when in Mel-

---

*One of the outcomes of the 1961 Official Secrets prosecution of the Admiralty clerk John Vassall (see p. 73) was the setting up by the Government of a tribunal of inquiry. Among those summoned to appear before this tribunal were two Fleet Street journalists, Mulholland and Foster, who were asked to disclose their sources for certain information they had published. Both journalists refused, citing the ethical code of their profession. As a result they were imprisoned for contempt of court. This episode was thought to be substantially reponsible for poisoning the relationship between the Press and the Macmillan government from 1962–1964.

bourne, I was astonished to receive the following telegram from my mother:

> Police very active in Yorkshire upsetting many constituents stop bad rumours growing as Alexander talks and you not there to answer stop Hugh and Goodie* still think prosecution unlikely but suggest you come home soonest.

I returned post haste from Australia, arriving in London on 2 March, and immediately learned the details of what had been going on in Yorkshire. It transpired that Special Branch detectives had been staying in an hotel at Thirsk for some days around 19 February and from there had carried out an extensive investigation. Police statements had been taken from all those present at General Alexander's dinner party. Detectives had called on neighbours in my village to ask questions about my movements on 21-22 December. Mrs Roy Smith, the chairman of the Thirsk and Malton Conservative Association, had been interrogated. The police had also investigated the constituency offices at Easingwold, making a careful inspection of the aged duplicating machine and taking away staples and samples of my handwriting. The twenty-year-old assistant secretary to the Conservative Association, Miss Judith Breese (who on the face of things had no connection whatsoever with the case) was cautioned and told she would be required to give evidence against me in court. She was later told by Chief Superintendent Pendered that it was necessary for her to give up her star part in a local play in order to be a prosecution witness at the Magistrates' Court hearing, though in fact she was never asked to do this and no statement from her was included in the prosecution depositions.

All these bizarre enquiries, which were carried out by Scotland Yard officers citing the Official Secrets Act, inevitably created considerable agitation in my hitherto tranquil constituency. This agitation was in no way abated by General Alexander who when asked by bewildered neighbours what the fuss was all about, recounted a version of his dinner party transaction of the Scott Report which was highly unfavourable to me. Thus when I returned to Yorkshire in the first week of March I found that a number of my most prominent political supporters were in a state of high panic about the extra-curricular activities of their candidate, and

*The Rt. Hon. Hugh Fraser MP and Lord Goodman.

it was only after I had contradicted General Alexander's account of the affair (producing letters and other documents in support of my denial) that local feelings began to change. After I had discussed the matter extensively in private with two key groups of constituents, the view prevailed that there must have been some sort of a misunderstanding between me and the General and that the whole affair was much ado about nothing. However, I was urged by some Yorkshire friends to counteract all possible constituency ill-effects from this misunderstanding by going to see General Alexander and soothing the matter down by personal conciliation.

As a result of this advice I telephoned General Alexander on the morning of 11 March and asked whether I could come to see him. He was very friendly, and promptly invited me to tea that afternoon. I arrived just after 5 p.m. at his home in Brandsby, was warmly greeted by Mrs Alexander and shown into the library. The General was already seated beside a blazing log fire and he waved me to an armchair the other side of the fireplace, all the other seats being covered with riding hats, horsewhips, jodhpurs, and other impedimenta of the fox hunt from which my host had just returned. We talked together for over an hour.

Seen in retrospect, this encounter was fraught with high comedy. General Alexander and I were by this stage wary antagonists, equally anxious to extricate ourselves from all Official Secrets Act problems. To this end we had both prepared separate and mutually hostile strategies which we were now putting into effect beneath the veneer of a mutually friendly conversation. My plan was to put a stop to rumbles of discontent in the constituency by getting General Alexander off my locally-vulnerable back and shifting him on to Hugh Fraser's politically invulnerable back. In order to achieve this I was as conciliatory as possible to the General. I apologised for having caused such a storm and for having allowed the Scott Report story to get politically out of control, although I stuck to my guns about the terms under which I had been given the document for journalistic purposes. I concealed from the General the truth about where the photo-copying had been done (thinking that the truth might lead to a police swoop on Yorkshire Television) putting the blame for this and for all other controversial aspects of the affair on to Hugh Fraser, a manoeuvre which Fraser himself had suggested I should employ.* But while I was indulging in these private verbal subtleties, General Alexander was perpetrating a far more effective trick of his own, for unbeknownst to me our entire tea-time conversation was being 'bugged' by a hidden tape-recorder. This device had been set up entirely on the General's initiative,† for although he had telephoned Sergeant Digby at Scotland Yard about an hour before I arrived, and subsequently played the tape over to the Special Branch seven days later, nevertheless it appears from the evidence given in court that Scotland Yard played no part in the planning or the arrangement of this trap.[1]

For my part I walked obliviously into General Alexander's tape-recorded ambush and although I was mildly surprised during our talk at the way in which my host occasionally raised his voice to protest his innocence as though he was addressing a public meeting, I had no idea whatsoever that we were talking on tape. It never occurred to me that General Alexander would be such a superior exponent of the art of self-extrication.

Aside from those parts of the conversation in which the General white-washed himself and blamed me, and I in turn white-washed myself and blamed Hugh Fraser, our talk consisted largely of a discussion on the chances of a prosecution and the political stir caused locally by gossip.‡ Our meeting ended on a reassuring but supremely ironical note when the General said to me in the friendliest possible way: 'I can assure you that I am not going to make any capital against you if you are worried about that.'

After this apparently air-clearing talk with General Alexander, my Official Secrets worries began to diminish. Almost nine weeks had elapsed since the publication of the Scott Report, there was talk of an early election, and the Nigerian civil war was fast fading from public memory. It seemed increasingly unlikely that any

*Hugh Fraser had made this suggestion partly to help me out of my constituency difficulties but more because of his own attitude to General Alexander. The two of them had clashed on the issue of Uli airstrip, which General Alexander wished to bomb despite the presence of relief planes. This was a repugnant view to a humanitarian sympathiser for Biafra. Fraser also knew from the police and Lord Goodman that Alexander had handed over my correspondence to Scotland Yard without my permission, and took a dim view of this behaviour.

†At the Old Bailey trial, General Alexander insisted that the bugging device had been installed on his wife's initiative.

‡For extracts from the transcript see Chapter 11.

Attorney-General or Prime Minister would, in these circumstances, sanction an Official Secrets prosecution of a matter as irrelevant to national security as the *Sunday Telegraph's* disclosures. The only indications that this might not be the case were the hints that had been dropped to my constituents by Chief Superintendent Pendered and my own possibly paranoiac belief (based on excessive electronic irregularities from my telephone and frequent sightings of men in mackintoshes strolling near my flat) that I was still under surveillance by the Special Branch.

Six days after my talk with General Alexander the presence of the men in mackintoshes became a reality. At about 9 a.m. on the morning of 17 March as I was going out of my flat in London to put some money in a parking ticket machine, a shiny black chauffeur-driven Wolseley drew up to the pavement and two familiar figures jumped out. They were Detective Chief Superintendent Pendered and Detective Sergeant Digby, one of whom handed me a piece of paper. It read:

> Information has been laid this day by Kenneth George Pendered, a Detective Chief Superintendent of the Metropolitan Police Force on behalf of the Director of Public Prosecutions, that you on the ninth day of January 1970 in the said city at 135 Fleet Street, London EC2 did receive a document entitled 'An Appreciation of the Nigerian Conflict', knowing or having reasonable grounds to believe that at the time you received it the said document was communicated to you in contravention of Section 2 (2) of the Official Secrets Act 1911.

The summons ended by commanding me to appear before the City Justices at the Mansion House on 22 April 'at 10.30 in the forenoon'.

Aftermath of the Summons

Soon after the issue of the summons, the case was engulfed in a tidal wave of publicity. Some of the press criticism of the prosecutions stretched the *sub judice* rules to new limits. First off the mark was *The Times,* which slammed the Official Secrets Act in a first leader of 18 March saying:

> The charges have been brought under Section 2 of the 1911 Act. This section covers any wrongful communication of information or the receipt of information which has been wrongfully communicated. It is so broad a clause that any newspaper is likely to be in breach of it in the ordinary course of its business, perhaps several times a day. We all sometimes have a public duty to act in breach of it. Any official information which is given to a newspaper by any servant of the Crown high or low, without an authority or a duty to communicate could in theory lead to a prosecution.

The *Evening Standard** of the same day continued this theme with the comment:

> The Act is so widely drafted and open to so many abuses that for a long time it has been assumed that many of its provisions were defunct. The only respect in which it is normally called into operation is in matters directly relating to the work of the national security services and defence and research establishments. The charges against the *Sunday Telegraph* and its editor

---

*I should make it clear that although I was a feature writer under contract to the *Evening Standard* at this time, the extensive editorial coverage given to the case was in no way contributed or directed by me.

and against Mr Jonathan Aitken do not fall into this category
... if the law officers have now decided to reactivate Section 2
(2) of the Official Secrets Act their action could constitute a
serious infringement of Press freedom to discuss matters that
could be of public interest.

These two editorial salvoes unleashed a flow of further criticism
in the press, and a particularly lively debate ensued in the correspondence columns of *The Times*. After the third prosecution had
been announced later that day against Colonel Douglas Cairns, the
former British Representative on the International Observer team
to Nigeria, it was noticed that the wording of this last summons
named Major-General H. T. Alexander as the person to whom
Cairns was accused of passing the Scott Report. This made it
obvious to the Press that the General had been a link in the chain
of communicators whose handling of the document eventually led
to the *Sunday Telegraph,* so when Scotland Yard announced that
no summons would be issued against Alexander, a fresh furore
broke out about the selectivity of the prosecutions. The *pièce de
résistance* in this controversy was a letter to *The Times* of 19
March from Hugh Fraser, which read:

Sir, – what goes on?
Your leader today rightly draws attention in general terms to
the public dangers involved in the indiscriminate use of Section
2 of the Official Secrets Act, 1911. But there is more to it than
that – a curious selectivity of prosecutions. An ex-Army officer,
a journalist and an editor are being prosecuted under that
section, the latter two for 'receiving' the Scott Report. But it is
well known that I, too, received this report, encouraged its publication in the *Sunday Telegraph,* published it over the BBC
and in the House of Commons and on platforms up and down
the country because, to put it bluntly, it showed that the House
of Commons and the public had on many occasions been misled
on many aspects of the Nigerian civil war by Government
spokesmen and the Foreign Secretary in particular.
What goes on?
Yours faithfully, Hugh Fraser
House of Commons, 18 March.

After this surprise intervention the flow of press criticism became a torrent again. Once more *The Times* led the field with a thunderous leader on 21 March entitled 'The Attorney-General's Discretion' which stated:

The Attorney-General's decision on whom to prosecute and whom not to prosecute on the Secrets case seems even more open to question now than it did when the charges were first made known. There seem to have been at least six recipients of the document or the information at one time or another of whom only two have been charged with receiving . . . If this is a correct view of the matter then the Attorney-General – whose integrity is of course not in question – has made a most serious error of judgment. The selection of the people charged raises the most serious doubts about his use of the discretion which is undeniably his.

On Sunday, 22 March, the *Sunday Telegraph* made its first comment on the case, stating with Olympian dignity:

Charges have been brought against this newspaper and its editor under the Official Secrets Act of 1911, concerning our publication on 11 January, just as Biafra was collapsing, of extracts from 'An Appreciation of the Nigerian Conflict'. This had been prepared by Colonel Robert E. Scott, defence adviser to the British High Commission in Lagos, on the eve of the Federal offensive. The charges, brought under Section 2 (2) of the Act, have evoked much comment on the serious issues raised for the freedom of the Press in view of the sweeping and vague nature of Section 2. These were powerfully posed in a leading article in *The Times* on Wednesday. Mr Hugh Fraser MP, who also received a copy of the same document to which he gave wide publicity, has drawn attention to the curious fact that he has not been summonsed. As the case is *sub judice*, all we can say at the moment is that this newspaper and its editor intend to defend themselves against the charges with the utmost vigour.*

*During the next few days, more and more leading articles or comments by legal and political columnists appeared expressing concern about the operation of the Official Secrets Act. Among these journals which gave the subject particularly extensive coverage were the *New Statesman*, the *New Law Journal*, the *Financial Times*, *The Times*, the *People*, the *Sunday Express*, the *Guardian*, the *Daily Mail*, the *Northern Echo*, the *Evening Standard*, the *Spectator*, the *Irish Times*, *Newsweek*, *Le Monde*, *Tribune*, the *New York Times*, *Peace News* and *Private Eye*. Some of these publications flagrantly violated the normal reporting rules of *sub judice*, and almost all of them sailed dangerously close to the wind on the question of contempt of court.

At this time various politicians began stirring up the hornets nest. Lord Foot, the Liberal peer, gave notice of a motion for a House of Lords debate calling attention to the Official Secrets Act 'with particular reference to the operation of Section 2 of the Official Secrets Act 1911'. Dame Irene Ward, the Conservative MP for Tynemouth, gave notice of her intention to present in the House of Commons a bill to amend the Official Secrets Act of 1911 'in such a way as to bring it into line with the practice of modern publicity and communications'. Also in the House of Commons Mr Marcus Lipton (Labour, Brixton) tabled a motion calling on the Attorney-General Sir Elwyn Jones to indicate what action he proposed to take over Mr Hugh Fraser. Several Conservative back benchers joined in the supplementaries, including Mr John Peyton (Yeovil) who asked the Leader of the House 'Do you think the Attorney-General would welcome an opportunity of making a statement clearing up the doubts because it does appear that some selectivity characterises proceedings under the Official Secrets Act?' Government spokesmen merely stone-walled such questions with the reply 'The matter is now *sub judice*'.

This consideration was not, however, preventing political figures from writing to *The Times*. Perhaps the most interesting of these was the former Conservative Attorney-General, Sir Lionel Heald QC, whose letter of 20 March claimed that *The Times* had been understating 'the vice of the Official Secrets Act'. Sir Lionel continued:

There is no doubt that the Act makes it a crime, without any possibility of a defence, to report the number of cups of tea consumed per week in a government department, or the details of a new carpet in a minister's room. This is because the offence is absolute. The Act contains no limitation as to materiality, substance, or public interest. It simply uses the clear and unambiguous words 'any information' ... The only protection against abuse under the Act as it stands is the requirement that the consent of the Attorney-General must be obtained before prosecution.

Another pertinent comment in the correspondence columns of *The Times* came from Mr Woodrow Wyatt MP, who wrote:

As that wise statesman General Gowon has decided on the highly civilised course of no trials in Nigeria following the collapse of the rebellion, why is it necessary to have one here?

All these political and journalistic excitements created an atmosphere of private sympathy for the defendants and public suspicion towards the prosecuting authorities.

National interest in the Scott Report case simmered down over the Easter holiday and Parliamentary recess, but the lull was shattered by the news of a courageous private gesture on the part of Lord Hartwell, the chairman and editor-in-chief of the *Sunday Telegraph*. In a signed front page article in the *Sunday Telegraph* of 12 April, Lord Hartwell revealed that he had written to the Attorney-General, Sir Elwyn Jones, two days after the paper's editor, Mr Brian Roberts, had received the Official Secrets Act summons. The point of the letter was in effect a polite request for a prosecution. The full text ran as follows:

March 19

Dear Sir Elwyn,

I am chairman and editor-in-chief of the *Sunday Telegraph*. When police officers first visited the editor of the *Sunday Telegraph* they informed him that they would also be questioning me in regard to the Nigerian report by Colonel Scott. They have not done so.

The editor has now been charged under the Official Secrets Act. I wish to inform you that, in my capacity as above, I take full responsibility. I was aware of the receipt of the document, of the attempt to establish its authenticity, and I personally fixed the sum of money which we were prepared to pay for it.

I am sending a copy of this letter to the Prime Minister in his capacity as Head of the Security Services.

Yours sincerely,
Hartwell

Four days later the Attorney-General replied:

March 23

Dear Lord Hartwell,

Thank you for your letter of 19 March sent to my private address. I have forwarded it to the Director of Public Prosecutions. In view of the last paragraph of your letter, I am copying this to the Prime Minister.

Yours sincerely,
F. Elwyn Jones

131

Lord Hartwell pointed out in his *Sunday Telegraph* article that throughout the three weeks since receiving the Attorney-General's letter 'I have had no further inquiry or communication, written or verbal'. Lord Hartwell's intervention, all the more audacious because it had initially been so discreet, triggered off a new explosion of public and private protest about the way the case was being conducted. A typically trenchant example of this was the *Evening Standard*'s leading article of 13 April whose penultimate paragraph read:

> The Government has chosen to prosecute under an antiquated section of an unsatisfactory Act, an editor rather than his editor-in-chief, a military adviser (a colonel) rather than a major-general and a junior Conservative candidate rather than a senior Conservative MP. When this case is settled, Parliament and the public will be entitled to the fullest explanation of why this revelation in particular was considered worthy of prosecution – and why these people were selected for summons.
> Until such time, people will continue to wonder: What goes on?

In the midst of these alarms and excursions, my solicitors received from the Director of Public Prosecutions office on 11 April a fifty-five-page folio of the statements by prosecution witnesses together with a wad of exhibits. From Colonel Scott's statement it transpired that no less than fifty-one copies of the report had been distributed, and that an unknown number of spare copies and spoilt sheets had also been duplicated. The distribution list in Lagos included the Press Officer of the British High Commission and the Commercial Counsellor, the Australian and Canadian High Commissioners, the Defense Attaché to the US Embassy (three copies), and the two British members of the International Observer team, Colonel Cairns and Major Gray. There was also a large overseas distribution list, mainly to Foreign Office and Ministry of Defence officials in London, although one copy went as far afield as Rio de Janeiro, to the former British High Commissioner in Lagos, Sir David Hunt. General Alexander was not included in any of Colonel Scott's distribution lists.

General Alexander, in his statement dated 18 March, said that he had received a copy of the Scott Report through the post from Colonel Cairns. Referring to the dinner party of 21 December, the General's statement continued:

During the meal the Nigerian situation was discussed. Jonathan Aitken disputed the ability of the Federal army to win the war. I have, since visiting Nigeria, been a supporter of the Federal Government cause. I found it impossible to convince him by my own argument and eventually said that if he did not believe me perhaps he would believe Bob Scott whom he knew. I said therefore that in strictest confidence I would allow him to read a paper I had received (I did not disclose how) provided that he treated it in strictest confidence. I knew that he had written articles on Nigeria suggesting an arms embargo and opposed to the Government policy. I hoped that my argument, supported by what Scott said, might do good by making him see the futility of his own argument. Before Aitken left the dinner party he asked if he could take the document home to read as it was so late. I said yes, so long as he returned it the next day and treated it as confidential as background to himself only. He gave me his assurance and I gave him the document.

General Alexander's statement ended:

I wish now to explain why I showed the document in question to Jonathan Aitken. He is prospective Conservative candidate for Thirsk and Malton, the constituency in which I live. As such I have had considerable contact with him and counted him as a personal trusted friend. I briefed him and gave him introductions before he went to Nigeria/Biafra; he had dined in my house on several occasions. In fact, I considered him to be a close trustworthy friend.

The General's statement (which included no mention of the bugged conversation with me on 11 March) was partially and somewhat vaguely corroborated by the statement of his son, David Alexander, but one intriguing omission from the prosecution case was the absence of statements from all the other people present at the dinner party. I knew that the Special Branch detectives had questioned every one of the General's guests. Could it be that none of them were able from their recollections to back up the Alexander story? This in fact proved to be the case, and we were later able to call four independent witnesses from the dinner party to give evidence for my defence.

The rest of the prosecution case against me consisted largely of formal identification evidence tracing the route of the document to the *Sunday Telegraph* and was not in dispute, while the exhibits included a copy of my 20 January letter to General Alexander, and a copy of the Attorney-General's fiat consenting to the prosecutions. The most astonishing part of the prosecution case against the *Sunday Telegraph* was the statement by Vice-Admiral Sir Norman Denning, KBE, CB, the secretary to the D-notice Committee. The Admiral confirmed that a summary of the Scott Report's contents had been read over to him paragraph by paragraph by an assistant editor of the *Sunday Telegraph,* Mr Gordon Brook-Shepherd. Denning's statement continued :

> I told him [Brook-Shepherd] that D-notices did not come into it as it was a report dealing with forces other than our own national forces and therefore did not imperil our own national security. But I did add that if it was a genuine document then it was subject to the Official Secrets Act.

If this was an accurate version of the conversation between Mr Brook-Shepherd and Sir Norman Denning, then it marked the collapse of the entire D-notice system. While the D-notice procedure is entirely voluntary and has no legal status, the whole point of it is to give newspapers clearance to publish defence information without fear of subsequent official reprisals. Until the Scott case, it used to be the view of all practitioners of the D-notice system, including Colonel Lohan the previous incumbent of Sir Norman Denning's office, that once a newspaper had submitted a sensitive story to the Secretary of the D-notice Committee and had received an assurance that a D-notice would not prohibit publication, then the newspaper was immune from prosecution under the Official Secrets Act if it printed that story. To be able to stop newspaper disclosures either by D-notices or by the Official Secrets Act gives modern Whitehall a power over the Press equivalent to Cardinal Morton's notorious fork over the aristocracy in the Middle Ages.

Studying the papers submitted by the Director of Public Prosecutions office, one felt impelled to ask why the Attorney-General had given his fiat for a government-ordained Official Secrets Act prosecution? Vice-Admiral Denning as Secretary of the D-notice Committee had confirmed that national security was not affected by the disclosure of the Scott Report. Colonel Scott's description of his own security arrangements and of his voluminous distribution list made it clear that the author of the document had no special qualms as to the report's security importance or diplomatic sensitivity. Nowhere in the prosecution's case was there any suggestion that damage had been done to British interests. Why then had the case been brought at all? There were a multiplicity of rumours in answer to this question which amounted to five main theories.

One theory was that we had been prosecuted as a retaliation for ministerial embarrassments. Undoubtedly the Scott Report showed that certain government spokesmen had made misleading and inaccurate statements about Britain's involvement in the Nigerian civil war. Could the case have been brought to hit back at journalists for exposing these ministers and to stop the exposure being repeated?

Another theory was that we were being prosecuted for party political reasons. At this time, a back bench Labour MP, Mr Wilfred Owen, was on remand in Brixton Prison awaiting trial on Official Secrets Act charges. Although he was eventually acquitted, the allegations against him involved the passing of so-called national security secrets to a Czechoslovakian diplomat and the resulting publicity had undoubtedly done some damage to the image of the Labour party. Could the possible technical breach of the Act in our case have been jacked up to a prosecution because having a Conservative candidate and a Conservative newspaper on Official Secrets charges seemed a convenient Tory quid pro quo for the Owen case?

A third theory was that we were being prosecuted as a result of diplomatic pressure. There was no doubt that the publication of Colonel Scott's less than polite sentiments on the efficiency of the Nigerian army had caused great umbrage to be taken by the top brass in the Federal Military Government. Against a background of growing Russian influence in Nigeria, the British High Commission might well have argued that a public trial for the culprits of the Scott Report leak would deflate the high dudgeon of Lagos officials and repair any damage to Anglo-Nigerian relations. Were we being slaughtered as sacrificial lambs in some international power game?

A fourth theory was that we were being prosecuted as a general warning to the whole of Fleet Street that leaks must stop. As happens with most governments nearing the end of a term of office, indiscretions from ministers and civil servants were, by early 1970, pouring into the Press like the waters of Niagara Falls. Some ministers and permanent secretaries were getting indignant at the lack of security, which was certainly worse than in any previous administration. Could the Scott Report prosecutions against the journalists concerned have been embarked on *'pour encourager les autres'*?

Every one of these hypotheses had its supporters. Staunch Conservatives, including many of my constituents, tended to believe in the theory of Party political revenge. Their credence in this was considerably strengthened when it became known that Mr Wilfred Owen's trial, which had been waiting for some five months to come to court, would begin on almost the same day as the Magistrates' Court hearing of the Scott Report case.

The Biafra Lobby, or what remained of it, inclined towards attributing the prosecutions entirely to Mr Michael Stewart. Old West Africa hands felt that the Foreign Office was endeavouring to placate General Gowon, while a few paranoiac journalists were convinced that the Government was about to do another 'Vassall prosecution' on the communications industry.

Listening to all this gossip and speculation, I developed my own fifth theory which I hold to this day. I believe that the Official Secrets Act prosecutions against Colonel Cairns, the *Sunday Telegraph,* its editor and myself were proceeded with because of confusion and over-reaction in the middle levels of the government machine. My information suggests that the scenario went something like this: after the leak and Colonel Scott's expulsion, officials at the British High Commission in Lagos were angry and upset. They filed bitter protests to the Foreign Office in London, stressing the great offence taken by Nigerian officials. The Foreign Office was no less enraged, and through its legal and intelligence departments pressed the Director of Public Prosecutions' Office for a searching investigation. The Director of Public Prosecutions' men in turn hotted up the Special Branch, which likewise went to great lengths to piece together a viable prosecution case. It must, for example, have been among all these officials, none of whom are at the top rank of government, that the extraordinary decisions were originally taken not to proceed against Lord Hartwell, Hugh Fraser and General Alexander, presumably because the eventual victims were more junior and therefore more vulnerable. In the final stages the papers on the case went before Sir Burke Trend, the Secretary of the Cabinet; Sir Norman Skelhorn, the Director of

Public Prosecutions; and Mr Harold Wilson, the Prime Minister, Sir Elwyn Jones, the Attorney-General. Any one of these high functionaries could have put a stop to the entire affair or at least could have avoided the absurdity of the selectivity of prosecutions, but in fact every member of this powerful quartet pressed for the case to go forward in its original state.

Whatever the reasons behind the plans for issuing the summonses, all the available evidence suggested that the prosecutions amounted to someone's misuse or misunderstanding of the Official Secrets Act, a view that was of small comfort to me on 22 April as I walked into the City of London's Guildhall Magistrates' Court to answer the charges against me.

At the Magistrates' Court

The case of *Regina v. Cairns, Aitken and Roberts* was opened for
the Crown at the Guildhall by Mr John Mathew, a senior
Treasury Counsel.* He began by saying the Attorney-General
had indicated that the matter was too serious to be dealt with summarily and so the magistrates would be asked to commit the defendants for trial at the Central Criminal Court. Mr Mathew
conceded that the case did not concern national security and that
the Crown had no evidence to relate the prosecution to the story
that General Ojukwu had been sent a copy of the Scott Report.
But he insisted that the publication of the report had 'seriously
endangered diplomatic relations with Nigeria', that the defendants
had disclosed the 'important military secrets of a Commonwealth
Power' and that the episode had 'repercussions of a very serious
nature'.

After outlining the case against Colonel Cairns with commend-
able restraint ('It is not suggested that this act of Colonel Cairns,
although contrary to the Official Secrets Act, was done with any
sinister motive. It was clearly sent in confidence to a trusted colleague.'), Mr Mathew launched a considerably more formidable
attack on me. In particular, he claimed that I had 'deliberately
dishonoured a promise' and told a 'deliberate and dishonourable
lie' in my dealings with General Alexander. Mr Mathew also made
the innuendo, which was amplified in newspaper headlines the

---

*John Mathew is now the second senior Treasury Counsel at the Central Crim-
inal Court, an appointment he has held since 1959. Treasury Counsel are retained
by the Crown as full-time state prosecutors. John Mathew's father, the late Sir
Theobald Mathew, was Director of Public Prosecutions from 1944–64.

next day, that the five hundred pounds fee paid by the *Sunday Telegraph* had been a factor in my motives for getting the document published. The evidence for all these allegations turned out to be slender. Not a single witness supported the claim that Anglo-Nigerian diplomatic relations had been endangered. Colonel Scott admitted there were 'no vital secrets in the report' except for the section of his predictions headed 'Aims and Intentions' which in any case had proved wildly inaccurate. General Alexander never at any stage alleged that I had made him 'a promise'. The 'deliberate and dishonourable lie' turned out to be an uncorroborated and confusingly related remark I was alleged to have made on the telephone to the General during the police enquiries. The innuendo of financial motivation was effectively destroyed by the prosecution evidence of Graham Watson, and the Crown did not again pursue this line of attack at any stage in the trial.

Mr Mathew's language about my behaviour looked even more unjustified when under cross-examination General Alexander conceded 'I am certainly prepared to accept there could have been a genuine misunderstanding between Mr Aitken and me on the evening of 21 December'.[1]

There is unfortunately no redress against an advocate who, in the privileged environment of a court room, pitches his allegations against a defendant too high. Barristers are normally scrupulously careful not to use words or suggestions stronger than those which appear in the statements before them, and it was regrettable that Mr John Mathew did not observe this practice. Personally I was shattered by the ferocity of his attack, but although it was suggested that some sort of formal complaint against the prosecution's opening should be lodged, and though Lord Goodman went so far as to draft a statement for me to read in court expressing criticism of the Crown's phrases, I was advised that even these mild forms of retaliation would, in the end, be counter-productive.

Apart from the manifest unfairness of the prosecution's opening speech and the ensuing bad publicity, the early phase of the hearing went well for the defence. The first highlight of the trial was the cross-examination of Colonel Scott by my counsel, Basil Wigoder QC, which lasted for two and a half days. Its purpose was to establish that the Scott Report contained 'no military secrets from start to finish' by proving that every single fact in the document was already public knowledge. A pro-Biafran author[2] and freelance journalist, Mrs Suzanne Cronje, had made a meticulous analysis of Scott's text and had been able to find a public reference to match virtually every one of the so-called secrets. These references were diligently assembled in a voluminous pile of press cuttings, magazines and books and were presented one by one to Colonel Scott who was asked to read them, then to re-read the relevant paragraph in the report, and then to answer the question whether he would agree that the information in the paragraph was public knowledge. There were ninety-one paragraphs in the report and each one seemed to need at least half a dozen press cuttings. These were individually unearthed from the files of Mrs Cronje, handed to Jeffrey Maunsell my solicitor, passed to Basil Wigoder, and passed on to a court room attendant who numbered them with an exhibit slip. This exhibit slip with press cutting attached was next given to the presiding magistrate, Sir Bernard Waley-Cohen, who signed it before finally passing the exhibit to Colonel Scott. This cumbersome procedure was complicated still further by the activities of the clerk of the court, Mr John Tratt, who will long live in my memory as a legendary figure in the folklore of British Justice.

Mr Tratt had the task of whispering the words of each witness into a dictaphone, whose tapes were transcribed and read as depositions at the end of each day's hearings. He also had the responsibility of advising the three lay magistrates on points of law and procedure, a duty which he freely interpreted. Indeed, by far the greater part of Mr Tratt's interruptions were in the category which lawyers politely describe as '*Obiter Dicta*', for he frequently broke into the speeches and questions of all the barristers on a wide variety of excuses, and was by no means averse to introducing a little courtroom wit. When a witness was asked to examine a press cutting exhibit taken from the French newspaper *Le Figaro*, Mr Tratt observed 'Figaro! Figaro! Anyone would think we were at the Opera.' Another typical comic moment occurred when Mr Tratt suggested that part of the case should be heard in camera on the grounds that the Scott Report was marked 'Secret'. Since the Scott Report had already been published to two million newspaper readers and was in any case marked 'Confidential', the barristers turned on the clerk with words of scathing sarcasm. However, Mr Tratt had the last laugh for he triumphantly produced his copy of the Scott Report on which some over-zealous official in the Director of Public Prosecutions office had indeed imposed the heavy black stamp of 'Secret' on top of the original word 'Confidential'. This absurd attempt to lock the secret door after the confidential horse had bolted was a timely reminder of the Civil Service penchant for over-classification.

Yet although Mr Tratt's interventions had their amusing side, his management of the dictaphone machine was open to more serious criticism, for the depositions on the evidences of several witnesses, particularly that of Colonel Scott, were found to be full of errors and omissions. At one point, Mr Tratt admitted that his machine had been 'posing some problems' to the typist who had been making the transcript and that he had filled in his own recollections of what was said. This brought a storm of protest from the lawyers and thereafter stringent measures were ordered by the magistrates to ensure the accuracy of the record.

Absolute accuracy certainly became essential towards the end of Colonel Scott's testimony, for after ploughing through the mountain of exhibits and agreeing that all but two or three paragraphs in his report were public knowledge, he made some very helpful admissions from the point of view of the defence. Besides conceding 'there is nothing in the report which was a vital secret' (apart from the section headed 'Aims and Intentions'), Colonel Scott revealed that in Lagos he had used his report to brief a press conference of journalists, many of whom were foreign. He added that at this conference 'substantial passages of my report would have been given verbatim as this was almost a briefing document'.[8] Colonel Scott's evidence ended with this revelation, which appeared to have established a new rule of precedent to the effect that officials may quote documents verbatim to journalists, but when journalists quote verbatim from the same documents they are liable to be prosecuted under the Official Secrets Act.

The next witness was Mr Graham Watson of Curtis Brown, who gave formal evidence about the passage of the document to the *Sunday Telegraph*. He caused considerable amusement in the court by declaring that the Scott Report had struck him as 'incredibly boring for most readers' and went on to say :

I definitely formed the impression that it was rather specialised and said so to Mr Aitken. I did in fact telephone him and said it was not of much commercial interest. He replied 'Don't worry about the money, go ahead and get it published' or words to that effect.[4]

Mr Watson confirmed that he had received instructions from me on 17 January about the money going to a Biafran charity and added under cross-examination:

To my knowledge he [Aitken] did support the Biafran cause. It was obvious to me his interest was totally a political one and not a financial one.[5]

The court at this point adjourned for ten days. When we re-assembled, the first witness was a senior Foreign Office official, Mr Johann Welser. His evidence related to a pre-publication conversation about the authenticity of the document with Mr Gordon Brook-Shepherd, an assistant editor of the *Sunday Telegraph,* but during a shrewd session of cross-examination by the *Telegraph's* counsel, Mr Jeremy Hutchinson QC, Mr Welser gave the court an interesting insight into the workings of officialdom's mind when he said:

This is the correct meaning of the term confidential, and I say this as an official of the Foreign Office: A government official who thought that the disclosure of a document might cause embarrassment to Her Majesty's Government might well classify it as confidential. Naturally I mean politically embarrassing. It is no business of any official to try or allow the Government to be embarrassed. That is what we are working for. Embarrassment and security are not really two different things.[6]

After Mr Welser had finished embarrassing the Crown lawyers, General Alexander entered the witness box. Three days earlier he had given the authorities his personal copy of the transcript of the conversation he had tape-recorded with me on 11 March. The arrival of this document as an addition to the prosecution's statements came to me as a great shock, for never in my wildest and most paranoiac nightmares had it crossed my mind that General Alexander might have invited me to tea at his home in order to trap me with a bugging device.

Although the transcript of this bugged conversation filled some thirty pages of police statement forms, most of it is extremely boring. It begins with Mrs Alexander withdrawing from the room, saying to her husband, 'Here he comes now in his blue sports car. Good luck darling! Good luck!' A moment or two later, I was ushered into the room and manoeuvred into the hot seat. The General and I then talked for about half an hour about our chances of being prosecuted; then he started pressing me for details of what had happened to the document:

Aitken: Well from you to me, from me to Hugh Fraser, Fraser to the *Sunday Telegraph*. As you know things just spiralled totally out of control.

Alexander: Who did the copying?

Aitken: The copying was done by an innocent third party – at Hugh Fraser's direction.

A little later on in the talk I added: 'Hugh very carelessly I think gives it to the *Sunday Telegraph,* without great strings attached. It's a misunderstanding between him and me, and I take the responsibility and must take the blame for it.'

It was the above passage in the tape recording which caused me the greatest discomfort, for the prosecution was quick to seize on these prevarications as evidence of my guilty mind. All that I could subsequently say in my defence was that Hugh Fraser had specifically invited me to put the blame on him and that I could not reveal the true identity of the photo-copier for fear that General Alexander might tell the police, who in turn might make life awkward for Mr Michael Deakin and Yorkshire Television. Nevertheless I was full of regret for my inaccurate statements, and could only reflect that there are probably few people who can stand the test of having their intimate conversations bugged and read out two months later in court.

Yet despite the embarrassment of these disclosures, on the crucial point of the terms under which I was given the Scott Report, the tape-recording proved fairly helpful. One vital passage of the transcript went as follows:

Alexander: I gave you this document in confidence. I would never have given it to you if I thought it was any other way, and nobody else had seen it. This very reason, that it was a confidential document and I wasn't going to show it to every Tom, Dick and

143

Harry and as far as I was concerned it was in confidence I mean I attach no significance to it at the time to the exact wording what I said to you, I mean I can't recall but I am quite clear in my mind and this is the thing that narks me, that I was clear in my mind that I gave you the document to read in confidence and let me have back and it would never enter my mind that the consequence would be that it would get copied.

Aitken: Well that's very fair, I mean, I will tell you what I thought, first of all I mean whether it's a genuine misunderstanding or whatever it is I was certainly not under the impression it was given to me under what might be called strict confidence but obviously what might be called in a confidential way, I mean I presumed it was given openly and in my recollection of the words there was not any great adjuration as to secrecy ... [interruption – telephone call] ... Well as I was saying I was sort of wondering why you had given me the document and seeing that it was very much a ... thing, obviously as a pro-Biafran myself I would reckon very much that the basic reason you gave it was to show the pro-Biafran gang how wrong they were, and if I had been absolutely left in control which I wasn't I would have used it as background information.

Alexander: This is what my recollection is that I gave it to you as background information and I expected you to use it as background information.

The General's admissions on this tape that he gave me the document 'as background information' and his statement that he attached 'no significance to it at the time to the exact wording what I said to you, I mean I can't recall' had considerable relevance to the receiving charge against me.

Section 2 of the Official Secrets Act 1911 specifies that the offence of receiving only occurs when the person who receives the information 'knows or has reasonable grounds to believe that the information is communicated to him in contravention of the said

Act.' If on 17 March the General could not recall what he had said when he gave me the document as background information, then since I was maintaining that the document had been given openly and without adjuration to confidence or secrecy, how could it be proved that I had reasonable grounds for believing that the Official Secrets Act was being contravened? This question was answered when General Alexander gave his evidence in the witness box, for he made some forceful additions to his police statement and to the version he had given in the tape-recording. He now claimed that 'over the port' we had argued about the Nigerian civil war, and that because he did not agree with my views he had offered to let me read the report. The General continued, stressing that the conversation took place in the dining room after the ladies had withdrawn :

> Well, I made three things clear to him [Aitken]. The first thing I made clear to him was that I didn't think I should be in possession of the document in any case. The second thing I made clear to him was that it was a classified confidential document, and the third thing I made clear to him, I said you can read this as background information in strict confidence. When I put the conditions to him he said Yes.[7]

Under a long and tortuous cross-examination from Basil Wigoder QC General Alexander somewhat reluctantly admitted that he knew I was a professional journalist and that he had given me letters of introduction and information about the civil war on several occasions. After much studying of certain letters and press cuttings which were handed up to him, he agreed under further questioning that he had known I was using his information in the press as background information. Nevertheless, General Alexander reiterated again and again: 'I keep on telling you that I never treated Jonathan Aitken as a journalist. I treated him as a friend and our prospective candidate.'[8] When Basil Wigoder gently suggested 'Calling him a friend of yours is putting it a bit high isn't it?' the General expostulated 'Nonsense! Look at the way he signs his letters – Yours ever, Jonathan – Dear Henry.... I'm fifty-eight and he's twenty-eight. It's hardly likely that a young man of twenty-eight unless he's a friend of mine would sign his letters in this manner.'[9] With the cross-examination growing more and more heated, particularly on the subject of whether the alleged conversation about keeping the report in strict confidence had taken place during the meal, over the port, in the drawing room or not at all, the Court rose for the day.

The following morning, Basil Wigoder QC made a surprise application for an adjournment after receiving a telephone call just before the court was about to sit. He told the magistrates: 'My solicitors have been offered certain information which it is clearly highly desirable to obtain and thoroughly check before use.'

I learnt later from my solicitors that the information related to General Alexander's evidence and had come from two sources, a retired army officer and a former Member of Parliament. However, the checking of these new disclosures was only part of the reason for the adjournment.

Unknown to the defendants, the defence and the prosecution lawyers had been talking about the case overnight and were trying to arrange a quick settlement of the whole affair. Later that morning I was offered the terms of the settlement deal. The Attorney-General was prepared to drop his demand for the committal for trial at the Central Criminal Court and would now allow the case to be dealt with summarily by the Magistrates – who by statute could not impose more than a fifty pound fine. In return, the defendants must plead guilty. The prosecution would publicly accept that the damage to Britain's diplomatic relations with Nigeria had been potential rather than actual, and would also accept that there was no question of my having been financially motivated towards publishing the Scott Report. In return, Basil Wigoder QC would have to withdraw the allegation he had earlier made in court on my behalf that the case was 'a simple political prosecution brought for political purposes'. After this we could all go home.

I was extremely reluctant to plead guilty to the charges, particularly as the case was going well for the defence. But I was strongly advised to accept the settlement on the grounds that a long battle in the High Court would be prolonged and expensive, and that despite the triviality of the affair the wording of the Act was so broad that the chances of an acquittal were no better than fifty-fifty anyway. I was distressed by this advice, but finally accepted it after consulting prominent constituents and getting their opinion that a fifty pound fine or less would be better than an unresolved case for my chances of survival as candidate.

146

Meanwhile, the *Sunday Telegraph* and its editor Mr Brian Roberts discussed the Crown's offer with their lawyers, and after a meeting which lasted long into the evening, they too reluctantly decided to accept the settlement. Although both I and Mr Roberts agonised over taking this decision (and to each other in court the next morning we privately expressed our mutual distress at having submitted) nevertheless we had separately concluded that the weight of advice from all sides was too heavy to resist. Thus the lions of the Press capitulated to the Crown's suggestion of a plea bargain, and it was left to the straightforward soldierly mind of Colonel Douglas Cairns to reject the terms of the deal.

In court the next morning a prolonged delay before the entry of the magistrates created a general atmosphere of bewilderment as to what was going on behind the scenes. In fact, chaos was reigning over the question of the settlement. The barristers were arguing in one room, the magistrates were receiving and sending back messages in another, while the Clerk of the Court, Mr John Tratt, shuttled backwards and forwards as plenipotentiary between the two. What exactly went wrong has never been made clear. It is thought that Colonel Cairns' counsel was holding out for improved terms, and that the magistrates were so amazed by this volte-face of the case that they baulked at the suggested arrangements. In any event, the end result was that the pre-arranged deal between the prosecution and the defence fell through, and the case continued. As things turned out, this was a most fortunate, if unexpected, outcome.

When the hearing resumed General Alexander came back into the box and continued his evidence. It lasted less than five minutes and was completely different in tone from the previous session of cross-examination. After saying that he was convinced that the Scott Report had been handed over in confidence, the General went on:

> I am certainly prepared to accept there could have been a genuine misunderstanding between Mr Aitken and me on the evening of 21 December and I greatly regret this case had to come to court. I would be very happy to shake hands with Mr Aitken and forget about the whole thing.[10]

After this unexpected turn of events, the defence lawyers decided not to continue cross-examining the General or any other prosecution witnesses, so the court merely accepted the rest of the Crown's case on the basis of written statements. Then the three defendants had the charges read to them, formally pleaded not guilty, and were asked if they had anything to say. I made the following statement from the well of the court :

> My motive for bringing the contents of the Scott Report to the attention of the British people was that this document contained definite evidence that Parliament and the public had been deliberately misled about the true nature and extent of this Government's controversial policy of supplying arms to the Federal Military Government of Nigeria during the Biafra war.
>
> When I received the Scott Report from General Alexander, who had given me information for journalistic purposes on many previous occasions, I was firmly under the impression that I was free to make use of it.
>
> I would like to make it clear that throughout this affair I have told no dishonourable lie, that I have broken no promise, that I have violated no confidence, that I have in no way acted dishonourably.
>
> If there was a misunderstanding between General Alexander and myself I regret it. I also regret that my actions have unintentionally caused such embarrassment and inconvenience to Colonel Scott and Colonel Cairns.
>
> I believe that this document was of vital public interest. In revealing it I was upholding the right of a free press to publish non-secret material affecting government policies.

In order to counteract the bad publicity emanating from the prosecution's unfair opening attack, it was decided that I should call some defence witnesses, starting with the Rt. Hon. Selwyn Lloyd MP, who gave character evidence for me. He was followed by four guests from General Alexander's dinner party.

First of these was Mrs Daphne Preston who said:

> At dinner I sat between General Alexander and Mr Aitken. I have no recollection of any conversation between them about Nigeria or Biafra.[11]

Next in the box was Colonel Geoffrey Preston, the only independent witness at the critical port-drinking session. He said:

> When taking port I think we closed up. I do not remember the

General saying he had in his possession a document which he thought he should not have. I do not remember the General saying to Jonathan Aitken that he could read the document as background information in strict confidence. From the time the ladies left until the men left to rejoin them I was with the men throughout. I feel sure I would have heard any conversation taking place in the room during that time. I have no recollection of any discussion about Nigeria or Biafra while we were taking port.[12]

Colonel and Mrs Preston were followed in court by Mr and Mrs A. D. Cliff, who had joined the General's party after dinner.

Mr Cliff confirmed that he had seen the document being 'quite openly'[13] handed over by General Alexander to me towards the end of the party when the only other people left in the room were Mrs Alexander, David Alexander and Mrs Cliff. Mrs Cliff explained that she had been sitting beside me on a sofa when General Alexander came over. She continued:

To the best of my recollection he handed the paper he had in his hand to Mr Aitken and said 'This is the paper I thought you would be interested to see, you see it is marked confidential, and I'll be pleased to have it back as soon as possible.' Mr Aitken said 'Thank you very much. I shall be interested to see it and I shall give it back to you as soon as possible.' Mr Aitken put it in his pocket. The piece of paper was handed over openly. No attempt was made to prevent me from seeing or hearing what was happening. I think the General was laughing at the time. I had no reason to suspect a criminal offence was being committed by anybody. Throughout the time I was there I heard no discussion about Nigeria or Biafra.'[14]

Although the evidence of three of these four Yorkshire defence witnesses conflicted with the testimony of General Alexander, the prosecuting counsel, Mr John Mathew, did not cross-examine any of them.

However, Mr Hugh Fraser's cross-examination was one of the liveliest episodes of the Magistrates' Court proceedings. During his evidence in chief Hugh Fraser outlined the circumstances in which he had received two copies of the Scott Report from me in Scotland, and went on to say:

149

I read the document and I found it of very great interest because it confirmed known facts denied by the Government to both Houses of Parliament. I could amplify this statement under six headings. Taking that view, I urged Mr Aitken to get the document maximum publicity. I thought the *Sunday Telegraph* would be the best paper because of its objective reporting of these methods. I told him I would ask for the document to be laid in the library of the House of Commons. The question of literary agent was not really discussed but Graham Watson was the obvious one, he being Mr Aitken's and my agent. Nothing was said about payment except that should there be payment it was to go to a Biafran charity . . . It did not cross my mind that communicating this document to a newspaper might be an offence under the Official Secrets Act. I did not put Mr Aitken on his guard that he might be breaking the Official Secrets Act as I did not regard this as an official document.'[15]

For the Crown, Mr John Mathew tried hard to shake Hugh Fraser from his position but to no avail. Asked if it was not obvious that there had been a security leak, Hugh Fraser replied: 'It was obvious there had been a leak of a document compromising to the Government.' After a volley of questions on the lines of 'Surely you must have known this was an official document?' the answer came back 'It was clearly written by an official but was not an official document, because it had no address, no addressee, no number and was not written on official paper . . . I thought it could have been a private circulation to friends of his [Scott's] in this country, including General Alexander.' Trying to ask about statements on the tape-recording of my meeting with General Alexander, Mr Mathew got the dusty reply: 'This came out of a tape-recording made by somebody who has turned Queen's Evidence and I regard it as unreliable.' After some forty minutes of this kind of stone-walling, Mr Mathew gave up.

The court then adjourned for a further ten days, during which election fever hotted up to a new pitch as freak Gallup polls predicted a Labour victory by an eight per cent landslide. On 18 May, Harold Wilson announced the dissolution of Parliament and a General Election for 18 June.

When the hearings were resumed on 20 May, the final defence witness was Michael Deakin of Yorkshire Television. He confirmed that I had brought the Scott Report to him on 22 December, and that we had discussed using the document as background information for a projected documentary programme on Biafra. He continued:

> Since there was only one copy of the document it seemed necessary it should be copied, so having asked Mr Aitken if it was agreeable to him I instructed my secretary to have copies made. Six copies were made. The decision to copy was mine, it was arrived at because Mr Aitken and I both needed copies. My Secretary unstapled the document, copies were made, and I restapled the document. No attempt was made to conceal the restapling, far from it, I had a small stapling machine and had to strike it repeatedly. Absolutely no suggestion was made by Mr Aitken that the document should be put back into its original condition. He did not ask for any payment for letting me have the document. After the copies were made I kept two copies and Mr Aitken kept four . . . It did not occur to me that this was a classified document or that I might be committing an offence under the Official Secrets Act if I used it. Nothing was said by Mr Aitken about any possible offence under the Official Secrets Act.'

Michael Deakin also revealed that all scripts for Yorkshire Television programmes are stamped 'Confidential' before they have been broadcast and ended his evidence by saying:

> As a result of the collapse of Biafra the programme was not made . . . but if in the interests of the attractiveness of the programme I had wanted to use extracts from the report, I should have had no hesitation whatsoever in doing so.[16]

After Michael Deakin's evidence, all that remained to be heard were submissions from the defence barristers and the magistrates' decision on whether or not to commit the defendants for trial. In fact, the magistrates had long ago made it clear from their comments that they were going to send the case on to a higher court, a fact which was acknowledged by Basil Wigoder QC when he said in his closing speech:

> It is unfortunate that when this case began the prosecution used words critical of Mr Aitken's behaviour, because it is now clear from the evidence, in particular that of Colonel Preston and

Mrs Cliff, that either General Alexander is mistaken in his recollection or that there was an unhappy misunderstanding at a dinner party. It is now clear that Mr Aitken behaved throughout as a gentleman of honour, a journalist of integrity who quite properly refused to disclose his sources to the *Sunday Telegraph*, and a politician of passionate beliefs who neither sought nor gained one penny by his activities in this matter.

Mr Wigoder said that nobody claimed the security of the state was in any way involved and that almost all of the contents of the Scott Report were common knowledge. 'The case could indeed be described as a storm in a port glass,' he added, ending by telling the magistrates:

You are concerned in the consideration and interpretation of Section 2 of the Official Secrets Act of 1911, an obscure and not easily comprehensible section. There are obviously matters of real public concern involved, in particular the position of a journalist who wishes information to be published of a non-secret nature as a contribution to legitimate political controversy. In all the circumstances, Mr Aitken considers that it is desirable in the general interest to obtain the ruling of a judge at the Central Criminal Court on these complex matters. He therefore does not desire submissions to be made on his behalf at this stage and would welcome a full investigation at a higher court.

Colonel Cairns having already reserved his defence, a statement was then made on behalf of the *Sunday Telegraph* which said that the newspaper and Mr Roberts had acted throughout in complete good faith and continued:

The report was published only after the most careful consideration of all the information available to them and in the belief that it was not an official document subject to the Official Secrets Act. They received it from a most reputable literary agent. They made inquiries of Mr Aitken and Mr Fraser. At no time was the fact that it had been obtained from General Alexander or the circumstances under which it was so obtained, disclosed to them. As a result of other inquiries they instituted, they had official confirmation that no question of national security would arise from publication. They knew that other copies were in existence and that the report and its contents were about to be revealed in the House of Commons. Responsibility for the decision to publish is accepted as fully now as when this investigation first began. Publication was undertaken in the interests of the public and in accordance with the high standards set by the *Sunday Telegraph*.

After these speeches, the Chairman of the Magistrates, Sir Bernard Waley-Cohen, made a short statement:

I want to emphasise that the court is not a political arena, nor in any respect is it the arbiter of social, moral or ethical proprieties. Nor does it fall within the court's responsibilities to decide whether any other person or persons should be facing similar charges. This court's sole concern is to decide if a *prima facie* case has been made out on the charges. On that clear issue the court is in no doubt.'

Sir Bernard then formally committed the defendants for trial at the next sessions of the Central Criminal Court and fixed bail at the agreeably moderate sum of ten pounds each.

The following day, 21 May, I was formally asked for my resignation as Parliamentary candidate for Thirsk and Malton. This request followed the 18 May announcement of sixty-eight-year-old Mr Robin Turton, the constituency's retiring MP, that he had withdrawn his resignation and was available for nomination as candidate. In my letter of resignation of the same day, I said I was glad that the issues on which I had lost the seat were of such national importance :

The right of a free Press to publish non-secret material affecting Government policy, the right of a political opponent to reveal information contradicting ministerial statements, and the whole question of the use of the Official Secrets Act are all matters of controversy which will endure long after the present election. They are particularly relevant to the present situation in which an increasing number of young people feel totally alienated from the political system because they believe governments often officially suppress the truth for political advantage.

It was now a matter for a judge and jury at the Old Bailey to decide whether the prosecutions over the Scott Report leak would prove a genuine crime against the state or a mere attempt to 'officially suppress the truth for political advantage'.

12

Trial at the Old Bailey

The dock of Court Number 1 at the Old Bailey looks and feels like a rather run-down municipal swimming baths. During this century, its walls of chipped white tiles, glass and wood, have guarded many of Britain's most notorious criminals, among them Dr Crippen, Lord Haw-Haw, Christie, Blake, Haigh, the Kray Brothers, and the Hoseins. Before proceedings began on the morning of 12 January 1971, this roll call of dishonour was recited to me several times by assorted wardens, court attendants, reporters and other knowledgeable spectators with such effect that by the time the usher shouted 'put up the prisoners', one almost had the feeling of being a temporary waxwork in Madame Tussaud's Chamber of Horrors.

The scene that greeted the three defendants as we walked up into the dock from the cells* was strangely theatrical. The judge Mr Justice Caulfield was being bowed into his judicial throne by an escort consisting of the Lord Mayor of London in full regalia and two City Aldermen wearing gold chains and fur robes. This procession was led by a sword-bearer holding aloft the sword of Justice, and an usher booming out the litany: 'Be upstanding in

*It is the normal rule at the Central Criminal Court that even those accused who are out on bail have to report to the cells an hour before proceedings begin, return to the cells for the lunch interval, and are not released again until after all the jury have departed from the court precincts. This rule was waived by Mr Justice Caulfield in our case, provided the defendants had lunch with their solicitors. Such a relaxation amazed the prison warders, who solemnly insisted that the 'prisoners' nevertheless went down to the cells a few seconds before the start of each session and came up into the dock from the subterranean staircase. Towards the end of the trial this symbolic piece of ritual was ended, and we were allowed to come and go from the dock by the ordinary door.

154

Court! All persons who have anything to do before my Lords the Queen's Justices of Oyer and Terminer and general Gaol delivery of jurisdiction of the Central Criminal Court, draw near and give your attendance – God Save the Queen.' The judge, who was carrying the black cap and a nosegay of flowers, then took his seat, after exchanging bows with the twelve bewigged barristers in the case, and the defendants. The next twenty minutes were spent in empanelling and swearing in the jury, seven of whom were formally challenged by defence counsel and replaced.

The Clerk of the Court then read the indictment* and asked 'Prisoners at the Bar, do you plead guilty or not guilty to these counts?' On receiving pleas of not guilty from Colonel Cairns, Mr Roberts and me, with Mr Jeremy Hutchinson QC entering the plea of not guilty on behalf of the *Sunday Telegraph* Limited, the case for the Crown was opened by Mr John Mathew.

THE CASE FOR THE PROSECUTION

Mr Mathew's four hour opening was markedly different in tone from his Magistrates' Court speech. This time he made no allegation that Britain's diplomatic relations with Nigeria had been endangered, did not claim that important military secrets of a Commonwealth power had been disclosed, and did not suggest that the Scott Report's publication had caused any serious repercussions. Instead he began with a cool dissertation on the Official Secrets Act 1911, saying of Section 2 : 'This section deals with the wrongful communication and receiving of information other than that covered by Section 1. It defines a wide range of

*The actual charges were as follows:

Colonel Douglas Jeffrey Cairns was accused of possessing on 16 December 1969 a confidential report 'An Appreciation of the Nigerian Conflict', and communicating it without authority to Major-General Henry Templer Alexander.

Jonathan William Patrick Aitken was accused of having received a confidential report on 21 December 1969, knowing or having reasonable grounds to believe, that it was communicated to him in contravention of the Official Secrets Act 1911, and that on 8 January 1970 he communicated the document to the *Sunday Telegraph*, to whom he was not authorised to do so.

Brian Richard Roberts and the Sunday Telegraph Limited were accused that on 9 January 1970 they received a confidential report knowing, or having reasonable grounds to believe, that it was communicated to them in contravention of the Official Secrets Act 1911.

Mr Roberts and the *Sunday Telegraph* were also accused that, having the report in their possession, they on 11 January 1970 communicated it to persons to whom they were not authorised to do so.

offences covering a multitude of sins—some serious and some much less serious. Normally the more confidential the facts the greater the offence, but the facts do not have to be confidential at all, although normally no prosecution would take place if they were not confidential.'

Mr Mathew explained to the jury that the meaning of confidential information was information whose unauthorised disclosure would be contrary to the interests of the State. In this case, Colonel Scott had written a diplomatic report to Her Majesty's Government in London assessing the Nigerian Civil War. 'In the submission of the Crown,' said Mr Mathew, 'it is most important that the preparation of uninhibited reports and assessments by representatives of the British Government in other countries should be one of the functions of diplomacy, and if reports from overseas provided by diplomats were made available for publication, the system of diplomacy, you may think, members of the jury, would break down. This applies even to facts in a report which had already been matters of general speculation.'

Mr Mathew then went on to outline the details of the case.

These were unchanged from the Magistrates' Court, but Mr Mathew's style of presentation was infinitely more restrained in manner and in language. As far as I was concerned, there were virtually none of the inflammatory epithets which had caused me so much private distress in April. Although at a later stage in the Old Bailey Trial, Mr John Mathew vigorously denied defence suggestions that the prosecutions had been politically motivated, I could not help reflecting that the sharp differences in tone between the Crown's emotive Guildhall opening and its low key Old Bailey opening might well have had something to do with the fact that a change of government had occurred in the intervening period.

Perhaps the most interesting parts of the Crown's recital of the facts were those in which Mr Mathew set out before the jury his reasons for alleging the essential ingredient of 'guilty knowledge' in the case of each defendant.

On the first count, Colonel Cairns was said to have been employed by the Crown and to have signed an Official Secrets Act declaration form making him aware of his obligations. When General Alexander had received the Scott Report from Cairns there was attached a covering letter saying 'Don't tell Bob Scott you have got a copy'. The Crown alleged that Colonel Cairns wrote this because he knew he had no authority to send on the report.

In the case against me, the Crown claimed that General Alexander's version of the dinner party conversation proved that I knew from the outset that I was being entrusted a classified document in strictest confidence. Further I had copied the report 'in an underhand way' and had clearly shown by my attempts to shift the blame on Hugh Fraser (in the tape recorded conversation of 11 March) that I was trying to cover up what I knew to have been my wrongdoing.

As for Mr Brian Roberts and the *Sunday Telegraph* Limited, they were alleged by the Crown to have deliberately ignored two clear warnings that they might be contravening the Official Secrets Act if they published the Scott Report. These warnings were said to have been given by Mr Johann Welser of the Foreign Office and Vice-Admiral Sir Norman Denning, the secretary of the D-notice Committee.

After the opening speech, the prosecution witnesses gave their evidence according to the pattern of the Magistrates' Court hearings, although there were some interesting variations and additions.

Colonel Scott in his evidence in chief said that he had finished off his report on 13 December 1969, 'in rather a hurry to catch the diplomatic bag to London at noon'. It was, he said 'one of hundreds of confidential documents which go out from the High Commission every month'. Colonel Scott was assisted in the final stages of the report's preparation by Colonel Cairns, who had been colouring in the red lines of the attached sketch map. Colonel Cairns himself had been given a copy (along with some forty-five to fifty other people) but General Alexander had not. Although Scott knew General Alexander well and had sent him at least one situation report before, Scott said he would not have given permission for General Alexander to be sent a copy of this report, 'because he was remote from the scene'.

However, under cross-examination from Colonel Cairns' counsel, Mr James Comyn QC, Colonel Scott agreed that a copy of the report had been sent to one person who was even more remote from the scene – Sir David Hunt, the former High Commissioner in Lagos, who was now British Ambassador in Rio de Janeiro. Colonel Scott also said that he would not have minded

Colonel Cairns passing on the gist of the report to General Alexander, and added 'by the gist I mean what was in it, not my name . . . the real point is that it would be non-attributable'.

This curious distinction between the contents of the document and the authorship of the document continued to be drawn throughout this evidence, and even the judge was at one stage heard to refer to 'the information in the report as opposed to the report *in toto*'. However, during the cross-examination of Colonel Scott by my counsel, the emphasis on the non-attributability of the report began to be undermined when Mr Basil Wigoder QC went into the details of the briefing Colonel Scott had given to a number of British and foreign journalists on 6 December 1969. Colonel Scott agreed that at this press conference his report was uppermost in his mind as it had only just been written. He admitted that the assembled journalists (some of whom as foreign nationals were not bound by the Official Secrets Acts) had therefore been given verbatim accounts of whole sections of the report, in some cases word for word.

Basil Wigoder then asked: 'You, as an experienced officer, quite obviously would never consider passing to the press either on an attributable or non-attributable basis, information the publication of which might embarrass the government?'

Colonel Scott : That is so.

Q : As I understand the way the case is now being put, it was not the publication of the information that embarrassed the government, it was the publication of your identity.

A : Yes, this is true.

Q : But your identity as its author was given out at the press conference?

A : You mean because I gave the conference?

Q : Yes, you did not wear a mask or pretend you were the hall porter?

A : No, they knew precisely who I was.

Q : What was happening was this. You were saying : 'Look, you can have the information. Look, you know I am the author, but please don't quote me'?

A: Yes, if you wish to put it in those words, I would agree there.

Colonel Scott seemed in a mood to agree with a great many of the defence counsel's points, and the court was thus mercifully spared a repeat of the two-and-a-half-day Magistrates' Court marathon of questions to prove that the vast majority of facts in the report were widely known before publication. The witness simply acknowledged that this was so.

On behalf of Mr Roberts and the *Sunday Telegraph,* Mr Jeremy Hutchinson QC asked Colonel Scott:

Q: We reach the position, do we not, that as far as the contents of the report are concerned, they cease to be confidential when they are conveyed to the press.

A: Under their name but not under mine.

The judge then intervened: 'The point Mr Hutchinson is making is this: That information once disclosed to the reporter ceases to be confidential and becomes public knowledge.'

Colonel Scott: Certainly.

Mr. Hutchinson: Thus what was confidential on Monday and subject to the Official Secrets Act, on Tuesday becomes public property.

A: That is so.

Mr Hutchinson then made the point that as far as the *Sunday Telegraph* was concerned, a number of copies were in circulation to members of the public before the *Telegraph*'s story was published. He continued:

Q: And if that document was going to be raised in the House of Commons the very next day by a Privy Councillor and ex-minister, the whole thing clearly would not be confidential?

A: I couldn't agree more.

After Colonel Scott, the next prosecution witness was General Alexander. He said that he had been 'surprised' to receive the Scott Report from Colonel Cairns, because it was classified and accompanied by a letter saying 'Please don't tell Bob Scott I have sent you a copy'. General Alexander had put the document away in the bottom drawer of a desk in his study, and took it out again to give it to me. He gave his account of the dinner party, again with particular emphasis on his three solemn conditions about the use of the document alleged to have been imposed on me and agreed to by me over the port. At one point in this part of his evidence the judge dramatically intervened to warn General Alexander that he need not answer any questions that might incriminate him over this alleged passing of an Official Secret. General Alexander replied: 'Yes, I would sooner tell the truth. I would prefer to answer the questions.' Later on in his evidence, when General Alexander had said he gave me the document 'on a confidential basis as a friend', the judge again intervened to ask: 'You had nothing in your mind to do anything wrong as regards an official document?' Alexander: 'None at all.' This answer later had profound significance when it came to the summing up.

Cross-examined by Mr James Comyn QC on behalf of Colonel Cairns, General Alexander paid tribute to his former colleague's honour and patriotism, and recalled occasions when he had despatched the Colonel to suppress mutinies in the Congo. He confirmed that he had asked Colonel Cairns to keep him fully informed on the situation in Nigeria, and that Colonel Cairns knew that this information was used by the General for lectures to such organisations as the Army Staff College. Describing his reactions when he received the Scott Report from Colonel Cairns, General Alexander said 'It never crossed my mind I was committing an offence'.

The cross-examination of General Alexander by my counsel, Basil Wigoder QC, produced its expected moments of friction. After a number of my articles had been produced in court as exhibits, General Alexander agreed that he knew me to be a pro-Biafran sympathiser, and a journalist writing regularly about Nigeria. He further agreed that he had on a number of occasions handed me information about the civil war, which with his knowledge and consent had been used by me on a non-attributable basis in my newspaper articles. However General Alexander added: 'I had a special relationship with Aitken. I was not dealing with

him as a second-class journalist but as a prospective Conservative
candidate and a friend.'

Cross-examined about the dinner party conversation, General
Alexander said that when he handed over the Scott Report, it
never crossed his mind that he was contravening the Official
Secrets Act, but nevertheless he had only given it to me under
strict conditions. Mr Wigoder then asked:

> Your final version of the matter is this : that you said over the
> port after dinner, 'I will let you have this document to look
> at on three specific conditions (1) I do not think I ought to be
> in possession of it anyway, (2) it is secret and confidential and
> (3) you can read it as background in strict confidence?'

A :   Correct. As I have said already, I considered
                    Aitken to be a trusted friend. I had helped
                    him smooth his path when there were diffi-
                    culties about his nomination as the Con-
                    servative candidate for my constituency. He
                    had accompanied my daughter to a dance.

Q :   I suggest you handed over the report in a
                    lighthearted and smiling way?

A :   Of course, it was a convivial dinner party.
                    We were all in good form, but I did remind
                    him that it was a confidential document.

Q :   It is obviously very easy on a convivial occa-
                    sion of this kind for there to be a mutual
                    misunderstanding between you and Mr
                    Aitken?

A :   It is perfectly possible, but as far as I am
                    concerned there was no misunderstanding.

At this point the cross-examination became somewhat rougher
when Basil Wigoder QC said to the General: 'I must suggest to you
that your evidence about these three conditions has been fortified
with the passage of time.' In support of this allegation, the defence
produced General Alexander's early statements to the police. In
the first of these, made on 23 January 1969, the General's only
reference to me was, 'there is one other personal friend of mine
whom I allowed to read the document. It would have been before
11 January this year'.

Asked by Basil Wigoder why this statement made no reference to the three conditions or to the 'in strictest confidence' claim, General Alexander replied: 'I was being very guarded and was giving the minimum information to the police because I did not want to say anything until I had Aitken's permission. There was no need to say at that time that it was given in confidence.'

The General was then asked about his letters to me of 19 and 22 January, his second police statement of 28 January, his tape-recorded conversation of 11 March and his final police statement of 18 March. None of these communications or statements, all of which were produced in evidence, mentioned the three strict conditions. Even the General's 18 March statement which was the basis of the prosecution's case confined itself to the claim: 'I said he could take the document away as long as he treated it in strictest confidence as background information for himself only.'

Mr Wigoder then asserted that it was clear that the three strict conditions (which had appeared for the first time at the Magistrates' Court hearing) had grown with the passage of time. General Alexander retorted, 'I don't agree. The important thing is that it was given in confidence. All the other things are irrelevant.'

Mr Wigoder then suggested that there might have been a misunderstanding between his client and the General, similar to the *Topic* article misunderstanding between the General and a journalist some years before. General Alexander replied that the two episodes were not at all similar.

The final stages of the cross-examination touched on General Alexander's actions and correspondence after the *Sunday Telegraph* published the Scott Report on 11 January.

Mr Wigoder: When you saw the *Sunday Telegraph* on 11 January 1970, you realised there had been a leak?

A: Yes.

Q: And you knew that Aitken was a journalist and a close friend of Hugh Fraser MP, whose name was all over the *Sunday Telegraph*?

A: Yes.

Q: Surely it must have crossed your mind that perhaps Aitken had something to do with the article?

A: No, I thought it quite impossible for it to be my copy of the report that had been used.

Q: Once it was realised that the Official Secrets Act was involved you took steps which it would be difficult for you to look back on with pride?

A: I do not think it is fair to say that. I may have acted with indiscretion in showing the report to Aitken, whom I considered a friend, but I do not consider I have done anything dishonourable throughout this case.

Q: I am not suggesting that you did. I am only suggesting that you, rather like Mr Aitken, took some steps to try to avoid being caught up in the web?

A: I did not want it to be known that Colonel Cairns had sent me a copy of the Scott report.

Asked about his reasons for bugging the tea party conversation on 11 March, General Alexander replied: 'The whole thing was very distasteful to me. I only agreed because my wife was having a nervous breakdown and insisted. My wife set up the tape-recorder. I did not like using it at all.'

In a short cross-examination from Mr Jeremy Hutchinson QC, General Alexander accepted that neither the *Sunday Telegraph* nor its editor had any idea that he was the original source of the Scott Report. The only other interesting point to emerge was that General Alexander had written a letter to the *Sunday Telegraph* on 21 January, ten days after the leak had been published. In this letter General Alexander fiercely criticised the newspaper for printing extracts from the Scott Report ('I can only assume that the document is genuine which to my mind makes it worse') and had some harsh words to say about contemporary journalists and journalism. The judge was later to make some trenchant comments about this letter in his summing up.

General Alexander, who was in the witness box for nearly six hours, was followed by his son David. His was expected to be a crucial piece of prosecution testimony, for twenty-six-year-old David Alexander was one of the four men present at the all import-ant port-drinking session at which the General claimed to have got my agreement to his three conditions. David Alexander said that an argument about the Nigerian situation had taken place over the port between his father and me. He continued: 'The point that was being discussed was whether the conflict could be ended quicker than was thought. My father couldn't convince Aitken. "Well", said my father, "if you don't accept what I say, perhaps you'll accept it from a report I have received." The report wasn't produced at that stage. My father made it clear that he could have the document for his own information as someone interested in the Nigerian situation. I don't know whether he said this then or when Aitken was leaving the house. It was a general impression that I had.'

Since David Alexander's general impression was a great deal weaker than the impressions of the General on the key points of conditions and words used, the defence made no cross-examination of the son, and he left the box after less than six minutes.

The next prosecution witness was Mr Graham Watson of Curtis Brown. He again gave formal evidence about receiving the document from me on 8 January, passing it to the *Sunday Telegraph*, negotiating the price of five hundred pounds, and carrying out my instructions of giving the money to charity. Tributes to Mr Watson and his agency flowed in from all sides, particularly from the *Sunday Telegraph*'s counsel, who was anxious to establish the complete normality and respectability of the transaction of the document from Curtis Brown Limited to the newspaper's features editor, Mr Ralph Thackeray. Mr Watson said he would never have offered the Scott Report to the *Sunday Telegraph* if he had thought for a moment that he might committing an offence. He had sought the advice of Mr Hugh Fraser MP, before forwarding the document and was convinced that everything was above board, on learning that the report was about to be raised in Parliament. Mr Jeremy Hutchinson QC then asked:

> Was anything said by Mr Fraser which caused you to think that you might be committing an offence against the Official Secrets Act if you offered the report to the *Sunday Telegraph*?
>
> Mr Watson : No, rather the contrary.
>
> The Judge : When you offered the report to the *Sunday Telegraph* you felt you were doing nothing wrong?
>
> A : That is so.

The significance of this evidence was that it effectively destroyed the charge against the *Sunday Telegraph* that they had received the document 'knowing or having reasonable grounds for believing that it had been communicated to them in contravention of the Official Secrets Act'. Indeed Mr Justice Caulfield eventually directed the jury that they must acquit on this count of the indictment.

The next two witnesses, Mr Johann Welser of the Foreign Office and Vice-Admiral Sir Norman Denning of the D-notice Committee, had been built up by the Crown's opening speech as the officials who had between them given 'two clear warnings' to the *Sunday Telegraph* about the Official Secrets Acts being contravened if the Scott Report was published. But under cross-examination from Mr Jeremy Hutchinson QC, it transpired that both these alleged warnings had been so vague as to be almost meaningless. Mr Welser, who was a middle-level official in the Information and Research department of the Foreign Office, said he had been 'somewhat horrified' when the assistant editor of the *Sunday Telegraph*, Mr Gordon Brook-Shepherd, showed him the Scott Report over lunch on 9 January. Mr Welser and Mr Brook-Shepherd were old friends, and during the meal they discussed whether the document might be a forgery because of certain unusual features such as its lack of a distribution list. Mr Welser continued: 'I said that if the document was genuine it would be much better if it was not published. I said I would go back to the Foreign Office to make enquiries and would try to find out whether we had the original document'. After an afternoon of worried discussions with officials in the West Africa department, Mr Welser rang Mr Brook-Shepherd. 'I told him that what he had got was almost certainly a copy of one of our documents. I said he ought not to have it and that it should not be for sale and ought not to be published because it was classified. Mr Brook-Shepherd said that as copies were in the hands of an MP and others, they were advised, probably by lawyers, that it would be all right to go ahead. I said all right, be it on you. It can't be helped, I'm very sorry. I was very sorry indeed because this should not have been published.'

At this point in the Crown's examination of Mr Welser, the prosecuting counsel, Mr John Mathew, made heroic efforts to get the witness to say something more, firing volleys of questions such

165

as: 'Did you detail any reasons as to why it should not be published?' 'No.' 'Was anything more said in this telephone conversation?' 'No.' 'Are you sure?' 'Yes, I think so.' 'Why did you think it was wrong to publish the report?'

Before the witness could answer, a wrangle broke out among counsel as to the admissibility of these questions, and the jury were made to withdraw for half an hour. In the ensuing discussion it was claimed that Mr Welser had said in his original police statement that he had warned Mr Brook-Shepherd that publication might lead to trouble with the Official Secrets Act, but he had now apparently forgotten his specific mention of the Act. When the jury came back, Mr Mathew made some more attempts to jolt the witness' memory but to no avail, and so the *Sunday Telegraph*'s first 'clear warning' about the Official Secrets Act sank into oblivion.

Mr Welser was then cross-examined, as the only Foreign Office representative in the case, for some two-and-a-half hours about the reasons and purposes for classifying and de-classifying confidential official information. This session became unbelievably confused and complicated as all counsel and the judge threw lengthy hypothetical questions at the unfortunate Mr Welser, who was clearly floundering way out of his depth as a suddenly created expert on the obscure problems of classification. Eventually the questioning broke down into farce, when Mr James Comyn QC asked:

Q : Would it be right to say that nowhere can we find any written rules about classifications?

A : Quite wrong.

Q : Then there are, are there, written rules about classification?

A : Yes, but they are probably themselves classified. (Loud and prolonged laughter in Court.)

Mr Comyn : We can end up in an Alice in Wonderland situation really.

After a much-needed weekend break from the Lewis Carroll pattern that the case was beginning to follow, the court resumed on Monday 18 January, to hear the evidence of Vice-Admiral Sir Norman Denning, the Secretary of the D-notice Committee.

After describing his role as adviser to the Press on news which might infringe national security, the witness gave an account of his telephone conversation with Mr Gordon Brook-Shepherd on 9 January about the nature of the Scott Report. Admiral Denning explained: 'Mr Brook-Shepherd said that from his own army experience he doubted very much whether it was an official document. He told me it had no distribution list on it and that the classification "confidential" was typed on it and not stamped. He gave me a short summary of the contents paragraph by paragraph. I told him that as it did not refer to our own national forces it did not affect our own national security and therefore D-notices were not concerned. But I did add that if it was a genuine official document it would be covered by the Official Secrets Act.'

Answering further questions from Mr John Mathew, the Admiral continued: 'Mr Brook-Shepherd seemed to be in a quandary so I told him that perhaps the Foreign and Commonwealth Office could throw some light on it. I said if he wished I would inform Sir Edward Peck*, who was the Foreign Office representative on my committee. Mr Brook-Shepherd seemed to welcome this so I said I would inform Sir Edward Peck and probably someone from the Foreign Office would communicate with him. I had no further communication with the *Sunday Telegraph* about this matter.' Cross-examined by Mr Jeremy Hutchinson QC, Admiral Denning agreed that he was not in any way a spokesman for the Government. He went on: 'I am not an authority as to what is or is not covered by the Official Secrets Act. D-notices are distinct from the Official Secrets Act, although they may of course cover the same matters.'

Mr Hutchinson asked:

> Is it right to say that you could not speak for the Government as to whether or not the Scott Report fell within the ambit of the Act?

A: That is true.

Q: If Sir Edward Peck of the Foreign Office took the view that publication might involve a breach of the Act, he could be expected to get in touch with the editor and tell him so?

A: Yes indeed. I could only inform him and leave him to take such action as would be necessary,

*Deputy Secretary, Foreign and Commonwealth Office.

> but I had expected him to get in touch with the editor.

Q : Because for the editor to make that difficult decision it is vital that he should be given as fully as possible, the official reasons for requiring suppression?

A : Most certainly. Within my own sphere, I have never asked for anything to be suppressed. I have been able to adjust the article so that the sensitive part is omitted or otherwise so that no damage is done.

These admissions by Admiral Denning that he himself had no authority to issue instructions about the Official Secrets Acts effectively destroyed the only remaining part of the Crown's claim that 'two clear warnings' about breaking the law had been received by the *Sunday Telegraph*. Already it was getting difficult to see how the prosecution against the newspaper could succeed, even though no defence had yet been presented.

The final witness for the Crown was Detective Chief Superintendent Pendered of Scotland Yard's Special Branch. He formally produced the fiats of Sir Elwyn Jones, the Attorney-General, authorising the prosecutions, and gave evidence of his interviews with Mr Roberts and Colonel Cairns and of his non-interview with me.

In cross-examination, Mr Basil Wigoder QC put in a few gentle digs about the selectivity of the prosecutions. He also highlighted the fact that the police, after questioning all the guests at General Alexander's dinner party, could only produce David Alexander to support the General's account, whereas the defence had produced four of the guests at the Magistrates' Court to contradict parts of the prosecution's story. But apart from drawing the jury's attention to these ironies of the case, the defence in no way challenged the police evidence. This closed the case for the prosecution.

THE LEGAL SUBMISSIONS

During the five days taken by the Crown to present the case for the prosecution, Mr Justice Caulfield had at various moments invited all counsel to assist him over the interpretation of the law.

This assistance, it was inferred, would be gratefully received at the end of the Crown evidence. Then, as expected, there took place a titanic legal battle between prosecution and defence counsel over the issue as to whether there was or was not a case to answer. These submissions lasted for two-and-a-half days and as the arguments dealt exclusively with points of law, they were held in the absence of the jury. This long session amounted to a first-class academic debate on legal theory, for the court listened to some of the best brains of the Criminal Bar clinically dissecting the delphic obscurities of the Official Secrets Act 1911.

These submissions, in the view of some observers, were directly responsible for the part of the judge's final summing up in which he urged that Section 2 of the 1911 Act should be 'pensioned off'. Indeed it is not too far fetched to say that the impetus for the present government's desire to change the law springs more from those two-and-a-half days of esoteric intellectual argument than from half a century of popular agitation by aggrieved Official Secrets Act victims. In the presence of legal luminaries from Whitehall (including the Director of Public Prosecutions, Sir Norman Skelhorn), Mr James Comyn QC, Mr Basil Wigoder QC and Mr Jeremy Hutchinson QC convincingly proved that not only the case under discussion, but also Section 2 of the 1911 Act, was a monstrous absurdity which had no right to exist in Britain of the 1970s. Although these submissions were at the time unreported (so as not to prejudice the minds of newspaper-reading jurors) and highly technical in their presentation, they deserve to be summarised on account of their fundamental importance to the future of Official Secrecy.

The main submission, put forward by both Mr Hutchinson and Mr Wigoder, was that Section 2 of the 1911 Statute only made sense if it referred back to the same kind of official information defined by Section 1 – i.e.: information prejudicial to the safety and interests of the State. This construction of the Act, it was argued, must have been what Parliament originally intended in 1911. Because of the repetition of certain phrases in the original Official Secrets Act of 1888, it was clear that Parliament had never intended that the receipt and communication of *all* official information should be a criminal offence. The 1911 legislators had voted for Section 1, because it dealt with active espionage and for Section 2 because it was meant to protect with lesser penalties

information, in the hands of unauthorised ordinary non-spy
citizens, which might if disclosed be useful to enemies. Section 2
was also intended to discipline civil servants, but as far as private
citizens were concerned, Section 2 only applied to information
relating to national security. Moreover the test of whether information was covered by Section 1 or 2 was an objective test to be
applied by the courts. The civil servant classifying a document
was expressing his own or his department's opinion, but this
opinion could not be unchallengeable by the courts. As Mr
Wigoder put it, 'If this Act applies automatically to all official
information, then that amounts to total censorship which Parliament could not have intended'.

As far as the defendants' positions were concerned, Mr Comyn
argued that Colonel Cairns was 'head of his own mission' in
Nigeria. He was not a servant of the Crown and he was not in any
way attached to the British High Commission. Colonel Cairns was
an officer brought out of retirement to take on a contract of service
with the British Government as a member of an international
team. In this job, he was entitled as an independent representative
to pass on information in confidence to his former superior, General
Alexander. On my behalf, Mr Wigoder argued that as a private
citizen, I could only be guilty of an offence under the Official
Secrets Act if there was a chain of guilty knowledge running from
Colonel Cairns to me. Section 2 ordains that a chain of guilty
knowledge must run either from a Crown servant who knows he
has broken the law, or from a person who has been entrusted
information in confidence by a Crown servant, and knowingly
breaks that confidence. But General Alexander had not been prosecuted, presumably in order to get his testimony as Queen's
Evidence. This non-prosecution meant that the chain had been
broken. Moreover, General Alexander, despite his emphasis on
conditions of strict confidence, had specifically stated that he did
not think *he* was doing anything wrong, or that *he* was breaking
the Official Secrets Act when he gave me the Scott Report. The
prosecution, if they wished to get a conviction against me, were
thus in the ridiculous position of having to admit that their star
witness was deliberately lying in the witness box when he said
'It didn't cross my mind that I was breaking the Act when I gave
the document to Aitken'. Unless the prosecution did a complete
volte-face and declared the General to be a dishonest witness on

this point, there could be no conviction against me since the Crown had produced not one scrap of evidence to show how I could have acquired guilty knowledge between the time of receiving the document at the dinner party on 21 December and communicating it to the *Sunday Telegraph* on 9 January.

On behalf of the *Sunday Telegraph* and its editor, Mr Jeremy Hutchinson QC pointed out that the newspaper had received the document not from me but from my literary agent, Mr Graham Watson of Curtis Brown Limited. Thus the newspaper could only get the guilty knowledge link from me (always assuming that I had it in the first place) if Mr Watson was in law 'a mere conduit pipe'. But since Mr Watson had himself made enquiries of others, had satisfied himself as to the propriety of passing on the document before he did so, and had negotiated the price, then as Mr Hutchinson put it: 'Mr Watson must be regarded as just about the most active conduit pipe ever conceived of.'

Mr Hutchinson also stressed that the enquiries made by the *Sunday Telegraph* of Mr Welser showed that guilty knowledge could not have been in their minds. If it had, they would never have asked a Foreign Office official for guidance.

Finally all defence counsel supported the argument that the Scott Report could not remain covered by the Official Secrets Act after it had been used to brief a press conference of journalists using verbatim extracts from the document.

Replying to these submissions on behalf of the Crown, Mr John Mathew battled with consummate skill, even though he was forced into several ultimately untenable positions.

He rejected the construction of the Act arguments, by declaring that the Crown regards all official information – whether classified or not – as covered by Section 2 of the Official Secrets Act. He added: 'The whole structure of government would fall down if people had complete freedom to communicate any document that was not a document useful to an enemy.'

Developing this point, Mr Mathew argued: 'A budget leak in relation to purchase tax could hardly be said to be of use to an enemy and yet it would be an outrage to our society if someone who received that information could use it as he wished.'

The Judge: Are you saying that if the *Sunday Telegraph*

	gets to hear of a budget leak, they cannot tell us on Sunday morning?
Mr Mathew :	No they could not.
The Judge :	I have a feeling they would. So really they have got to get their instructions from a Ministry?
Mr Mathew :	They are not entitled to communicate that information without authority.
The Judge :	This is one of the fundamental points of the case.

Dealing with submissions on behalf of Colonel Cairns, Mr Mathew agreed that his status under the Crown was a matter for the jury. Colonel Scott had stated that Cairns was not authorised by him to send a copy of the report to General Alexander, and that was enough.

The Judge :	Are you saying that if an official stamps a document confidential and says no-one at all is authorised to receive it, then a person who passes it on automatically commits an offence?
Mr Mathew :	Yes.

Mr Mathew accepted that a chain of guilty knowledge would have to run from official sources through to me, Mr Roberts and the *Sunday Telegraph* but said that the chain could begin either with Colonel Cairns or with General Alexander. General Alexander would in either circumstance have to be technically guilty of an offence, but he had in fact virtually admitted this himself by saying: 'I told Aitken I did not think I should be in possession of the document.'

As for the *Sunday Telegraph* and Mr Roberts, Mr Mathew contended that there had been no receipt in law by Mr Thackeray (the features editor) from Mr Watson. The receipt was by Mr Roberts on behalf of the newspaper. Mr Roberts must have known as soon as he read it that he was holding a document covered by the Official Secrets Act, and before he communicated it to his readers he received more information from Mr Welser and Admiral Denning which should have indicated that he was unlawfully in possession of the report.

Rejecting the defence's claim that the confidentiality of the Scott

Report had been lifted by Colonel Scott's press briefing, Mr Mathew replied that the case was not about the information in the report, it was about the report itself.

At the end of Mr Mathew's reply, the defence counsel all made their final rebuttals. The central issue of the construction of the Act argument was dealt with by Mr Wigoder who said: 'The Crown objects to the defence construction of the Act because it would mean that a member of the public can communicate any official information which would not be useful to an enemy. In the view of the defence this would be an entirely proper result, and one which Parliament originally intended. As for Mr Mathew's argument that the defence construction would cause the whole structure of government to break down, this must surely be wrong because action can still be taken against the civil servants who disclose the information in the first place.'

After some thirteen hours of such arguments the moment came for the judge to give his ruling on whether or not there was a case to answer. Mr Justice Caulfield did so in just eighteen words: 'I find that there is a case to go to the jury on each count against each accused.'

The brevity of this ruling startled all the barristers, for the judge had been expected to elucidate the law at some length. In fact when it came to the summing up, it was clear that Mr Justice Caulfield accepted many of the defence's submissions but evidently wished the case to be decided in open court by a jury. However, this judicial view of the case was not immediately apparent, and and at the time there was general despondency in the defence camp that two and a half expensive days had been used to no apparent avail. Yet the lasting importance of these exhaustive legal submissions was that the Crown was forced to spell out at length, officialdom's true view of the scope of the Official Secrets Acts. Since Mr John Mathew had at his elbow during this part of the trial a battery of Whitehall legal experts, it can confidently be assumed that he spoke with the authentic voice of the establishment. But the arguments he was forced to propagate were so outrageous in terms of the basic British freedoms of speech and communication, that these submissions may well have done more than anything else to hasten the downfall of the Official Secrets Act.

THE DEFENCE

As soon as the judge had ruled that all defendants had a case to answer, Mr James Comyn QC rose to open for the defence of Colonel Cairns. In a splendid flourish of Hibernian oratory, he declared: 'In my submission this prosecution should never have been brought at all. There are no secrets involved in it from start to finish. It is a petty and a trumpery matter, a storm in a teacup, or perhaps one should say a storm in a wineglass and that is where it should have been left.'

In the witness box Colonel Cairns, after being taken by his counsel through his long history of military service, said he had been released from his post as a cashier in Barclays Bank, Windsor to serve in Nigeria as a British representative on the International Team of Military Observers under General Alexander. After General Alexander had returned to Britain, Colonel Cairns kept the General fully informed as to what was happening in the war. 'It was my belief,' said Colonel Cairns, 'that General Alexander was lecturing widely in support of the Government's policy. I thought he was an unofficial envoy of the Foreign Office and of the Government.'

Mr Comyn then asked his client:

	In everything that you did, were you acting as you believed in the interests of Britain?
A:	Yes.
Q:	What did you think of the General's loyalty to this country?
A:	Absolutely unquestioned.
The Judge:	You took those matters into consideration before you sent him Colonel Scott's report? You used your best judgement?
A:	Yes.
Mr Comyn:	Did you contemplate that you were handing it to some unauthorised person?
A:	No, I considered that he was bound by the Official Secrets Act, the same as I was.
Q:	Did it ever cross your mind that you might be breaking the Official Secrets Act when you sent General Alexander a copy of the Scott Report?
A:	Never.

Q :   Did you think it your duty, in the interest of the
            state, to communicate it to General Alexander?
A :   I did.
Q :   Would you consider it your duty to do the same
            again in the interest of the state?
The Judge : Forget about this trial. Put yourself back to 13
            December 1970.
A :   I would do the same again, my Lord.

Colonel Cairns was then questioned by Mr John Mathew on
behalf of the Prosecution.

Q :   This report was a highly sensitive document, was
            it not?
A :   I don't disagree with that.
Q :   And one whose publication might affect this
            country's relations with Nigeria.
A :   Yes.
Q :   The fact of the matter is, Colonel Cairns, you
            broke the rules. You knew perfectly well you were
            doing something you should not have done in
            sending General Alexander that report?
A :   Sir, I cannot agree. I did not contemplate that
            General Alexander would pass on the document.
Q :   Who were you to decide that you could send
            this report to General Alexander?
The Judge : Throw your shoulders back, Colonel, and tell the
            jury who you were.
A :   I was the Senior British Member of the Inter-
            national Observer team.
The Judge : And you thought you were doing your duty in
            sending the report?
A :   Yes, my Lord.

Asked by Mr Mathew why when he had sent the report to
General Alexander, Colonel Cairns had written in a covering letter
'Please don't tell Bob Scott that you have got a copy', the reply
was: 'I thought he might write to Scott to comment, and as a
matter of friendship and courtesy to Scott I wanted first to tell
him I had sent General Henry* a copy.'

*Cairns' nickname for General Alexander.

175

The principal witness for Colonel Cairns' defence was Brigadier Sir Bernard Fergusson, GCMG, GCVO, DSO, OBE, the former Governor-General of New Zealand. Equipped with monocle, moustache and military bearing, this imposing figure ('his appearance may linger in your memory for years' the judge later told the jury) explained to the court that he had been the Senior British Member of the International Military Observer Team immediately after General Alexander. Colonel Cairns had then been his deputy. Sir Bernard paid high tributes to Colonel Cairns, saying his loyalty was 'absolutely unimpeachable'. During cross-examination by Mr Mathew, Sir Bernard was asked:

Q :   Would you have felt free to send a classified document such as the Scott Report to any person you thought fit to see it without obtaining the permission of the author?

A :   Well, I might have done.

The Judge : In other words you would have used you commonsense and discretion, bearing in mind the person to whom you were sending it?

A :   Yes, my Lord.

During re-examination, Mr James Comyn asked Sir Bernard:

Q :   Would you be prepared to say Colonel Cairns was wrong in sending the report to General Alexander?

A :   Bearing in mind what General Alexander was doing, making speeches and the like, which we all knew, and also the very long and close association between the two of them, I feel in my own mind it was morally all right.

A final touch of light relief was provided by Colonel Cairns' last defence witness, Major Paul Gray. He had been Cairns' deputy on the Observer Team and had come into Colonel Scott's office on 7 December to help with the final stapling together of the report and the colouring in of the red lines on the map. Giving his account of the conversation that morning, Major Gray said: 'I remember Colonel Scott saying that he had marked his report confidential in order to ensure a wide distribution' – The Judge : 'Well he certainly achieved that.' (Laughter).

Opening the case for my defence, Mr Basil Wigoder QC told the jury that I had been waiting for twelve weary months to answer the charges and the attacks on my honour and integrity. 'These have been based on the entirely unsupported, uncorroborated and unreliable recollection of one witness, General Alexander, as to what took place in one conversation at a dinner party. Mr Aitken went off to that dinner party looking forward to his consommé and his cutlets, and found by way of dessert that General Alexander had stuffed into his pocket, contrary to his hopes and expectations, a confidential document which turned out to be a time-bomb. The General's latest account of the conversation that night has very little in common with the first accounts he gave of it to the police. The evidence of the son, David Alexander, makes it perfectly clear that nothing remotely resembling his father's version took place. You will have no doubt that when Mr Aitken left the General's house that night, he felt completely free to use the document he had been given, except that he was not free to reveal the General as his source.'

Mr Wigoder then outlined the evidence that he was going to call and explained the various defences that I would plead. Before the jury could convict me, they would have to be sure the General was committing a crime and passing on his own guilty knowledge to me. The sheer absurdity of that proposition against the background of the evidence would already be apparent. Secondly the jury would hear that before it was decided to publish the Scott Report, Mr Aitken and Mr Hugh Fraser MP reached the decision that they were fully entitled to draw the attention of the public to the contents of that document, as it confirmed that their suspicions that inaccurate and misleading statements had been made in Parliament by Mr Wilson, then Prime Minister, and Mr Michael Stewart, the Foreign Secretary; that was the duty of any citizen. If the jury were satisfied that these misleading statements made it his client's duty in the interests of the State to communicate the Scott Report to the public through the *Sunday Telegraph,* then they must acquit. Dealing with my inaccurate statements on the tape-recording which the prosecution had emphasised so heavily, Mr Wigoder said: 'Analysing the behaviour of the General and Mr Aitken after the storm broke doesn't really give you any guidance whether they were really guilty people who had committed an offence. They were both beating a retreat as quickly as they could. When it comes to beating a retreat Mr Aitken has a great deal to learn from a former Major-General.'

After Mr Wigoder's opening, I went into the witness box and remained there for over six hours. First I was led through a general resumé of my political and journalistic career, and my views on the Nigerian civil war. Asked about my relationship with General Alexander, I replied: 'We were on friendly terms, particularly because we both shared a common interest, perhaps even a common obsession, about the Nigerian civil war. We both had differing points of view. He knew a great deal of the Federal point of view. I knew a certain amount of the Biafran point of view and we exchanged information. The General was really my main source of information for my articles, and gave me a great deal as well as documents. He showed me maps and was extremely helpful. We met at least once a month.'

Asked if I was free to publish the information from the General, I replied:

'Yes, but there was an understanding I was not going to embarrass him by disclosing him as my source. It was a gentleman's agreement.'

Mr Wigoder then questioned me about the dinner party, and I emphatically denied General Alexander's account of the three conditions. I then told the full story of what had happened, as described in Chapters 8 and 9 of this book. On the embarrassing issue of the tape-recording, I expressed regret at having panicked and made untruthful statements shifting the blame for the leak on to Mr Hugh Fraser MP, but pointed out that Mr Fraser had said beforehand: 'When you see the General, shovel all the blame on me. I'm not vulnerable in your constituency.'

After telling the court about the *Topic* affair in 1962, I said that I felt unable to be frank with General Alexander 'because I was afraid that I might become the General's second journalistic victim'. The final part of Mr Wigoder's examination of me went as follows:

Q :   When you received that report did you know or did you have reasonable grounds for believing that it was being communicated to you in contravention of the Official Secrets Act?

A :   I certainly knew no such thing.

Q :   When you left the General's house what did you
      think you were entitled to do with it?

A :   I believed this document had been given to me
      because the General was helping me in my journa-
      listic work and that I could make use of it for
      journalistic purposes.

Q :   Did it occur to you that General Alexander might
      have committed an offence by passing his copy
      of the report to you?

A :   Never.

Q :   When you agreed to the report being photo-
      copied at Yorkshire Television did you think you
      were doing anything shameful?

A :   Absolutely not. Photocopying research documents
      is a matter of routine in a television station.

Q :   In taking the decision to communicate the docu-
      ment to the *Sunday Telegraph* did you think you
      were doing anything shameful.

A :   Absolutely not – completely the reverse.

Cross-examining me on behalf of the Crown, Mr John Mathew
tried hard to shake me from my refusal to accept the General's
account of the three conditions but received only negative
answers. Eventually he put it bluntly:

Q :   You are really saying, are you not, that General
      Alexander in order to cover his tracks, has in-
      vented this story that he handed you the docu-
      ment in confidence.

A :   I'm afraid I am saying exactly that.

Q :   So that is the straight issue between you.

A :   Yes.

Q :   If you had been given the document in confi-
      dence, you would never have passed it on, or
      copied it, or caused it to be published.

A :   No I wouldn't.

Q :   And if the General had said he had no right to
      be in possession of it and was only lending it to
      you in strict confidence you would have known
      that he had no lawful right to pass it on.

A :   I question your use of the word lawful. He might
      just have been asked by a friend not to pass it on.

Anyway the General never said that so we are
talking about a hypothetical situation.

Mr Mathew retorted: 'We are if your evidence is correct. We are
not if General Alexander's evidence is correct.' Faced with this
impasse, Mr Mathew launched an onslaught on my credibility as
a witness, and fiercely attacked me for telling lies on the tape-
recording. He went on:

Q: When you saw General Alexander at his house,
       the time the tape-recording was made, you went
       there with the object of shovelling the blame on
       to someone else for your own private motives,
       mainly in the constituency?

A: That is correct.

Q: Are you now trying to shovel the blame on to
       someone else, namely the General?

A: Not at all.

Mr Mathew then suggested that I had only discovered about
the General's previous repudiation of the *Topic* journalist since
the case had begun and was rushing it forward as an excuse. I
denied this, explaining that when working as a reporter on the
Evening Standard I had looked through General Alexander's
press cuttings in 1966 when he was in the news over a family
matter and had then seen the national press coverage of the *Topic*
affair. With Mr Mathew getting more and more heated as I
refused to agree with his suggestions that the tape-recording of
11 March 1970 proved that I had a guilty mind on 21 December
1969, the cross-examination ended. It had been a painful ordeal,
but one which had not materially advanced the Crown's case.

My defence witnesses began by following the pattern of the
Magistrates' Court. Mr Michael Deakin testified about the
openness with which I had brought him the report at Yorkshire
Television and described the routine nature of the photocopying.
Colonel Preston said he couldn't remember a word of the General's
three conditions over the port. Mrs Cliff repeated almost verbatim
her Magistrates' Court account of the casual handing-over of
the document on the sofa, while Mr Cliff produced the most
felicitous phrase of the day when he described the General's entry
into the drawing room carrying the Scott Report: 'He came into

the room waving the paper around quite openly – like one might wave a race card.'

The Judge : 'You would take more care of a race card, wouldn't you?' (Laughter).

The liveliest defence witness, predictably enough, was Mr Hugh Fraser. He was called on the morning of the eleventh day of the trial, having spent the previous evening at an all-night sitting at the House of Commons voting on the Industrial Relations Bill.

Despite this lack of sleep, Hugh Fraser was in no mood to pull punches. In his evidence in chief he described how I had brought the Scott Report to his home in Scotland.

Mr Basil Wigoder then asked:

> With your experience as a Privy Councillor and a minister did it ever occur to you that the document might have been handed over in contravention of the Official Secrets Act?

A : No it did not. I imagined that a general would not hand over an official document to a journalist.

Q : Did you regard it as an official document?

A: No. I regarded it as a document issued by an official but not as an official document because it had been handed around by people like General Alexander who were propagandists for the Nigerian Government in England.

Q : As a result of your discussion with Mr Aitken what decision did you take about the document?

A : That the maximum use should be made of the document, first by handing it to the Press and secondly by my putting down a series of Parliamentary questions and pressing for an emergency debate when the House reassembled. I wanted to change government policy.

The Judge : Putting it another way, you were wanting to make a rumpus?

A : Yes, my Lord.

Mr Wigoder : What view did you form as the relevance of the Scott Report in relation to statements in the House of Commons about arms supplies to Nigeria?

181

A :   I thought it proved certain ministers' statements to be outrageously mendacious.

At this point the defence produced large numbers of volumes of Hansard from which Mr Fraser read out extracts of ministers' speeches. He then compared these statements with paragraphs in the Scott Report. A number of discrepancies were alleged. The most important of these was the discrepancy between the Foreign Secretary's statement that Britain was supplying only fifteen per cent of Nigeria's arms, and the Scott Report's figures which indicated that Britain had been supplying over eighty per cent approximately of Nigeria's arms*. Dealing with events after the *Sunday Telegraph's* publication of the story, Hugh Fraser corroborated my evidence that he had given me *carte blanche* to put the blame on him when seeing General Alexander. He ended by reading aloud his 'What Goes On' letter to *The Times* of 18 March in which he had complained about the 'curious selectivity of prosecutions'. The reading of this letter was like a red rag to a bull so far as the Crown lawyers were concerned, and Mr John Mathew really let fly on his cross-examination.

Q :   When the police came to see you, you refused to answer questions?

A :   I did not want to incriminate anyone being attacked through an abuse of the Official Secrets Act for political purposes.

Q :   The Official Secrets Act at that time was not being used, let alone abused. No one was being attacked. Chief Superintendent Pendered wanted to see if you could help the police. Why did you not answer his questions?

A :   I first agreed to see Mr Pendered. But when I heard that Mr Aitken had been cautioned under the Official Secrets Act, I came to the conclusion that the Government was abusing its powers to persecute individuals and I wanted no part of it.

Q :   How can you say that after you yourself put down a question about security in the Lagos High Commission?

*See Chapter 8 for details.

A: I have very strong views about how the Official Secrets Act can be used by the executive.

Q: Having said nothing to the police so that they had no knowledge of your part in this matter, you wrote a letter to *The Times* which said in terms – Why haven't I been prosecuted? What do you think the reactions to your letter would have been if you had added a PS – 'but of course when the police came to see me about the matter I said nothing'.

A: I would have added a PPS – 'when the police came to see Mr Aitken, he said not a thing'.

In re-examination, the first question put by Mr Basil Wigoder to Hugh Fraser was:

After you had written your letter to *The Times* and it had been published, did the police ever come back to see you?

A: No.

Hugh Fraser was not the only former minister of the Crown to give evidence in my defence, for Lord Chalfont, who had been a Minister of State in the Foreign Office during the whole of the Labour Government's term of office, came forward as an expert witness to testify about the unusual appearance of the Scott Report. After telling the court about his own experience of seeing official documents during his previous careers as a Regular Army Officer, and as Defence Correspondent of *The Times,* Lord Chalfont agreed that he would have been surprised by the lack of an official stamp or crest anywhere on the Scott Report; by the absence of a cover sheet or distribution list; and by the lack of an address or addressee.

Mr Wigoder then asked:

What would have been your first reaction as a journalist on seeing the Scott Report?

A: I would have been very puzzled by it. I think my first impression would have been that it was a private document written as a mind-clearing exercise.

G

Q :   And if you had received the document from a retired general?

A :   That would strengthen this impression. I would have been very surprised to receive it from someone not serving. Journalists being naturally suspicious I might have thought it was a joke, a hoax, or a fake.

At a moment in the case when the Crown was leaning heavily on the appearance of the Scott Report as *ipso facto* proof of guilty knowledge on the part of anyone who handled it, this expert testimony proved most helpful to the defence. Coming forward to give such evidence must have required no small degree of political courage from Lord Chalfont, for his Labour ex-ministerial colleagues (particularly those in the Foreign Office) were the very people who had launched the original prosecutions.

The case for my defence was rounded off by the testimony of two distinguished character witnesses. First came Mr Charles Wintour, the editor of the *London Evening Standard,* for whom I had worked since 1966. He spoke of my good reputation in the profession, pointing out that he had never received any complaints about my professional ethics nor any legal problems arising from my work. He added: 'I did not know he was offering the report to the *Sunday Telegraph,* but under the terms of his free-lance contract he was free to offer articles to other publications.'

My final, and somewhat spectacular, character witness was the Speaker of the House of Commons, the Rt. Hon. Selwyn Lloyd. He had been elected to his new office only twelve days earlier, and his tail-coated appearance in the witness-box of the Old Bailey set a remarkable new legal precedent. Examined on my behalf by Mr John Lloyd-Eley QC, the Speaker said:

In 1965 until early 1966, Mr Aitken was my private secretary. At that time I was the Opposition spokesman on Commonwealth affairs and in pursuance of those duties I went to Australia, New Zealand and Rhodesia accompanied by Mr Aitken. I had conversations with prime ministers of these countries and Mr Aitken was present when matters of great confidence were discussed, particularly in Rhodesia. At the time, he was also a part-time journalist, but he never disclosed any of the matters discussed . . . I had and have complete confidence in his trustworthiness. I regard him as a man of the highest integrity and

I still believe he has a very considerable political future before him.

After this generous evidence had been given by The Speaker, Mr Jeremy Hutchinson QC opened the case for the *Sunday Telegraph*.

He began by saying that he wanted the jury to come down to earth from the diversions of the case. 'You have been taken through the realms of politics, dinner parties, port, Federal and Biafra lobbies, Yorkshire Television, Hansard and the House of Commons. Now I ask you to come back to the realities of the workings of an efficient and successful Sunday newspaper, and to consider the basic allegation – namely that Mr Roberts and the *Sunday Telegraph* acted in a criminal manner during January 1970.'

After pointing out that the case against the *Sunday Telegraph* could only be considered if General Alexander had acted criminally in passing the document to me, Mr Hutchinson stressed that the *Sunday Telegraph* had received the document innocently and had printed it in good faith believing that copies were already in circulation and that publication was in the public interest. Before publication, the assistant editor Mr Brook-Shepherd had consulted his contact at the Foreign Office and had received only the vaguest murmurs of concern on a personal basis. The Government had known for two days that the newspaper had the document and was going to publish it. Mr Hutchinson continued:

If the Foreign and Commonwealth Office thought publication would embarrass this country's relations with Nigeria and would therefore be against the interests of the State, why did it not say so at the time? Why did not one of its senior officials pick up a telephone and say to the editor: 'Please do not publish because it is not in the interests of the State that you should'?

Stressing that the *Sunday Telegraph*'s interest in the document was entirely based on humanitarian and public interest reasons, Mr Hutchinson went to great lengths to disassociate his clients from the political motives of Hugh Fraser and myself, saying:

The *Sunday Telegraph* is not the political poodle of either Mr Aitken or Mr Fraser. It is now clear that the newspaper was

185

quite innocently caught up in the tangled political web which these gentlemen had woven in Yorkshire, Scotland, and London.

Explaining the *Sunday Telegraph*'s somewhat flamboyant presentation of the original Scott Report story on 11 January 1970, Mr Hutchinson declared:

The report was of course dressed up for the paper's readers. Maybe it was overdressed, but the document was full of great stodgy passages and you may feel a suet pudding is very much improved by a dash of golden syrup, but not in this case with Aitken and Fraser and the manufacturers. It was dressed up with a certain degree of journalistic licence, but it was never thought that the Official Secrets Act could possibly have covered this document, and it was published in good faith.

The first witness for the *Sunday Telegraph* was the paper's features editor, Mr Ralph Thackeray. He gave evidence of receiving the Scott Report from Mr Graham Watson. The document, he said, was accompanied by a short 'blurb' (in fact my précis notes) which summarised the report's contents and stated that pro-Biafran circles in London were aware of the Scott Report's existence, that it had been seen by certain MPs, among them Mr Hugh Fraser, and that questions were to be asked about it in Parliament.

The second, and perhaps the most important of the *Sunday Telegraph*'s witnesses was Mr Gordon Brook-Shepherd. He was the assistant editor who according to the Crown's opening speech had received 'two clear warnings' that publication might contravene the Official Secrets Act. He was also the editorial writer who had composed the 'overdressed' front page article accompanying the report's text.

Describing his conversations with his old friend and Foreign Office contact Mr Johann Welser, Mr Brook-Shepherd said that they had discussed the authenticity of the report and nothing more. The idea of the Official Secrets Act prohibiting publication had not arisen. All that Mr Welser had said was that he 'hoped the report would not be published'.

Mr Brook-Shepherd continued: 'I asked him what would be the reaction of the news department of the Foreign Office, and Mr Welser told me he thought their official reply would be – 'no

comment, which is a standard reply from the news department.'
Mr Hutchinson then asked:

	During these conversations, was Mr Welser speaking to you in his private capacity as a friend?
A :	Yes indeed. At no time did he as it were put on his bowler hat, brandish his umbrella and say I'm speaking now to you officially.
The Judge :	What difference would it have made if he had?
A :	It would have meant that I would have placed a different value on the Government's response . . . Had even an under-secretary telephoned and spoken on behalf of the Foreign Office, it would have put a totally different complexion on the matter.

In recounting his telephone conversation with Admiral Denning, Mr Brook-Shepherd denied that the Admiral had ever said that the document was covered by the Official Secrets Act. He continued:

I do not remember that. I think he said it should not be published without authority . . . To us Admiral Denning was the personification of the Officials Secrets Act and once he had washed his hands of it by saying that no question of national security was involved, I dismissed it from my mind.

Mr Brook-Shepherd agreed with the prosecution that he had dressed up the news story on the front and back pages using plenty of journalistic licence, but said his use of phrases like 'secret report' had not meant to indicate that security had been breached.

The Judge :	You used a dash of syrup.
Mr Brook-Shepherd :	I would prefer the word spice.
The Judge :	Syrup flows more gently.

Re-examined by Mr Hutchinson, Mr Brook-Shepherd said it had never entered his head that the report had been obtained in contravention of the Official Secrets Act. On the subject of the so-called 'warnings' from government officials, Mr Brook-Shepherd claimed that no such warnings were ever issued: 'All we got was the old boy unofficial network all the time. Half of our

time we live with a Government trying to persuade us not to publish something which we think we ought to. The other half of our
time we spend resisting attempts by the Government to get us to
print things we are not interested in.' The Judge : 'It is a wonder
you produce a newspaper at all.' (Laughter).

The final evidence for the *Sunday Telegraph* was given by the
newspaper's sixty-four-year-old editor Mr Brian Roberts. Entering the witness box on the thirteenth day of the trial, Mr Roberts
said that there were three main considerations which led to his
decision to publish the Scott Report.

The first was that he considered it was the task of the Press to
disclose, within the law, information on matters of public interest.
The report dealt with matters which at that time were of intense
and continuing public interest. He thought that as the document
had been cleared on the grounds of security, publication was within
the law. 'At no time thereafter did it occur to me that publication
would infringe the Official Secrets Act. We have not yet got censorship in this country.'

The second main consideration was that the word 'confidential'
was meaningless unless it was confidential to someone. 'Anyone
can write the word "confidential" on a paper from motives good
or bad, selfish or disinterested, if he does not wish it to become
known. There was no indication whatsoever on the Scott Report as
to whom it was to be confidential.'

The third consideration was that whatever confidentiality the
report had originally possessed, it was entirely negated by the
knowledge that it was already in the hands of an MP, and others,
and that questions about it were being tabled in Parliament.

Mr Roberts added that in taking the decision to publish he
had been unaffected by political considerations and had 'no
interest in beating Mr Fraser's political drum'.

As far as the government was concerned, Mr Roberts said that
if the Foreign Office had considered the publication of the report
to be detrimental to British national interests, he would have expected to receive representatives at a very high level. 'I thought
that possibly the Permanent Secretary, Sir Denis Greenhill, or the
Foreign Secretary, Mr Michael Stewart, would telephone Lord
Hartwell (editor-in-chief, *Sunday Telegraph*) or myself and say
"Look, publication of this report will damage national interests.
We will tell you off the record why." '

Mr Roberts added: 'If they had done that an entirely different situation would have arisen. We would have given it serious consideration, even if it meant losing an edition of the paper while we took the report out.'

Questioned by the prosecuting counsel, Mr John Mathew, Mr Roberts agreed that the paper had used 'journalistic licence' in presenting the story on the newspaper's front and back pages.

Q : Your story was designed to make it look as though the report had got through a security net.

A : It had got through a net, but I do not think it was a security net.

Q : Why did you complain of the document's 'hopelessly inadequate classification' on the back page?

A : I meant that if it was a State document then the classification was inadequate.

Pointing to certain passages in the story, Mr Mathew claimed that the ordinary reader would draw the conclusion that there had been a serious breakdown of security in Lagos. Mr Roberts replied: 'We were merely reporting on the questions tabled in the House by Mr Hugh Fraser.'

Mr Roberts was questioned by the Judge about the scope of the Official Secrets Act, which he had earlier agreed 'hovered like a vulture over Fleet Street'.

The Judge : In fairness to you and possibly other editors, would this be a fair summary of the situation – that when documents do not affect national security an editor can be in a great quandary at a critical time on whether to publish or not?

Mr Roberts : Yes.

The Judge : And whatever assistance you seek from government circles, ultimately the decision has to be made by the editor?

Mr Roberts : Yes, and there is the added difficulty that apart from security there is no one designated to advise editors on the Official Secrets Act.

The Judge : The D-notice is really a co-operative voluntary affair between the Press, broadcasting and other public media and the Government so that all are

co-operating in a desire to avoid damage to the
State.

Mr Roberts : Exactly.

The Judge : And speaking generally editors do not want to
damage national interests.

Mr Roberts : Of course not.

The Judge : Equally you had no desire to be in the dock for a
month on an Official Secrets charge.

Mr Roberts : The role of martyr is not congenial to me.

Mr Robert's evidence ended the case for all the defendants, and
there now remained only the closing speeches by counsel.

In his final address on behalf of the Crown, Mr John Mathew
began by telling the jury:

You have heard allegations that this case is a political prosecution, but we do not have political trials in this country. The
judiciary and all those who help in the administration of justice
are wholly independent of politics for the purposes of the law.
It is not so in all countries, but thank God it is here. Mr Aitken
may like to think he is being hounded by angry politicians
whom he attempted to expose, but perhaps you may think that
he sees himself in a rather more important role than in fact he
merits.

After explaining to the jury that it was not their task to criticise
the Official Secrets Act but instead to decide whether offences had
been committed under the Act, Mr Mathew said of Colonel
Cairns:

One can only look for sympathy for the Colonel in his predica-
ment. You may well find that he has been placed in his position
because of the irresponsibility of others. But the one undisputed
fact of this case, whatever you may think of it as an offence
under the Official Secrets Act, is that his was the action which
started the whole of this unhappy chain of events. Obviously
he thought no harm could ever result from passing the document on to his trusted friend General Alexander. But was it
for Colonel Cairns to judge? This is what rules are for.

Dealing with the charges against the *Sunday Telegraph* and its
editor, Mr Mathew told the jury:

You should hesitate for an eternity before convicting Mr Roberts and the *Sunday Telegraph* of receiving the report knowing it to be in contravention of the Act. The inquiries they made after receiving it from a most reputable agency indicate their good faith, and you may feel that you would have to stretch the evidence to an absurd extent to find them guilty of this charge . . . but by the time they came to communicate this report to the public, the situation was rather different. If you look at the article of 11 January you may feel that it has been presented on the basis that there has been a security leak of a highly confidential document. You may think that this represented the true state of mind of these defendants when they published this document.

Turning to me, Mr Mathew suddenly introduced a startling new motive for my actions.

Was his use of this document really to show up ministers for their misleading statements? Or wouldn't it be more accurate to say that Mr Aitken wanted to make mischief for the British Government in its diplomatic relations with Nigeria – as much mischief as possible?

Mr Basil Wigoder QC indignantly intervened to say that this question of wishing to disrupt Anglo-Nigerian relations had never been suggested to me when I was in the witness box, and should not be so unfairly introduced in a closing speech.

The Judge: Mr Wigoder, I hesitate to give a ruling on this point. You can deal with these matters when it comes to your turn. My advice to you is to hold your horses – and then let 'em go.

Mr Wigoder took this judicial advice to heart, for his final address to the jury was the longest, liveliest and most eloquent of the closing speeches. He began in a highly satirical vein.

This case has been called The Queen against Aitken. I am tempted to call it the Queen of Hearts against Aitken, for if ever there was an Alice in Wonderland trial then this is it. The prosecution's arguments have become, as Alice said 'curiouser and curiouser', and now Mr Mathew has taken over the role of the Queen of Hearts, shouting 'Off with his head,

Off with his head!' presumably in the hope that if this was said often enough then you, members of the jury, will come to believe that Mr Aitken has done something criminal.

But the Queen of Hearts also said to Alice 'I dare say you have not had any breakfast. I can sometimes believe as many as six impossible things before breakfast.' Members of the jury, if you examine the prosecution case carefully and with commonsense, you will see that it involves you in believing one impossible thing after another.

Mr Wigoder then turned scornfully on the prosecution's suggestion that I had seen myself in an excessively self-important role.

It lies ill in the prosecution's mouth to say that Mr Aitken has exaggerated his own importance, for it was the prosecution who chose whom to put in the dock. The Crown had to choose between Colonel Cairns and Major-General Henry Alexander, who was an important person. And they chose the colonel. They had to choose between Mr Aitken, the prospective parliamentary candidate and Mr Hugh Fraser, a former Minister and a Privy Councillor. They chose Mr Aitken.

They had to choose between Mr Roberts, the editor of the *Sunday Telegraph*, and Lord Hartwell, the proprietor of that newspaper and a distinguished Press baron, who had publicly admitted his responsibility for publication of the Scott Report. They chose Mr Roberts. You may think, members of the jury, that there has been a deliberate and utterly unfair selection process of those whom the Crown has decided to prosecute.

On the subject of the transaction of the Scott Report from General Alexander to me at the dinner party Mr Wigoder commented:

I suppose if anyone is going to impute moral blame, one might be forgiven for saying the chap who hands the document to the journalist is the man. But the prosecution are not suggesting that General Alexander should be prosecuted.

If General Alexander thought he was committing an offence under the Act, would he not at least have put the document in an envelope and asked Mr Aitken to step outside the drawing-room?

The whole of the background events of the dinner party

make it perfectly plain that at the time the General was perfectly happy about having the document from Colonel Cairns and perfectly happy for Mr Aitken to see it and use it for journalistic purposes.

Referring to the question of motive, Mr Wigoder said that I could have had no possible motive for wishing to jeopardise my own political career by deliberately breaking the Official Secrets Act. The Crown had now accepted that no-one ever intended to make a single penny out of the publication of the Scott Report. What other motive was there? The only thing approaching a motive was Mr Mathew's suggestion that I was seeking deliberately to upset Anglo-Nigerian diplomatic relations.

This was a mean, nasty and unworthy imputation, rushed forward in desperation in the Prosecution's closing speech, and never suggested to my client in the witness box. There is not a shred of evidence to support such a motive.

All the evidence, Mr Wigoder continued, pointed to the conclusion that both Mr Fraser and I had been sincere in saying that we thought the public ought to hear about the true facts of arms supplies to Nigeria. The public was entitled to know that ministers of the Crown had been making statements inconsistent with what was contained in the Scott Report.

It is not for civil servants and ministers of the Crown, however eminent they may be, to dictate to us the people on what may or may not be published. It is for the individual to consider if he has a duty in the interests of the State and it is for a jury to decide if the individual has acted reasonably and honestly in taking the course that he did. Journalists and the Press have an unfettered right to exercise their own judgement as to what information they publish, however embarrassing it might be to civil servants and ministers of the Crown. The crucial issue in this case is the right of the people to know. I suggest it is both the right and duty of a good journalist and a great newspaper to embarrass the Government. That is what they are for.

After reviewing the rest of the evidence in detail, and citing the Radcliffe Report and a judgement of the Press Council to show that journalists are not expected to suppress information marked 'confidential', Mr Wigoder's speech rose to a crescendo of angry criticism of the former Attorney-General, Sir Elwyn Jones, who had authorised the prosecutions. 'One cannot blind oneself to the fact that the Attorney-General is an MP, a politician, and a member of the Cabinet, and you may think in a case of this sort the political aspects were discussed and were borne in mind,' Mr Wigoder declared.

Mr Mathew was right when he had said: 'We do not have political trials in this country. Nobody is tried for their political beliefs.' But, said Mr Wigoder, that was a far cry from saying there could never be a case in which there was a political motivation for bringing a prosecution.

The jury might think it was inevitable from the facts in this case that this was a political prosecution which had indeed been brought for political purposes.

Those purposes were twofold [Mr Wigoder continued]. First it was necessary to offer up sacrificial lambs to appease the momentary indignation of some Nigerian officials, who had long ago forgotten about the whole matter and secondly, it was necessary to offer up sacrificial lambs to appease the wounded feelings of party politicians in this country who found themselves rendered vulnerable by the activities of an intelligent journalist of a great newspaper. Quite obviously, if you are going to select sacrificial lambs you try to select those who will struggle the least. I can only say on behalf of Mr Aitken that he proposes not only to struggle, he proposes to bite back and he asks you through me to free him altogether from the role for which he has been singled out by this prosecution.

Mr Wigoder's five hour speech was widely praised by the Press and moved one octogenarian listener in court to make a favourable comparison with a great closing address he had heard from Marshall Hall.*

The remaining counsel, if not quite so impassioned as Mr Wigoder, were no less effective on behalf of their clients. Mr James Comyn QC raised the already high feelings of sympathy for Colonel Cairns, when he said:

*Edward Marshall Hall QC, 1858–1927, was widely recognised to be one of the greatest orators ever heard at the Criminal Bar.

Members of the jury, you have listened for nearly three weeks to a multitude of words and you may think that the misconceived prosecution has crumbled and disintegrated against all four defendants. You may think that this whole case is much ado about nothing but that is not how the accused look at it. Consider what the stain of a conviction would mean to Colonel Cairns. First, there is his honour, which stands so high. Then there is his Army pension, which might or might not be affected, although one sincerely hopes not. There is his civilian job with Barclays Bank, where he is employed in a responsible financial capacity which involves secrets and confidences. How is he going to stand even with the most benign employers if he carries a conviction under the Official Secrets Act?

Mr Comyn said this was an example of how the small man was always attacked. He asked: 'Why do we not have General Alexander and the Rt. Hon. Hugh Fraser MP, in the dock?'

Mr Comyn ended: 'This case is a farce and has had nearly a three week run. It is high time the run finished, and let us hope it is not revived. On grounds of commonsense, in law, and on any honourable approach I ask the members of the jury to find Colonel Cairns not guilty.'

In his brief closing speech for the *Sunday Telegraph* and Mr Roberts, Mr Jeremy Hutchinson QC reminded the jury that they need no longer consider the receiving charge against his clients. On the communicating charge, Mr Hutchinson said that the newspaper had showed the report to the Foreign and Commonwealth Office and never at any time were they officially and authoritatively told that there was a good reason for not publishing it. The report had been cleared from the point of national security and Admiral Sir Norman Denning, responsible for advising the Press on security, had said he would get in touch with authoritative people in the Foreign Office and that no doubt the Foreign Office people would get in touch with the *Sunday Telegraph*. But no such person ever did.

In those circumstances the editor, exercising his responsibility and his honest appreciation of all the circumstances, decided to publish the report.

'What on earth more can a responsible newspaper do?' asked Mr Hutchinson. 'One of the most astonishing facts of this case is that all the way through we have never heard a word from the Crown as to why no official word was passed to the newspaper and its distinguished editor. It has never been explained why it was wholly blanketed in an official fog.'

Referring to an earlier remark in th proceedings about the Official Secrets Act hovering like a vulture over Fleet Street Mr Hutchinson ended:

> You have heard of vultures in this case, but you may think that these gentlemen of the Foreign and Commonwealth Office acted like a lot of old hens, fluttering their feathers in their Whitehall coops, pecking away at their classifications, and that when the truth began to leak upon them, they ran to their traditional range, the deep litter house – the Official Secrets Act. – And for all we know they are still there.

With this felicitous simile the closing speeches finished, and after a short adjournment the judge commenced his summing up.

13

Summing Up

Mr Justice Caulfield began his summing up ten minutes after noon on the sixteenth day of the trial. When he finished on the seventeenth day after speaking for six-and-a-half hours, he had effectively recast Britain's laws of Official Secrecy. Because the Government subsequently initiated certain moves which will undoubtedly at some stage produce legislative reform of the Official Secrets Act, Mr Justice Caulfield's judgement has assumed an historic as well as a contemporary importance, and extracts from it deserve to be quoted in full.

The judge began by stressing that the courts are independent of politics and of the executive government. Dealing with the suggestion that the trial had been politically inspired he said:

It may well be that prosecutions under this Act can serve as a convenient and reasonable substitute for a political trial, with the added advantage of achieving the same end without incurring the implied odium. Nevertheless I urge you most strongly to dismiss from your minds, now that this Court is seized of the matter, any political prejudice one way or the other.

Turning to the issue of press freedom, the Judge continued:

It may well be that this trial is important to the Press of this country. We all recognise, do we not, that the opinion-forming and informing media like the Press must not be muzzled. The warning bark, you may think, is necessary to help in maintaining a free society. If the Press is the watch-dog of freedom, and the fangs of the watch-dog are drawn, all that will ensue

197

is a whimper, possibly a whine, but no bite. And the Press so muzzled, you may think, becomes no more than the tenement of the political poor.

Mr Justice Caulfield then told the jury that their task was to decide whether any one of the defendants had criminally gone beyond the limits of communication permitted by Section 2 of the Official Secrets Act 1911. He added the comment:

The 1911 Act achieves its sixtieth birthday on 22 August this year. This case, if it does nothing more, may well alert those who govern us at least to consider, if they have the time, whether or not Section 2 of this Act has reached retirement age and should be pensioned off, being replaced by a section that will enable men like Colonel Cairns, Mr Aitken and Mr Roberts and other editors of journals to determine without any great difficulty whether a communication by any one of them or a certain piece of information originating from an official source, and not concerned in the slightest with national security, is going to put them in peril of being enclosed in a dock and facing a criminal charge.

After these dramatic preliminary observations, the judge summarised the evidence in the case of Colonel Cairns, going into voluminous detail as to whether Colonel Cairns received the report by virtue of his contract under the Crown, and whether in receipt he was authorised to send it on to whom he thought fit. Directing the jury that they must make up their own minds on this, and not necessarily accept the evidence of Colonel Scott that Colonel Cairns had no authority to pass on the report, the judge continued:

If Parliament had wanted to say that only civil servants or serving officers such as Colonel Scott, or his seniors, had the power to forbid – on the facts of this case, that is all that we are dealing with – communication by Colonel Cairns to a person such as General Alexander, Parliament could have said so

The summing up then turned towards the issue of who was originally responsible for the leak:

Mr Mathew said there has been an enormous conflagration, that is the publication of this confidential report by the *Sunday*

Telegraph, which started from a little fire that was lit by Colonel Cairns. Now if there has been a conflagration, it was Colonel Scott, wasn't it, who sent that document outside the diplomatic service in the British High Commission to Colonel Cairns. It may well be, members of the jury, you'll conclude that it was that action that started any fire, if there was a fire. This isn't a condemnation of Colonel Scott. Nobody has suggested he has done anything wrong. But that is how, you may think, this document eventually got into circulation. You might think that, if a British High Commission wishes to avoid the escape of a document, they can avoid it perfectly easily; and there was no reason, was there, on the evidence given by the Crown why Colonel Cairns shouldn't particularly be given that document? Colonel Cairns didn't ask for it, and you might conclude that it was handed to him in a very loose sort of way.

At this stage, Mr Justice Caulfield devoted over an hour of his speech to the position of General Alexander in the case. He pointed out that in law none of the defendants in the dock could be guilty of their alleged offences unless the General was guilty also. If Colonel Cairns was not guilty, then the remaining defendants could still be guilty provided General Alexander was the guilty party who had been entrusted the document in confidence by a servant of the Crown and had criminally passed it on. He told the Jury:

You should be on your guard because the prosecution has chosen to prosecute Cairns and not prosecute Alexander, but has utilized General Alexander as a witness against Aitken and the other defendants. If General Alexander had been prosecuted, members of the jury, as well, and had been in that dock, much of the prosecution evidence could not have been given against Aitken. If you find Colonel Cairns not guilty it forces the prosecution – in order even to begin to find a case in law against Aitken – to put forward Alexander as a person who has broken the law and has criminally communicated the report . . . Well, members of the jury, if that appears to you to be a farce you can say so by your verdict in the Jonathan Aitken case. In, I trust, plain language, you can't possibly proceed even to consider a case against Mr Aitken or Mr Roberts or the *Sunday*

199

Telegraph unless the Crown has convinced you that General Alexander has contravened the Act.

The Judge then spent a considerable time reviewing General Alexander's state of mind at the time when he handed over the report to me. Several early letters and police statements of the General's were read out. None of them indicated that the General had a guilty mind. As much as ten days after publication when General Alexander wrote on 21 January to the *Sunday Telegraph* telling them that journalists had no code of conduct and that 'any responsible person reading this document would be filled with disgust at the lack of taste shown in publishing it' – even at this stage, there was no evidence of guilty knowledge.

As the Judge put it:

Now, members of the jury, you make of that letter what you want; but the man who wrote that letter, members of the jury, had published the document himself to Mr Aitken, who was the prospective candidate for the division of Malton and Thirsk. Now, why do I alert your minds on this particular letter? Well, General Alexander is criticising the *Sunday Telegraph* for telling us about the document, but he makes no mention of the fact that he himself had published it to Mr Aitken, who was the prospective candidate, and you might wonder, members of the jury, what the difference is in publication. There isn't a limited circle, members of the jury, once a document is free to circulate, in which the document can only be read. I am not putting this against General Alexander. I am merely alerting your minds to the fact that General Alexander himself didn't think he had done anything wrong, and I am not suggesting you should conclude that he had.

The judge then read General Alexander's police statement of 28 January, which was the first of his statements in which the 'handed over in strictest confidence' claim appeared. He continued:

Now, members of the jury, I suggest you be realistic about this matter of General Alexander. Might this be the position? That by the 28 January, with the police on the scene, the General was getting very worried; and in fairness to Mr Wigoder's client – and Mr Wigoder has made a special point of this, in this way : he says the General has really fortified his evidence – and it is a matter for you – by the 28 January, was the General perturbed, because in that statement of 28 January, compared with his statement on the twenty-third, he is then saying Aitken had this document, but he had it in the strictest confidence. Is that a true position? It is a matter for you to decide, members of the jury.

Mr Justice Caulfield went on:

The Crown has put forward General Alexander as an honest witness. You will form your own view. Your view may be that once the fuss began and the balloon went up General Alexander didn't want to implicate himself; and, in fairness to him, implicate anybody else either; but you may think he became perturbed once the police were on the scene. Of course, members of the jury, when the police start to make inquiries about cases or about a possible crime, there are some people – perhaps the most respectable and elegant people – who get very worried and think that a crime has necessarily been committed. But might it be, members of the jury, that General Alexander was unnecessarily perturbed about the police inquiries? If he hadn't any worry – and he may not have needed to have a worry – couldn't he have said then to the police, 'Yes, Colonel Cairns sent the Report to me. I didn't think anything about it at the time. There was nothing secret in it. All the facts were known to the public that were contained in it, and on 21 December when I had a dinner party at which the local prospective Conservative candidate, Jonathan Aitken, was present we had an argument together about Nigeria. I couldn't convince Aitken that he was wrong, so I said to him, "Well, look, I have had a report from Bob Scott – from Colonel Cairns, rather – and this will convince you." So I lent it to him, in all good faith, to convince him that his views on the Nigerian conflict were all wrong. I told him he could use it as background information, and I pointed out to him that the document was marked "confidential".' Members of the jury, if he had said that to the police, you might think that may well be a fairly accurate summary of what happened at the dinner party. I am not saying it is. I am not putting the conclusion into your minds; but if General Alexander had said that – which you may well think

201

to be the truth – is he saying to the police, 'I was acting with a criminal mind. I was breaking the Official Secrets Act. I was conscious of what I was doing, and I knew it was wrong'?

After pointing out to the jury that yet another illogicality in the prosecution's case was that General Alexander had himself said that he did not believe he was breaking the Official Secrets Act when he handed over the report, the judge came to the dinner party. He summarised with scrupulous fairness the conflicting evidence of what was said or not said, emphasising that the jury might think that David Alexander's evidence was not as strong as his father's account of the three conditions. He went on:

> You may think, members of the jury, the Crown case is founded on what was said at a jolly dinner party. Are you surprised there is a conflict about what was said? Can you be sure about what was said?

On the subject of the tape-recording, Mr Justice Caulfield seemed inclined to be lenient towards my attempts to shift blame on to Hugh Fraser:

> You might think that Aitken went along to see the General not to attempt to stave off any prosecution but to save his safe seat. It would seem from the evidence of Aitken and Fraser that Aitken was going along to the General to shovel all the blame on to Fraser. What had Fraser to lose by receiving this heavy burden as regards responsibility for this particular document? You might think that Fraser felt himself in a rather fortified position and you might think that he hadn't very much to lose, but poor old Aitken had plenty to lose.

After summarising the statements in the tape-recording, the judge mildly observed that my untruthful remarks in this context did not necessarily prove guilt and that they may well have been unnecessary anyway in this case.

Coming to the case against the *Sunday Telegraph* and Mr Brian Roberts, Mr Justice Caulfield swiftly disposed of the receiving charge:

> Mr Mathew, in his final speech, asked you to pause for an eternity before convicting the editor or the *Sunday Telegraph* on this count. Well, you needn't pause at all, members of the

jury. I direct you as a matter of law that there is no evidence to support a conviction of either the *Sunday Telegraph* or Brian Roberts on this particular count. You must, on my direction, return a verdict of not guilty in favour of Mr Roberts and the *Sunday Telegraph* on this count.

On the communicating charge, the judge said the jury must decide whether the *Sunday Telegraph* had published the document knowing it to be in contravention of the Official Secrets Act. Referring to the evidence given by the two key prosecution witnesses, Vice-Admiral Sir Norman Denning and Mr Johann Welser, the summing up continued:

You may accept all their evidence. You may conclude they were most honest witnesses. The point you've got to appreciate, and it's pretty simple, is this: Mr Welser and Vice-Admiral Denning are not the judges as to whether there should be publication of an official document. You are. In other words you are the judges not of what should be published, but this particular issue in this case. Mr Welser's advice not to publish and Vice-Admiral Denning's advice not to publish are beside the point... You must work on the basis, members of the jury, that there is no censorship in this country. There is no duty in law, I want to make this absolutely plain, there is no duty in law for any editor or any newspaper to go running to Whitehall to get permission to print an article or to print news.

Dealing with Mr Robert's evidence, the judge said:

You may think it abundantly clear that he utilised the best member of his staff to check the document's authenticity. In those circumstances the editor, having made his enquiries, came to a decision to publish – which he says was an honest decision. How, in those circumstances, members of the jury, can you say that to his knowledge Mr Roberts was doing something he knew to be unlawful?

Mr Justice Caulfield ended his six-and-a-half-hour summing up with this comment:

We've had a vast amount of evidence in this case. You've had some long speeches, and I, too, have had to give you a long summing-up. It may well be during the course of the case you have said to yourselves, 'Well, really, we can't see the wood for the trees.' Members of the jury, you might pause and ask yourselves whether there are any trees at all, and what you might have seen, when you look at the whole of the evidence and what you have been told in this case, is that really there is only a desert, it's a barren waste; and that this prosecution perhaps has been put before you in this way : that once a document emanating from an official source is stamped 'confidential' that therefore anybody who handles the document is breaking the law. I hope I have explained to you in my directions in law that that is not the law.

14

Epilogue

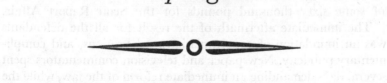

The jury retired to consider their verdicts and were out for two hours and eleven minutes. Some of this time was taken up by lunch in the jury room, and by a delay caused by the temporary re-allocation of Court Number 1 for the preliminaries of a murder case. But eventually the ten men and two women, whose impassive faces had become so familiar, returned to their jury box. At 3.21 p.m. on the seventeenth day of the trial, the bespectacled foreman of the jury rose and in answer to the Clerk of the Court uttered the miraculous words 'not guilty' to each and every one of the counts on the indictment.

Even though this result had been expected, it is impossible to describe the overwhelming sense of relief experienced by the defendants and their supporters. By 3.22 p.m. as we stepped out of the dock, a ripple of applause ran round the court and the atmosphere felt supercharged with emotion. The next few moments were taken up with defence counsel applying for costs on behalf of their clients. It was not expected that these applications would succeed for in criminal trials costs against the prosecution are almost never awarded unless it has been found that there is no case to answer or some other freak circumstances have occurred. Nevertheless Mr Justice Caulfield decided to end the case with yet another humiliating blow to the prosecuting authorities, and he ordered that the costs of each defendant should be paid out of public funds. Final figures are not available at the time of writing, but it has been estimated that the costs of Mr Roberts and the *Sunday Telegraph* would amount to approximately twenty thousand pounds, that my costs would total around twelve thousand pounds, and that Colonel Cairns' costs would be about ten thousand pounds. Add to these sums the costs of the Crown (who employed approximately six full-time lawyers on the case), the Court expenses, and the expenditure on the police investigation, and it must be assumed that the British taxpayer is footing a bill of some sixty thousand pounds for the Scott Report Affair.

The immediate aftermath of the result for all the defendants was an inundation of congratulations, celebrations, and complimentary publicity. Newspaper and television commentators spent several days demanding an immediate reform of the law, while the Government, on the night of the verdict, let it be known that it would take steps to review the Act. Two weeks later the Home Secretary announced that he was setting up a special Committee of Inquiry, under the chairmanship of Lord Franks, to examine the workings of Section 2 of the Official Secrets Act 1911.

Mr Brian Roberts has since been awarded a gold medal by the Institute of Journalists for his defence of press freedom. Colonel Cairns has been to Buckingham Palace to be invested by the Queen with the OBE he was awarded for services in Nigeria. I have spent the weeks after the verdict in writing this book as a contribution to the coming debate over the future of Official Secrecy.

In purely personal terms, the case underlined for me the truth of the Duke of Wellington's dictum that 'nothing except a battle lost can be half so melancholy as a battle won'. Despite the eventual triumph, the strains, stresses and disruptive effects of being involved for over a year in fiercely contested criminal proceedings amounted to a thoroughly undesirable ordeal. But if the results of this one battle cause an eventual victory in the war for freedom of speech against the dark forces of bureaucratic over-secrecy then the ordeal will seem very much worthwhile. For if meaningful law reforms of the the Official Secrets Act are passed, no journalist or private citizen will ever again in Britain face criminal charges for publishing official information which is merely embarrassing or inconvenient to the government of the day.

Part Three

Part Three

15

The Future of Official Secrecy

The Scott Report Affair has ensured that Britain's laws and customs of Official Secrecy will never be the same again. The historic summing up of Mr Justice Caulfield has left the Official Secrets Act of 1911 so maimed as to be unrecognisable. The notorious Section 2 is in ruins. Into this vacuum the Government have sent the esteemed figure of Lord Franks and a Committee of Inquiry to investigate the possibilities for amending the existing legislation. Although this committee's terms of reference are too limited (they have been instructed by the Home Secretary only to review Section 2) it seems almost inevitable that their recommendations together with the ensuing Parliamentary debates, will result in some change to the present law. Whether these changes will be substantial or minimal remains to be seen, but in view of the coming controversy over the future of the Official Secrets Acts, it seems appropriate to round off this book with a few thoughts on bringing about a meaningful reform of this unsatisfactory law.

The key to the future of Official Secrecy is in its past, for only by taking into account the evolving relationship between Government and governed can one see the way ahead for a more open system of communications in affairs of state.

Until the late nineteenth century, the internal power of the British State was both limited and in the hands of the few. Democracy was restricted. Parliament sat for five months a year and the mass political parties were only beginning to come into existence. Communications were slow and national newspapers were in their infancy. Government intervention and activity was, with income tax at sixpence in the pound, minuscule. Official business was transacted by a few hundred clerks in Whitehall, often nepotically recruited. In short, Government was a club, and as such relied on the discretion of its members to preserve its secrets.

The Marvin leak of Lord Salisbury's Anglo-Russian treaty in 1878 was a sharp indication that the club had expanded its membership to include some less reliable characters.

This realisation, coupled with the growing complexity of Government and the increasing threat of hostilities in Europe, led to the passing of the Official Secrets Acts of 1888 and 1911. After the First World War, Government became more complex and more extended. With this development a new estate of highly qualified and dedicated permanent civil servants emerged. To these, as to the Phanariot Greeks in the Ottoman Empire, more and more power inevitably fell. Government ceased to be a club and became instead a fortress city. The Official Secrets Acts of 1911 and 1920 were the watch-dogs at its gates, guarding against the escape of any information which might be prejudicial to the safety and the interests of the State. Although these watchdogs occasionally nipped those responsible for harmless indiscretions (as in the Somerset House Wills case of 1932 and the Compton Mackenzie case of 1933) and thereby brought the law into mild disrepute, the principle that criminal penalties should be imposed on those who disclosed government information remained largely unchallenged.

The reason for this lack of challenge was that the activities inside the fortress city were still comparatively restricted and often of high importance in terms of national and international security. London was still the capital of a great empire, Britain remained a global military power, and Europe was teetering on the brink of another war. Moreover the Government spokesmen of the day paid lip-service to the convention (occasionally abused) that the watch-dogs of the Official Secrets Acts would only be unleashed in cases of real or potential espionage.

After the Second World War, and five years of socialistic reforms introduced by the 1945 Labour administration, the activities of Government underwent a dramatic expansion. Bureaucracy burst through the walls of the fortress city and sprawled like a vast megalopolis into innumerable unexpected areas of the national consciousness.

Today, over half of Britain's economic life is being directly or indirectly controlled from Whitehall. Leviathan straddles the Thames. The interests and therefore security of the State can be claimed to be of almost total ramification.

As a result of this transformation the watch-dogs of Official Secrecy are no longer confined to the comparatively simple task of guarding Government's inner citadel of military security. Instead they roam the back streets of Government's megalopolis, growling menacingly at all forms of unauthorised communication between officialdom and the public. The same legal teeth that in 1911 were sharpened to prevent information on the movements of battleships falling into the hands of enemy agents were sixty years later being bared to prevent gossip about maladministration of the welfare services falling into the hands of national newspapers. This trend has brought about a situation worthy of Parkinson's Law, whereby the pressures towards tighter Official Secrecy grow in inverse proportion to the diminishing number of secrets worth guarding.

But while the apparatus of Government and its attendant emphasis on secrecy has expanded to monster proportions, the control exercised by Parliament and ministers has remained static and limited. This is a potentially dangerous situation, but fortunately no nation's public life has been freer of scandal or abuse than Britain's. The probity of the civil service and the omnipresence of Treasury Control have prevented anything more untoward this century than the so-called Marconi scandal of 1912. Nothing comparable to an affaire Stavisky or a Teapot Dome has tarnished any British administration in living memory. Nevertheless, the power of the State machine has increased, is increasing and ought to be kept under more careful surveillance. Politicians, supposedly elected to perform this supervisory role, simply cannot keep pace with the complexity of modern bureaucracy. In the case of the Crichel Down Affair, there was total ministerial ignorance. The same could be said of thousands of other single policy issues. Of course individual abuses may be righted by individual MPs or by the Ombudsman, but on broader matters of policy, both backbenchers and ministers are more and more in the hands of civil servants.

The absence of effective checks and controls on the activities of the contemporary Civil Service has recently lead to demands for 'more open government'. This presumably means giving journalists and other interested members of the public the opportunity to scrutinise the workings of Government more closely by delving for official information without fear of obstruction or prosecution under the powers of the Official Secrets Act. When this idea was seriously mooted under the previous Labour Government, the Civil Service responded with a White Paper, published in June 1969, entitled 'Information and the Public Interest'.

The stonewalling nature of this document can be summarised by quoting one sentence from its own text: 'The Official Secrets Acts are not in any way a barrier to greater openness in Government business', and one sentence from a letter to *The Times* by an eminent critic, Professor H. W. R. Wade QC, of St John's College, Oxford, who claimed that the White Paper had 'observed in a pained tone that the Official Secrets Acts were much misunderstood since they did not prohibit disclosures which were officially authorised – as if this were some wonderful blessing'.

Thus 'Information and the Public Interest', after reviewing the problem of striking a balance between the natural secrecy of the state machine and the 'need of the public to know', came down heavily in favour of preserving the status quo. The only check on Whitehall remains the privileged investigatory role of Parliament. Unfortunately, it is the privilege of a man to see in a darkened room.

Not only is the time of Parliament limited, its standing and select committees of investigation are cumbersome and, except in the case of the Public Accounts Committee, generally ineffective. The time has come when checks on the executive must seek reinforcement elsewhere. Thanks to the improved intellectual and technical sophistication of the press, radio and television, public communicators and commentators are now ready and able to take on a share of this responsibility.

Given adequate access to the facts, 'the Fourth Estate' could soon become a serious participatory influence on the processes of Government. Too often today the media's coverage of public affairs is superficial or trivial, placing undue reliance for its serious political content on the carefully-processed lobby briefings and official leaks. A changeover to the American system, whereby journalists may freely research into government information and have lawful access to many kinds of government documents, would surely lead to a much higher quality of political journalism in

Britain. Such an alteration of the present restrictions on contemporary reporting would certainly keep the public better informed about the workings of Whitehall, while Whitehall itself would be more critically watched than at any time in the last thirty years. Such an innovation might well create a completely new relationship between Government and governed.

A sweeping reform of this nature can only be carried out by means of drastic legislative amendments to the Official Secrets Acts. If there were ever any doubts as to the blanket prohibition on receiving and communicating government information that the law now imposes, these were removed during the unreported legal submissions in the middle of the Scott Report trial at the Old Bailey in January 1971. Replying to the defence speeches claiming that there was no case to answer, the Prosecuting Counsel, Mr John Mathew, declared that the Crown regards all official information – whether classified or not – as covered by the Official Secrets Act. Arguing that the only exception is official information about trivia, Mr Mathew went on: 'The whole structure of government would fall down if people had complete freedom to communicate any official document.'

If this is going to be the line taken by officialdom's establishment during the coming debates in and outside Parliament about the future of the Official Secrets Acts, then it is a line which is easily destroyed by international comparisons with the methods other democracies use to protect their Official Secrets.

The United States has nothing remotely comparable to Britain's Official Secrets Acts. The Government can prosecute spies or aiders and abbettors of espionage under the Espionage Statutes and the Internal Security Acts, but proceedings under these laws have never been taken against a journalist or a talkative official who disclosed information to the Press. In moments of national emergency (such as the Cuban missile crisis of 1962) the White House has been known to issue guidelines to the media, but these come in the form of requests and if ignored the only sanction that can be enforced against the offending journalists is the revocation of their White House press accreditation cards. The worst thing that can happen to an indiscreet US official is that he can be disciplined or dismissed under the rules of professional conduct, but even these strictures do not apply after his service has ended.

Moreover, the United States gives its citizens positive powers of

213

inquiry into official records. The Freedom of Information Act (1967) entitles any member of the public to inspect the files of any Federal Government Department or Agency, subject only to nine specific exceptions covering such matters as defence, foreign policy, trade secrets, medical histories, and personal privacy. In 1969, a US federal judge applied this Act in upholding the claim of a consumers' union to see the results of a government research programme for testing hearing aids. The American citizen thus has the lawful right to a great deal of official information which it would be a crime for a British citizen to disclose or receive. This has not happened by accident. The United States Government still regards one of its duties, in the words of President Kennedy as 'to give information'.[1] Although such a liberal attitude leads to a certain amount of sensitive, and sometimes even secret, information being published in the Press, Americans appear to prefer the balance of public curiosity versus official secrecy being heavily weighted in the public's favour. The dangers of this situation are that America's enemies must from time to time obtain amazing windfalls of knowledge about matters relevant to military security from published sources. Indeed Admiral Hyman Rickover of the US Navy once complained that foreign spies interested in the inner construction details of the Polaris submarine need only buy a plastic model for \$3.95.[2] This kind of complaint has been more seriously reechoed on several occasions in the last four years when the media disclosed compromising military information about the war in Vietnam. Yet despite any damage that may be done by these occasional breaches of security, the obvious benefit is that the American people know far more than the British people about the methods by which decisions affecting the way they are governed are taken and implemented. With a bureaucratic machine as vast as the US Federal Government, it is clearly essential to have some sort of additional check on the activities of the civil servants over and above the modest controls imposed by the enquiries of Congressional Committees. That the American public themselves should, through the Press and television, have acquired this watch-dog function, is surely the mark of a secure and free democracy.

Although the United States is far and away the most open Government in the free world, enforced restrictions on the reporting of non-secret official information do not appear to exist in any democratic society other than Britain. In France, journalists are free to write any story about government affairs that they wish. However, if the Quai d'Orsay considers that information harmful to France's national security has been published, then preliminary legal proceedings will be instituted against the journalist and his newspaper. The matter thereafter rests with an instructing magistrate who formally applies to the National Defence Council for an opinion as to whether or not national security has been violated. The magistrate is not bound by that opinion, but if he accepts it the final step is for the defendants to be formally charged and ordered to stand trial before the Court of State Security. This cumbersome procedure has so many 'fail-safe' devices likely to prevent the unnecessary prosecution of minor transgressors, that it has not been invoked for twelve years. The last time it was used was in 1959 when the scientific correspondent of a leading Paris newspaper disclosed that the first nuclear explosion tests in the Sahara desert were about to take place. After a hearing by a magistrate, the journalist concerned was not in fact charged before the Court of State Security, and the only ill-effect that befell him was the revocation of his press accreditation card to the Ministry of Defence.

Germany likewise places no restrictions on what the media can report, but the Federal Public Prosecutor may take action if there has been a clear breach of state security. The only case in the 1960s concerned an article in *Der Spiegel,* giving details of a NATO exercise, and for this the paper's Defence Correspondent was successfully prosecuted.

Sweden has the most relaxed procedures of any European country when it comes to protecting government information, for private citizens, under a law similar to the US Freedom of Information Act, have right of access to all but a very few categories of official documents. If the Press unearth secrets in these prohibited categories and publish them, they will be prosecuted only for violations of military security. In a recent Swedish incident where the Press disclosed some budget secrets, there were no prosecutions.

The only possible exception to the rule that no democracy except Britain prohibits the publication of official information not affecting national security concerns Australia, for Section 70 of the Commonwealth of Australia's Crimes Act 1914–66 makes it an offence against the State for a government official to publish or communicate without authority 'any fact or document which comes to his knowledge or into his possession by virtue of his office'.

But this offence, which carries a maximum penalty of two years' imprisonment, applies only to serving or retired civil servants. Private citizens can only be prosecuted for disclosures of information 'prejudicial to the safety or defence of the Commonwealth or a part of the Queen's dominions' (Crimes Acts, Section 76). Official Secrets cases in Australia are extremely rare, the only recent example being a 1969 prosecution which resulted in a humiliating rebuff for the Crown. In this case a government official, Pratt, was accused of communicating information about the Government's trade and tariff policies to a well-known Canberra journalist, Mr Max Newton. The Canberra magistrate ruled at first instance that there was no case to answer, thereby implicitly upholding the view that Australia's laws of Official Secrecy apply exclusively to breaches of security even where civil servants are concerned.

From these few international examples, it can be seen that Britain's methods of protecting government information are the most draconian in the free world. Other countries permit a reasonable degree of freedom for the receipt and communication of certain kinds of official material and it is absurd to argue that 'the whole structure of government would fall down' if similar freedom existed in Britain. After all, civil servants of all nationalities are by nature a highly discreet species and do not normally leak sensitive stories about their work to reporters even if the criminal law of the country concerned does not prohibit such conduct. An indiscreet official can in any case always be disciplined or dismissed under internal regulations. If Britain was to abolish immediately those sections of the Official Secrets Acts which have no connection with national security, the effect would not be a flood of embarrassing revelations pouring from Whitehall to Fleet Street. The only important result would be that journalists would feel free to make direct enquiries about the workings of Government to civil servants, while the civil servants would in turn be uninhibited about answering those enquiries with factual information, both verbal and documentary, which did not impinge on national security. This would undoubtedly amount to 'more open government' and would be a great improvement on the present unsatisfactory information bottlenecks of government department press offices. There is no substitute for direct journalistic access to the civil servants who are in charge of the subjects the public wants to know about. One possible by-product of such an adjustment might be a weakening of the closely-guarded anonymity of the Civil Service. This is in any case slowly breaking down as the informed public becomes increasingly aware that the distinction between senior politicians and top civil servants is a meaningless one in terms of power and influence. In the United States, key officials such as Mr Mac-George Bundy, Mr Walt Rostow, and Dr Henry Kissinger have for some time received almost as much attention from the media as have their political masters. There is no good reason why such realism should not apply in Britain.

Having thus outlined the need for more open government on historical, international, and contemporary grounds, one comes to the final problem of what to do about the reform of the Official Secrets Acts of 1911 and 1920. These statutes remain the ark of the covenant from which all the present prohibitions and practices of secrecy flow. D-notices, leak procedures, lobby briefings, positive vettings, press officers' records of ministers' conversations, and all the impedimenta of contemporary censorship derive directly or indirectly from these two ill-considered Acts of Parliament. How can they best be amended?

There are three main suggestions currently in circulation. The first of these advocates that the law of Official Secrets should be left amidst the hopeless ruins in which it now stands following Mr Justice Caulfield's demolition work in his Old Bailey judgement of 3 February 1971. The main effect in law of that summing up was to withdraw the test of whether or not a piece of information or document is an official secret away from the civil servants who originally imposed the classification, and to transfer the responsibility for that test to the courts. As the judge put it:

> This prosecution perhaps has been put before you in this way: that once a document emanating from an official source is stamped 'confidential' that therefore anybody who handles the document is breaking the law. I hope I have explained to you in my directions in law that that is not the law.

Some commentators have hailed these words as the destruction of the Civil Service's hitherto unquestioned right to impose the imprimatur of official secrecy on information which is not connected with national security. The dangers of attempting to

introduce legislation which will improve on the Caulfield doctrine
have been lucidly expressed by Mr Richard Crossman in the *New
Statesman* of 11 February 1971 when he wrote in his 'Crux'
column:

> I am amazed by the naive enthusiasm with which it is now
> being argued that the Act should be scrapped and replaced by
> a new statute. A delight in secrecy and a passion for keeping the
> public in the dark still dominates Whitehall ... What makes
> anyone imagine that if Whitehall gets the chance it won't pro-
> duce a young mastiff to replace the toothless old watch-dog?

Despite such fears, there are greater problems in continuing
with the unchanged 1911 and 1920 Acts. The doctrine of judicial
precedent makes it possible at any time for the Court of Criminal
Appeal or the House of Lords to overrule Mr Justice Caulfield's
line in some subsequent trial. More importantly, unless Parliament brings in statutory reforms, the psychological barriers to
'open government' will remain as tightly secured as ever, even
though there is now a judge-made loophole to allow journalists to
get the occasional scoop without punishment.

This last objection applies to the second widely canvassed idea
for reforming the law. This suggests that the Acts should be left
more or less unaltered save for one important amendment which
would provide the right for a defendant to plead that it was in the
national and public interest for the information to be published.
Such a modest change would certainly not bring about more open
government. Moreover it is impossible to know how the courts
will eventually interpret the ambiguous concept of 'the national
and public interest'.

An indication of the difficulties such a defence might present
occurred during my own trial at the Old Bailey. I pleaded as one
line of defence that it was my 'duty in the interests of the State' to
communicate the Scott Report to a national newspaper, and in
support of this I was able to show that the document proved that
ministers had been misleading Parliament in their statements about
arms supplies to Nigeria. The Crown even went so far as to accept
this evidence, although only where small arms were concerned.
Nevertheless, Mr Justice Caulfield, in his otherwise immensely

favourable summing up, appeared to be discounting this particular line of Defence when he said:

> Granting them [Aitken and Fraser] their fullest sincerity, has Mr Aitken any grounds for saying, as he does say, that he felt it was his duty in the interests of the State to communicate the Scott Report to the *Sunday Telegraph*? Notice, members of the jury, the words of the Act are 'in the interests of the state' and not necessarily in the interests of any particular faction.

The only point of including this quotation from the summing up is this. If one learned High Court judge is able to look unsympathetically on a claim that information has been published out of duty in the interests of the State even when the information concerned shows that ministers have been deceiving the public on a matter as serious as arms supplies to a civil war, how much more unsympathetic may some judges and juries be when information is claimed to have been published 'in the national interest' without any evidence of ministerial duplicity or other special circumstances. On the face of it a defence of 'published in the national interest' seems far too uncertain in its outcome, and may leave journalists and civil servants just as much in jeopardy from the wide jaws of the Official Secrets Acts as they were before this amendment was added.

A third and much more drastic suggestion for reform is that the most effective legislative amendment to the Official Secrets Acts should take the form of a one-clause bill abolishing Section 2 of the 1911 Statute. This simple proposal has more merit than the two previous ideas for it would confine the Official Secrets Acts solely to the disclosure of information prejudicial to the safety of the State, and would thereby leave the way clear for the elusive ideal of 'more open government'. Yet although such a reform would no doubt delight Fleet Street, it is argued with some justification even by the most liberal elements in Whitehall that there are certain kinds of official information which have no connection with national security yet whose disclosure would be profoundly damaging to the national interest. This category of information might include such matters as budget secrets, trade secrets, and national currency arrangements. There would be no protection by the criminal law for any of these if Section 2 of the 1911 Act was abolished outright with no alternative legislation in its place. Suppose for example a Treasury civil servant leaked the information that the pound was going to be devalued in a week's time. The damage done to the national interest by a disclosure of this kind would be enormous, so much so that some sort of special legal powers to deter and punish such leaks by officials might well be necessary.

Since the three principal suggestions for reform all contain certain serious defects, it seems that amending the Official Secrets Acts is going to be a much more complicated operation than is generally recognised. What any new legislation should set out to achieve is first the safeguarding of vitally important state secrets relevant either to national security or to one or two other carefully defined special categories. Secondly the unfettering of the press and public from the unreasonable blanket restrictions on freedom of communication which the present law imposes. Thirdly the creation of an 'open government' situation which will give individual citizens and the mass media ready access to certain kinds of official information, thereby enabling the public to keep a watchdog eye on the ever-increasing activities of the State. All these objectives could be attained by two legislative innovations, beginning first with limiting the scope of the Official Secrets Acts.

Section 1 of the 1911 Official Secrets Act, which is a widely drafted prohibition on all espionage activities 'prejudicial to the safety and interests of the State' should be retained in its present form, with one important clarification to the wording. The phrase 'safety and interests of the State', which is too broad in its possible interpretations, should be replaced by the more specific phrase used in Section 78 of the Commonwealth of Australia Crimes Act – 'safety or defence of the State'. This last wording is quite sufficient to ensure the conviction of all spies and traitors.

Section 2 of the 1911 Act should be completely abolished. The evils that have resulted from the vague and obscure nature of this section are now too notorious to need further comment.

Section 8 of the 1911 Act needs an important amendment, for this is the clause which states that Official Secrets prosecutions cannot be brought unless accompanied by the formal consent and fiat of the Attorney-General. As has already been argued in Chapter 6, this requirement places the Attorney in a most invidious position and provides no safeguard whatever to the liberty of the subject. Moreover, since Sir Elwyn Jones made his much-criticised blunders over the prosecutions in the Scott Report case, anxieties about the political bias of Law Officers have increased a hundredfold. As Mr Justice Caulfield put it: 'It may well be that prosecutions under this Act can serve as a convenient and reasonable substitute for a political trial.' Such anxieties will linger over Sir Elwyn's successors for at least a generation. The way to remove them is to hand the power of decision-making on Official Secrets Prosecutions to the Director of Public Prosecutions. In practical terms, such a change will make little difference, for the Director of Public Prosecutions will inevitably consult the Law Officers, and possibly even the Cabinet, in cases involving national security. His task will also be made far easier if the amended law contains more precise definitions of offences. But in terms of presentation the Director of Public Prosecutions will be immune from suspicions of political partiality and invulnerable to pressure from ministers. Never again will a respected legal publication be able to say, as the *New Law Journal* said on 14 May 1970: 'Prosecution under the Official Secrets Acts depends entirely on the length of an Attorney-General's foot.' Because it is important that justice must be seen to be done without any consideration of politics, it is essential, given the present disrepute into which the Attorney's discretion has fallen, that Section 8 should be redrafted transferring the power of initiating proceedings to the Director of Public Prosecutions.

Apart from these major changes, the Official Secrets Acts of 1911 and 1920 could benefit from several minor 'tidying up' amendments by expert Parliamentary draftsmen aware of the need for clarity in modern criminal legislation. These minor changes need not be detailed here, but taken in conjunction with the more drastic amendments mentioned earlier, the net result of all of these reforms would be to strengthen, rather than to relax, the protection given to vitally important state secrets. Injustices and anomalies which arose from the obscurity of the original Acts would vanish, as would suspicion of political bias by the Government of the day. The Official Secrets Acts would then return to their original purposes of protecting the state against the perpetrators, aiders, and abettors of espionage.

221

Although there is no need for Britain's laws of Official Secrecy to go beyond matters of espionage, the above-mentioned reform of the existing legislation does not achieve two of the main law reform objectives outlined earlier. One of these was the creation of 'more open government', the other was the protecting of certain kinds of nationally important secrets, such as the budget, which do not affect security.

Both these objectives could be achieved by a second legislative innovation – a completely new Act of Parliament, along the lines of the US Freedom of Information Act. It could appropriately be titled the Civil Service Information Act, for it would deal with the rightful and wrongful communication of information by the Civil Service to the public.

Section 1 of this projected Civil Service Information Act should simply state that it is the duty of all servants of the Government to give the public the maximum possible information about the processes of Government, the only exceptions being information specifically excluded by the reformed Official Secrets Acts or by subsequent clauses in the Civil Service Information Act.

Section 2 of the Act should follow closely the pattern of the US Information Act – i.e. it should ordain that individual citizens can be given access to certain records of Government departments, subject to a number of exceptions including defence, foreign policy, trade and economic secrets, and matters of personal privacy. These exceptions must be carefully defined in the Act.

Section 3 of this Civil Service Information Act should specifically prohibit civil servants from communicating secret information relating to national security, the budget and national currency arrangement. A breach of this section could be punishable by either a fine, dismissal from the government service, up to two years' imprisonment, or any combination of these penalties.

The advantage of a Civil Service Information Act of this sort is that its positive clauses would effectively create an 'open government' situation in Britain, while its prohibitive clauses would deter and if necessary punish serious indiscretions by officials in a position of trust. Meanwhile the much more formidable Official Secrets Act would be back in its originally intended role as the severe guardian against breaches of national security through espionage. There is no ideal solution to the problems of Official Secrecy, but one which strikes a fair balance between tight security for important national secrets and open government for those areas of official administration about which the public has a right to know, is surely the best of compromises in an imperfect world.

POSTSCRIPT

Since the above text was printed, the attention of the world has been sharply directed to the conflict between Press freedom and Official Secrecy by the furore over the *New York Times* decision to publish extracts from a secret Pentagon study on the Vietnam war.

The study consisted of a 3,000-page report (classified 'Top Secret-Sensitive') appended to 4,000 pages of official documents (variously classified 'Secret' or 'Top Secret'). It was commissioned in 1967 by the then US Secretary for Defense, Robert S. McNamara, to assess the reasons and the decision-making processes leading up to America's involvement in Vietnam. Among the most sensitive revelations were those parts of the report which showed that President Johnson had intensified the covert warfare against North Vietnam and had begun planning to wage overt war on a massive scale by the spring of 1964 – several months before Congress was informed of the true nature of the US military activity and commitment.

After the *New York Times* had published three instalments of extracts from the Pentagon study on 13–15 June 1971, the Nixon administration embarked on a series of civil actions to prevent further publication of any of the material. At the time of writing, the legal battle is complex and confused, but the net result of the latest court rulings in New York and Washington is that no further extracts have been published. On behalf of the United States, Secretary of State William S. Rogers has argued that publication of the study violated national security regulations and caused 'a great deal of difficulty' in relations with foreign governments. The *New York Times* has based its case on the First

Amendment's right to a free Press, and has pointed out that publication represents the revelation of recent history rather than the violation of current national security, since none of the disclosures in the Pentagon study relate to events after 1968.

The present legal impasse seems unlikely to be broken until the civil case reaches the US Supreme Court. In the meantime the administration is reported to be considering criminal prosecutions against the *New York Times*, certain members of its staff, and also against Dr Daniel Ellsberg, a professor at the Massachusetts Institute of Technology, who has identified himself as the Pentagon official responsible for the leak.

Although it is premature to draw any long-term conclusions from this remarkable American *cause célèbre*, certain provisional judgments may be attempted.

First it is clear that the publication of the Pentagon's Vietnam study marks a watershed in the history of the relations between the US Government and Press, for the precedents laid down by this affair are likely to be of lasting importance. Secondly it has become apparent that the 'open government' concept of American society has grown so open that the authorities are almost empty-handed in a crisis of this nature, for it is obvious from the chaotic legal battles so far that the United States Government has no real apparatus to deal with the problem of publication of national security information. Thirdly there seems to be extraordinary contradictions between the US constitution (notably the First Amendment) and the existing US laws governing espionage and national security. These are now in urgent need of clarification.

There has thus arisen a fascinating paradox between the Official Secrecy situations on both sides of the Atlantic. For just as the Scott Report Affair seems to be on the point of bringing about more flexible laws and official attitudes towards the control of Britain's government information, so the McNamara Report Affair seems likely to create tighter legal procedures for controlling the same kind of information in the United States. In the best of all possible worlds both nations should probably move closer towards each other's position on this complicated problem, and be prepared to learn from one another's mistakes.

Notes

CHAPTER 1. HOW THE ACT BEGAN

1 Charles Marvin, *Our Public Offices*, London, 1879, pp. 247–8.
2 Robert Blake, *Disraeli*, London, 1966, pp. 623–5 and 648.
3 Marvin, *op. cit.* p. 193.
4 *Ibid.*, p. 258.
5 *Ibid.*, p. 267.
6 *Ibid.*, p. 272.
7 *Ibid.*, p. 280.
8 *Ibid.*, p. 281.
9 Hansard, 3 June 1878, col. 1061.
10 Marvin, *op. cit.*, p. 287.
11 *Ibid.*, p. 281.
12 B. H. Sumner, *Russia and the Balkans*, Oxford, 1937, p. 88.
13 Robert Blake, *op cit.*, p. 649.
14 24 of Vict. Cap. 96 Sect. 20.
15 Horace Wyndham, *A Victorian Parade*, London, 1934, p. 48.
16 *Ibid.*, p. 56.
17 *The Globe*, 12 July 1878.
18 A. J. Balfour, *Chapters of Autobiography*, London, 1930, p. 117.

CHAPTER 2. THE PASSING OF THE ACTS

1 Hansard, 28 March 1889, col. 1110.
2 *Ibid.*
3 Hansard, 20 June 1889, cols. 322–3.
4 Hansard, 11 July 1889, col. 85.
5 *R. v. Doe* 1902.
6 Hansard, 26 June 1896, col. 471.
7 Hansard, 21 May 1908, col. 518.
8 Hansard, 11 May 1908, col. 178.
9 John Bulloch, M.I.5, pp. 80–88, London, 1963.

10 Winston S. Churchill, *The World Crisis*, London, 1939, p. 49.
11 *Ibid.*, p. 51.
12 Hansard, 17 July 1911, col. 642.
13 *Ibid.*, col. 644.
14 *Ibid.*, col. 647.
15 Hansard, 18 August, 1911, col. 2253.
16 1 & 2 Geo. 5. Ch. 28.
17 *R. v. Parrott* 1913, 8 Criminal Appeal Reports 186.
18 Cabinet Meeting, 29 January 1920, Cab. 23/20 p. 61.
19 Hansard, 25 June 1920, col. 896.
20 Hansard, 3 December 1920, col. 1539.
21 *Ibid.*, col. 1543.
22 Ibid., col. 1546.
23 *Ibid.*, col. 1571–3.
24 *Ibid.*, col. 1551.
25 *Ibid.*, col. 1562.
26 *Ibid.*, col. 1668.

CHAPTER 3. THE PRESS AND OFFICIAL SECRETS
 1 Hansard, 12 May 1930, col. 1447.
 2 Sir Gordon Hewart, Hansard, 3 and 16 December 1920, *passim.*
 3 *Lewis & Cattle*, 1938, 2 Kings Bench, 454.
 4 Hansard, 24 May 1938, col. 1047.
 5 Hansard, 24 June 1948, col. 1695.
 6 Chapman Pincher, London 1968, *Press Freedom & National Security Journalism Today*, vol. 1 no. 2 1968 p. 39.
 7 *Ibid.*, p. 39.
 8 Duncan Sandys to the author, 7 December 1970.
 9 *Daily Mail*, 11 May 1961.
10 Pincher, *op. cit.*, p. 40.
11 *Daily Mail*, 27 August 1965.
12 *Daily Sketch*, 20 January 1966.
13 *Evening News*, 14 December 1966.
14 *Evening Standard*, 16 December 1966.
15 *Peace News*, 16 January 1970.
16 *Peace News*, 13 March 1970.
17 *The Times*, 2 August 1965.
18 *Daily Mirror*, 9 February 1968.
19 *Sunday Express*, 5 November 1966.
20 Hansard, 29 May 1963, col. 904.
21 *The Law and The Press*, Stevens, London, 1965.
22 *The Times*, 11 May 1938.

23 *Daily Express*, 13 May 1966.
24 *The People*, 8 September 1968.
25 *Sunday Express*, 5 March 1967.
26 *Daily Telegraph*, 20 January 1970.
27 *Daily Telegraph*, 8 January 1969.

CHAPTER 4. HISTORIANS AND THE ACTS

1 *Daily Telegraph*, 4 July 1935.
2 *Observer Magazine*, 22 November 1970.
3 Sir Compton Mackenzie, *My Life and Times*, London, 1968, Octave 7, p. 91.
4 *The Times*, 13 January 1933.
5 *Evening Standard*, 31 January 1951.
6 *The Times*, 19 November 1970.
7 *Ibid.*
8 Hansard, 11 December 1962, col. 203.
9 Hansard, 8 November 1962, col. 1153.
10 See note 8.

CHAPTER 5. THE PRIVILEGED POLITICIANS

1 Sir Compton Mackenzie, *My Life and Times*, London, 1968, Octave 7 p. 84.
2 Hansard, 10 June 1936 col. 206.
3 Hansard, 10 June, col. 207.
4 Hansard, 5 December 1938, col. 899.
5 Report of Select Committee, 8 June 1938.
6 Winston S. Churchill, *The Gathering Storm*, London, 1948, p. 63.
7 Hansard, 22 February 1923, col. 1235.
8 Hansard, 1 August 1946, col. 1207.
9 Hansard, 25 February 1960, col. 572.
10 Randolph S. Churchill, *The Fight for the Tory Leadership*, London, 1963, p. 126.
11 *Crisis in the Civil Service*, edited by Hugh Thomas, London, 1968, p. 121.
12 *Sunday Telegraph*, 27 September 1970.

CHAPTER 6. A LAW IN DISREPUTE

1 Professor David Williams, *Not in the Public Interest*, London, 1965, p. 38.

CHAPTER 7. BACKGROUND TO THE SCOTT REPORT AFFAIR

1 Quoted in *Time* Magazine, 1 September 1967.
2 *Time* Magazine, 13 June 1966.
3 Frederick Forsyth, *The Biafra Story*, London, 1969, p. 144.
4 Private Information to the author from a Labour ex-minister.
5 See the *Economist*, 9 May 1970.
6 Guildhall Magistrates' Court Depositions, p. 33.
7 Guildhall Magistrates' Court Depositions, p. 29.
8 Interview with the author, 7 November 1970.
9 Hansard, 29 January 1968, col. 600.
10 Hansard, 16 May 1968, cols. 1397–8.
11 Hansard, 19 July 1969, col. 1603.
12 Hansard, 9 December 1969, col. 276.

CHAPTER 8. ANATOMY OF A SCOOP

1 Hansard, 8 December 1969, col. 49, and 2 April 1969, col. 496.
2 House of Commons, 12 June 1968, Hansard, col. 297.
3 House of Commons, 9 December 1969, Hansard, col. 279.
4 Scott Report, p. 12.

CHAPTER 9. SCOTLAND YARD INVESTIGATES

1 Guildhall Magistrates' Court Depositions, pp. 54–5.

CHAPTER 11. AT THE MAGISTRATES' COURT

1 Guildhall Magistrates' Court Depositions, p. 71.
2 Co-author with Auberon Waugh of *Biafra, Britain's Shame*, London, 1969.
3 Guildhall Magistrates' Court Depositions, p. 29.
4 *Ibid.*, p. 35.
5 *Ibid.*, p. 35.
6 *Ibid.*, p. 39.
7 *Ibid.*, p. 53.
8 *Ibid.*, p. 65.
9 *Ibid.*, p. 67.
10 *Ibid.*, p. 71.
11 *Ibid.*, p. 113.
12 *Ibid.*, p. 123.
13 *Ibid.*, p. 124.
14 *Ibid.*, p. 129.

15 *Ibid.*, p. 135.
16 *Ibid.*, pp. 144–5.

CHAPTER 15. THE FUTURE OF OFFICIAL SECRECY
 1 Press Conference, 18 August 1962.
 2 *The Times*, 15 June 1967.

Index

231